MW01244240

DOOBLE TONGUE

DOOBLE TONGUE

Scots, Burns, Contradiction

Jeffrey Skoblow

DELAWARE

Newark: University of Delaware Press
London: Associated University Presses

Associated University Presses
440 Forsgate Drive
Cranbury, NJ 08512

Associated University Presses
16 Barter Street
London WC1A 2AH, England

Associated University Presses
P.O. Box 338, Port Credit
Mississauga, Ontario
Canada L5G 4L8

The paper used in this publication meets the requirements of the American National Standard for Permanence of Paper for Printed Library Materials Z39.48-1984.

Library of Congress Cataloging-in-Publication Data

Skoblow, Jeffrey.
    Dooble tongue : Scots, Burns, contradiction / Jeffrey Skoblow.
      p.   cm.
    Includes bibliographical references (p.   ) and index.
    ISBN 0-87413-728-4 (alk. paper)
    1. Scots poetry—History and criticism.   2. Burns, Robert, 1759–1796—Criticism and interpretation.   3. Language and culture—Scotland.
    4.   Contradiction in literature.   5. Scotland—In literature.   6. Scots language—Style.   I. Title.

PR8561 .S55   2001
821.009′9411—dc21   00-061547

PRINTED IN THE UNITED STATES OF AMERICA

for my
lovely Mary, dearie O
and Hanamori Flo

The scholar sharpens the teeth of the poet.
The poet rises
furious and clear in the morning light
He shows the scholar's face and not the poet's.
                              —I. C. Smith

Singing responses order otherwise.
                    —Norman MacCaig

Poor bodies hae nothing but mowe.
                    —Robert Burns

Contents

Note

I must first premise [that these observations] are intirely my
own, and consequently [may appear ill d]igested, nay perhaps
to an unpre[judiced critic so]me of them may appear absurd:
[but I am writing] to a Friend.
—Burns, to William Niven, 29 July 1780

SOME SORT OF APOLOGY FOR THE WORK THAT FOLLOWS MAY BE
called for. This book, especially in the long section on Burns, vio-
lates certain standards of academic decorum, because I have tried
(or have felt compelled) to find a voice with which to speak a sub-
ject defined, in part, by the violation of various standards of deco-
rum: academic, aesthetic, linguistic, social, sexual, political. I have
had to find a kind of dooble tongue of my own, at once within and
without the conventional bounds of literary analysis—to keep my
troth with Burns.

The book is organized as a series of long improvisations, themes
and motifs coming and going and returning, a musical form as
much as a critical one. (Whether or not it makes a harmonious
sound is another question.) I have assumed my subject to be essen-
tially unspeakable, and I have sought, in some measure, to defami-
liarize the landscape.

The approach perhaps resembles more closely a nineteenth-cen-
tury appreciation of Burns than a twentieth-century report on tex-
tual findings—though my language is not the language of the
nineteenth century and what I appreciate not what that century
appreciated.

While I have borne in mind the book's most likely reader-
ship—an anonymous few among my academic colleagues—I have
also been writing here to various friends, teachers and students (a
shifting audience, shifting sometimes within a single sentence),
and have indulged the personal impulse with rather more liberty
than is perhaps customary. My relation to audience may thus be
roughly analogous to Burns's chiefly Scottish situation: writing
poems for friends and then offering them to Edinburgh and Lon-

9

don, in effect inviting the anonymous public to look over his shoulder, to eavesdrop on his private poetic conversation.

Literary criticism, as it has come down to us, almost never takes such a stance, and has grown increasingly reluctant to be deliberative and self-conscious in its choice of form. Literary criticism rarely considers its own form as a function of the material it treats, but, rather, characteristically slices whatever material it treats into a more or less standardized form fashioned for the professional culture of Litcrit consumers. But one speaks—or may usefully speak—otherwise (doobly) as well. I have tried, with this work, to imagine an audience that may not exist.

> Nothing can be more contemptible than to suppose Public RECORDS to be True.
> —Blake

ᔭ   ᔭ   ᔭ

Some acknowledgements:

Parts of this work, slightly altered, have appeared previously: "Perverse Pleasures in the Archive: W. N. Herbert's 'Horse Island' " and "*Sharawaggi*: Crawford and Herbert Meet the Incubus" in *Scottish Literary Journal* (vol. 23, no. 2, 1996, and vol. 25, no. 2, 1998, respectively); "Dr. Currie, C'est Moi" in *Studies in Scottish Literature* (vol. 30, 1998); and "Resisting the Powers of Calculation: A Bard's Politics" in *Critical Essays on Robert Burns*, edited by Carol McGuirk (G. K. Hall, 1998). "Dr. Currie, C'est Moi" is the text of a talk I gave at a conference on "Robert Burns and Literary Nationalism" held at the University of South Carolina, Columbia, in 1996, organized by G. Ross Roy and Patrick Scott. Two other talks have drawn on material here as well: "Hugh MacDiarmid: Monologos and Its Discontents," delivered at the convention of the Modern Language Association in 1998, as part of a session on "The British Pocket Epic" organized by Nigel Alderman; and "Herbert's Laurel and Crawford's Burns: Postmodern Scotlands," at the conference on "Scotland at Home and Abroad: Culture, Community, and Nation" organized by Leith Davis, Jack Little, and Stephen Duguid at Simon Fraser University's new Centre for Scottish Studies, in 2000.

For permission to reprint material, I am grateful to the following: W. N. Herbert for "Horse Island;" Robert Crawford, W. N. Herbert, and Edinburgh University Press, for *Sharawaggi*; and both Carcanet Press Ltd. and New Directions Publishing Corp., for

Selected Poetry (1992) by Hugh MacDiarmid, ed. Alan Riach and Michael Grieve.

I am grateful to Southern Illinois University at Edwardsville for a sabbatical leave and for two Summer Research Fellowships, and to the National Endowment for the Humanities for a Summer Stipend; all of this support was indispensable to the completion of my work. At SIU Edwardsville, too, I specifically would like to thank Alice Farley, Chair of the Department of English, David Steinberg, Associate Dean of the College of Arts and Sciences, and Steve Hansen, Dean of the Graduate School, for arranging a subvention grant to cover some of the production costs involved in the publication of this book.

My thanks to Robert Crawford and Douglas Dunn for lunch in St. Andrews one day in the early stages of this project, and to Robert, again, and Bill Herbert, for correspondence, corrections, confirmations, and encouragement later on; to Tom Leonard for drinks and conversation in Glasgow; to the staffs of the Mitchell Library in Glasgow, the National Library in Edinburgh, and the Burns Cottage in Alloway; and to the many proprietors of bed-and-breakfast establishments across Scotland—in particular Dave and Nan Demeral in Ayr—who helped to make my stay in that country such a warm pleasure.

Jerome McGann and Carol McGuirk read the entire book in manuscript and offered their invaluable enthusiasms, suggestions, and questions, saving me from much (though perhaps not all) foolishness: my deep thanks to both. Many other friends and colleagues have also offered much welcome assistance: thanks are happily due to Lynn Casmier-Paz, Anthony Cross, Ashley Dean, Allison Funk, John Harvey, Naka Ishii, Lloyd Kropp, Ted Leinwand, Tino Paz, Tina Redd, Isaiah Smithson, Richard Stack, Jack Voller, and Donald Wesling, for reading portions of the manuscript, often in very rough form, and letting me know what made sense to them, as well as for sharing with me their confusions (and illuminating my own); to the Arts League Players of Edwardsville, a community theater group—in particular to John Harvey, again, and Kevin Beyer—for instruction, collaboration, and fellowship in the arts of performance; to Jim Funkhouser for a rare old LP and to Patricia Talbert for a new CD of *The Merry Muses of Caledonia*, and to Eric Barnett and John Abbott (of the SIU Edwardsville Archive) for a rare old text of that work; to all the folks at Left Bank Books in St. Louis, especially Phil Barron, for satisfying my persistent appetite for peculiar and often inaccessible texts; to Steve Moiles and Linda Jaworski-Moiles, for the *Illustrated Family Burns*

they picked up at a central Illinois flea market; to Greg Conroy
and Terry Groce for signing up to study Burns with me; to Nancy
Ruff for talking to me about Gavin Douglas many years ago; to
Alex Babione for computer assistance on many occasions franti-
cally requested and always calmly delivered; and to Julien Yoseloff
and Christine Retz at Associated University Presses for their pa-
tience with my many questions. To my brother, for a lifetime of
music and brotherhood, my sister for sisterhood, and my parents
for setting me up and turning me loose: all my love and gratitude.
And to Mary and Hana, *como siempre . . . todo.*

DOOBLE TONGUE

Tuning Up: In Con Sub Re Versions

When I matriculate in the Herald's Office, I intend that my
supporters shall be two Sloths, my crest a Slow-worm, and my
motto "Deil tak the foremost."

—Burns

1

Something of an Incubus:
W. N. Herbert and Robert Crawford

Sen for the deid remeid is none,
Best is that we for dede dispone,
Eftir our deid that lif may we;
   Timor mortis conturbat me.

—William Dunbar

It was a matter of tracking down every manifestation of the multiple processes, the confusion of indicators, that have ultimately woven for a people, which had at its disposal so many officials and individuals, the web of nothingness in which it is ensnared today.

—Edouard Glissant

either I'm nobody, or I'm a nation.

—Derek Walcott

To come at Scottish literature primarily as an explicit meditation on Scottish culture, and only secondarily in terms of whatever other concerns Scottish authors may have, is to approach this material in (at the very least) a problematic manner. No doubt the inclination to do so is in part a function of coming at the subject from the perspective of an outsider—in my case, an American perspective. From such a perspective one approaches the Scottish almost necessarily (given the linguistic, bibliographic, and curricular politics of our shared and unshared histories) *through* the English, or through an experience of the British that is heavily defined by that term's commonplace misapplication as a synonym for the English.[1] Scottish culture appears thus a priori a culture of the Other (not simply *an* other culture, like Italian or what have you, but a culture overdetermined in relation to its *own* Other, the English— one of *my* own Others, too, as an American) and the literature of that culture not readily approached without seeing first and foremost Scotland (which is to say, in part, not England) written there. Not so much then Scottish literature itself (with all its varied concerns) as the Sign of Scotland, not the object but the identity of the object, the abstraction of its definitive markers: this, to a certain extent necessarily, is the object under view. And from this perspective indeed a kind of historical and national anxiety, at least a pointed preoccupation with national identity, seems the most salient feature of Scottish literature: an anxiety lit by phosphorescent zeal, full up with loss and persistent in the faith of exhumation (like the ancient stones of Callanish on the far Isle of Lewis, revealed standing still, during the reign of Queen Victoria, under millennia of peat bog).

Putting it another way: the "Scottish," from this perspective defined both by simple distance and by complex historical patterns of domination and subordination, is a category that refers primarily to itself, whatever else it may aspire to refer to; it is *marked* in the sense that linguists speak of marked and unmarked terms—not the one we claim to know and can afford, in some degree, to take for granted, but the Other. What is problematic about this—about seeing a literature or a culture in terms of the unmarked and the marked, the norm and the other—is that such a formulation shapes the underlying structure of any systematic prejudice. At its worst such a view sustains the most pernicious effects of England's domination over its northern neighbors. Whatever the Scots may do, from this vantage, has no meaning but to identify them as Scots—a reading informed by the rudimentary and dehumanizing logic of racism.

But this problematic point of departure is not entirely a function of foreign vantage. More troublesome still is the fact that Scottish culture has been bound for so long and in such politically charged ways to English culture that the context of this relation has come to seem definitive—not only from an exogenous but also from an indigenous perspective: a perspective in either case defined by alienation. (In Scottish literature, as in Rimbaud, "I" is another.) This situation, of course, is far from unique: from the perspective of Freud, Fanon, the Frankfurt School, and feminist theory, among others, the notions of introjection and self-alienation have become familiar staples of critical thought, shaping fundamental assumptions about identity and political resistance. What Scottish culture has to offer this discussion is perhaps the longest running case

> (Thae wha sing lyk this
> ur exiles ivrywhaur.)
> —W. N. Herbert

study of the problem on the scale of a national literature. And what this discussion has to offer Scottish literature is, problematically but unavoidably, the only place to begin.

I begin here, then, with an examination of the question of Scottish cultural self-consciousness. And although my ultimate focus is on the work of Robert Burns as that work relates to—and, I will argue, contests—the dominant traditions of British (or perhaps here I should say English) Romanticism, I will begin here too with an examination of contemporary, twentieth-century Scottish work. In doing so I hope to establish the continuity of an alternative tradition to the English, an alternative frame of reference within which the nature and importance of Burns's work might be made intelligible, and without which that work remains—as in fact it has remained, for the most part—little more than a kind of heroic curio.

In other words, if, as David Daiches claims in his influential study of Burns, "his work represented the last brilliant flare-up of a Scottish literary tradition that had been developing for centuries and that in the eighteenth century was in its final disintegrating phase,"[2] then the study of Burns would seem to be an occasion for lamentation or nostalgic testimonial—an occasion for eulogy of one kind or another—but little else: goodnight, sweet heaven-taught ploughman, we hardly knew ye, may flights of angels fill your cup. . . . I wish to argue, rather, that Burns's work represents a crucial moment in a living tradition, in the context of British Romanticism a kind of return of the repressed, associated at the current moment with that range of phenomena loosely (and problematically) grouped under the sign of the postmodern: a contestatory sub-tradition not limited to the Scottish dimension of British literature but highlighted there, informed by Scotland's broader struggle for political and cultural identity. More simply, I wish to argue that to understand the contemporary literary scene in Scotland is to understand the situation that Burns confronted two hundred years ago: the situation (the problem) of writing *Poems, Chiefly in the Scottish Dialect* in the context of Scottish resistance to English power.

One more note by way of beginning. I assume in most of my readers (of English) not only a general lack of familiarity but also a reluctance to engage with the cultural materials of this study—that is, not with the ideas and so forth, as sketched above and elaborated below, which our contemporary critical vogue has made commonplace enough, but with the *materials* per se. These are odd texts in several senses: their language (from the perspective of the reader of English) to varying degrees of intensity "not quite English," a language that both beckons with kinship and resists recognition. I will accommodate the needs of such readers, I hope, to the degree that it is possible to do so. But I hope (utopically) as well to resist reducing Scottish literature either to an appendage of English or to an exemplum of contemporary critical fashion, so I may also make certain demands of such readers at odds with the accommodation of their needs; that is, I will ask (beginning with Exhibit A below) for an encounter with this material not reducible to any readily apparent domesticating scheme, or in which I may not provide sufficiently explicit orientation. (I hope for orientation—and not domesticating scheme—to emerge from this encounter with the texts, rather than presenting texts too wholly controlled by my own overt and covert critical manipulations: or to tip the scales a bit at least from their usual balance in this regard.) I will present material that establishes, I hope, the dialectical nature and importance of cultural self-consciousness in Scottish literature, but that also makes its own divergent claims on our attention. Perhaps this is a commonplace observation. In any event, I ask the reader to come to this material without seeking to make it—and without asking me to make it—too familiar too quickly. We are, after all (I am, at least—and you?) crossing a border here: what do we find on the other side? That is the question.

In W. N. Herbert's "Horse Island" (1993), Horse Island is clearly a figure for Scotland as a whole.[3] It is also, even more pointedly, a figure for some place that is *not* Scotland. "Horse Island," in short, represents both Herbert's engagement and rejection of Scottish national identity anxiety—in either case an acknowledgement that this issue is the first given, the premise to be either engaged or rejected but not to be denied: we are either in Scotland or quite definitively not in Scotland, but we are nowhere else. The story begins: "When I crossed the small strip of causeway separating Horse Island from the rest of Scotland, I had a fleeting sense of leaving, not just one country, but one dimension, and entering another." To be separated from "the rest of Scotland" is to be, of course, still within that land, and in any case a causeway does not separate but join: for Herbert, though, in this case, or for his narrator Mr. Osmond Dips, the causeway separates and he finds himself emphatically to be Someplace Else. Or so at least it seems. Needless to say this sort of travel is impossible, and in any case, in reality, there is no causeway between Horse Island and the Scottish mainland. We are, on this crossing, in a world of (among other things) opposites that mirror one another.

"I felt light-headed," says Dips, "as though on a mountain-top rather than—literally—at sea level." This curious relation—being in a place that is two places at once, or neither one nor the other place—is both entirely substantial, as much so as dizziness on a mountaintop or the literality of sea level, and quite insubstantial, as lightheadedness suggests as well, and as "a fleeting sense" indicates. Scotland and not-Scotland are curiously, ambiguously related, and the ambiguity of the relation is a matter of determinate presence and of insubstantial, passing notice: on the one hand not quite to be credited, on the other not possible to avoid. "It would not be long," at any rate, "before the tide would sweep back into the narrow channel, and water had already begun to shine between the stones": what has been joined is already in the process of re-separating, and what re-separated rejoined. And although this process may be assumed to repeat itself as naturally as the ebb and flow of the tide, for Mr. Dips there is, apparently, no turning back.

A dooble world.

Horse Island is "in" Scotland—off the coast northwest of Ullapool, in the lea of Wester Ross—but it is Scotland, or some version of it, that we find in "Horse Island." We might say that what Horse Island (or at least "Horse Island") represents is a Scotland that is *not*: perhaps a utopian or dystopian vision, or perhaps both at once, but certainly an alternative vision. What distinguishes the place first is, as Dips puts it, "this manic sense of energy," and as the place is defined at the opening in relation to "the *rest* of Scotland," this may be a clue as to the nature of the relation: Horse Island is Scotland unrestful, or even Scotland raised from the dead. Whether Osmond Dips comes here for his holiday to rest in peace or to energize himself, or both, is another of the story's doubled uncertainties.

(Herbert discusses writing in Scots in an "Author's Note" to *Dundee Doldrums* [1991], in terms of "the buried life of that unfortunate tongue, and how, in one given instance, it was exhumed." But *Dundee Doldrums* is only part exhumation, and part invention; an "experiment," like Victor Frankenstein's, on the body of the Scots tongue, involving the galvanization of what seemed never more to be—the "merely antiquarian," "a subject tongue, persecuted into rural corners and forgotten"—and what never was in the first place—"my first work in Scots." A dooble tongue in more than one sense.)[4]

"Horse Island," as it turns out, *is* in fact a place where the dead walk, or at least, in a manner of speaking, talk, and where the living, in complementary fashion, are quite fantastically preoccupied

(preoccupied being exactly the word) with what has already
been—to the extent that they treat even the present and future as
purely archival matter. This is still again Scotland as we know it—
Scotland of the Immortal Memory and of Dundee, "a place," in
Herbert's phrase, "where nothing happened with deadening in-
tensity"[5]—and again not that Scotland, where "The whole atmo-
sphere of modern life, / particularly urban life, has no past,"[6] and
where the dead may haunt us but most emphatically do not them-
selves live: "Deid's deid," "Sen for the deid remeid is none . . ."
(Dunbar).[7]

Who is dead and who is living turns out to be precisely the ques-
tion that "Horse Island" turns upon.

> Upon my arrival in the village I was examined by the Doctor and the
> Magistrate. Notes were taken as to my occupation, date of birth, height,
> weight and the colour of my eyes; all the usual passport stuff. Then the
> samples were taken. Small squares were cut from each item of clothing
> and gummed to my form. Snippets of hair, blood and urine samples,
> even some excrement (I had been advised by the tourist board in Ulla-
> pool not to "go" before I went, as it were). Most of these items were
> placed in little cubic compartments in a plastic tray that was then fro-
> zen. I had politely but insistently to refuse the doctor's requests for "a
> wee drappie sperm."

As it were: not to "go" until after he's gone, Dips prefigures here
the curious status of Horse Island's dead (to which we'll come in a
moment): this seems, in fact, to be "another dimension," although
it is not clear, given the hedging reference to a passport, whether
this is also in fact "another country." Call it the subjunctive. (At the
same time the pun on "go" suggests that to go to Horse Island is
to go to the toilet: with reference to this place, to have gone is to
have located oneself in "this manic sense of energy," the excre-
mental as last bastion of the energetic. Further, to locate oneself in
this unlikely—not to say unpleasant—connection is to locate one-
self at once in one's body and beyond it, in its detached and pre-
served traces.) The specimens of Mr. Dips are appended to his
"form"—that is, to the paper representation of his (as it were) vital
statistics—or cubed in plastic and frozen. To refuse in this setting
to produce a semen sample either denies the future or insists on
preserving it from the catalog of what has already been: at least
some part of some future, or some fantasy of or desire for one. It
is, in "Horse Island," impossible to tell. Future or no future, living
or dead, going or not yet having gone, holiday or evacuation,
bodily form or paper form, Scotland or Notland: each of these op-

positions is governed and held in thorough equipoise by the sub-
junctive mood.

Of course the might-be or should-have-been of the subjunctive
is what the Islanders in their archival zeal appear most concerned
to master: "If we didna make every effort to assimilate aa the mate-
rial relevant tae ony given subject, then we might be forced tae ex-
perience its consequences, however far-fetched." And so the
cataloging continues.

> I then signed a document which stated in English, Scots, Gaelic and
> neo-Latin, that any drawn, painted or photographed images, cuttings
> of plants, clippings of the local paper or any literary work found on
> Horse Island, as well as any writings I might do, should all be listed on
> my departure. If at all possible, copies should be deposited with the
> Chief Archivist.
>
> The magistrate now pressed another small card into my hand. It had
> my name and home address on it, as well as a picture of me crossing
> the causeway (which I had not been aware of being taken).
>
> I was then photographed an extraordinary number of times: straight
> passport, then casual, then as the photographer imagined me (as Na-
> poleon, for some reason), then with the doctor examining my genitals
> (I thought at the time that this might have been revenge for refusing
> the semen sample), then with the magistrate apparently condemning
> me to death, then shaking hands with the Assistant Archivist, shaking
> hands with the Town Geographer and, at last, a group shot on the steps
> of the Incomers Building.
>
> I stepped down onto the main street of the village (indeed its only
> street) in a complete daze.

The present and the future here are entirely spoken for by the fe-
tishists of the past, and the past gathered with absolute rigor (and
wacky fancy) toward some unknowable future. To escape the expe-
rience of consequences: the archivists' zeal is a kind of necrophilia,
an embrace of or surrender to what is done, done for, done in,
going, or gone—a necrophiliac's dream of inoculation against Life.
This is again a matter of both Scotland and not: a place in which it
is possible for "nothing" to happen "with deadening intensity" and
a place where the past is adored (or devoured) rather than ignored
or patronized. Dips here is subjected at once to a mastery of the
uncertain and to uncertainty run rampant.

(In a daze: but whether this daze proceeds from a subjective or
an objective source is itself, as we might expect by now, quite un-
clear:

I was unable to focus much on my surroundings, as the paving-stones and the walls of the houses all glittered intensely in the late light. I couldn't tell if this was some quality of the stone, or my own slightly dazzled state of mind.

Even the question of who is the zealous cataloguer here is an open—or rather, doubled—one. Dips complains ["You people compartmentalize everything. You itemize butter dishes, you scalp strangers, you reduce the world to a list of lists!"] and asks one of his hosts, "Where does it come from, your energy?" He is asked in return, "The real question is, where do you lose yours?" and told that "It's because your energies are so low that you resort to compartmentalizing everything." Dips, the visitor from Scotland, is *of* Horse Island and the most alien presence there.)

The Islanders' obsession with what is *done*—which is to say, with what is finished and what might not yet be, the "consequences, however far-fetched"—is not a matter of choice. They call it "the Tendency":

Maist people date the Tendency tae the first Statistical Account and an unusually enthusiastic minister called McIlwraith, but it wid be prudent to note that a bardic college was maintained on the site of Kinawe for mony hundreds of years afore that, and the poets of Gaelic Scotland were trained tae perform considerable mnemonic feats.

The bar in the hotel where Dips puts up is "full of portraits, both of regulars and hosts, stretching back across the generations," and, of the living locals drinking there, "few . . . were distinguishable in any way from their predecessors. Had the walls been lined with little mirrors, the effect would have been much the same. . . . In fact there was one figure (I got up and peered closely at a faded interior) who looked rather like me, reading by a lamp in the middle of the last century." The site of "Horse Island" is the perpetual present historical tense.

Thus if Dips is dazed and maddened by the Islanders' utter absorption in the world as "*objet trouvé*," as something done and ready to be known, he is panicked at the possibility of the reverse—that there is *no* past, that nothing or no one here is *ever* done. Studying the hotel restaurant's menu, he notes that "Burns, too, had apparently stayed in the hotel, and had left a small stanza on 'Mrs Semphill's Bannocks'" ("something about 'slappin' doon the farls' and flour flying about like powder from the buttocks of a fine lady") and—what "stretched even Kinawe's bounds of credibility"—that "the kitchen maintains a twenty-four hour service." (We are here again both nowhere conceivable but Scotland and not conceivably in Scotland at all.) The kitchen is "located in some indeterminate space behind the reception booth, and connected to the dining room by a long corridor," "dimly lit"—as available and remote as Horse Island itself—and when Dips arrives he hears a voice from behind the door: " 'Mrs Semphill, Mrs Semphill,' she was saying, 'Ur these roastit enough yet?' " "A sensation of stark terror flooded over me," he notes, "and I was gone in a second, before even thinking why." Back in his room, he calms himself "a little, concluding that of course it was a small island, and family names persisted, and, what's more, it was quite likely a descendent of Burns's cook would be working here still"; but he can't quite shake "the little nerve thrumming in my brain 'So what made ye jump, then?' "

The past of "Horse Island," ferociously tamed, as it were, in advance of itself, labelled, listed, and frozen for posterity, simply won't stay put. How very Scottish, we might say, or how very not. (All pasts are quite literally unavoidable by definition, but this one is more so.) The dead of this place lie in a "combined cemetery and sculpture park," the "two little towns of stone [facing] each other across a narrow valley"—although "it would have been hard to tell the two apart," so it might be more precise to say that the valley joins rather than separates the two, Death and Art, like another (imaginary) causeway. As it happens, "the haill clanjamfrie was swappit over, fifty years ago" by the Chief Archivist, who "decided one fine day that the symbolism was jist as interesting the ither weys aboot"; on another occasion the "Toun Photographer" is said to have exhumed some Victorian corpses, "got all the relevant bodies thegither in appropriate costume, transported them to the theatre," and photographed one "Lady Croma's soirée," a historical fact of a kind ("She held a salon every Thursday evenin" back in the 1870s)—the "picter" being then printed "in the *Chronicle* as though it hud jist happened."

And then, climactically, Dips visits "The Archive itself." The building looks to be "a cross between Greek temple and Scottish bungalow"—rather hard to picture—and is "set on a rectangular grassy mound which suggested much material was stored below ground." The main hall is "full of the inevitable glass cases, here displaying ordinary household objects from every period of the village's history," and Dips notes that "At least in these surroundings, the appearance of a museum was not unsuitable"—but this comfort is short-lived, as he immediately comes upon what the Assistant Archivist calls "our Unnatural History section," in which animals are positioned to display human foibles. Here was a recreation of a pub, with a drunken rabbit floundering on the floor while the landlord, a capercaillie, stood over him threateningly. Mice and rat regulars studied their pint pots carefully, ignoring the fracas.[8]

From Unnatural History then (a "Victorian genre," Dips notes), the all-powerful Chief Archivist leads us "down a stair" ("I noticed it had no bannisters"),[9] "deeper into the Archive" to "a section where the lights worked properly and the floor did not lean to one side or descend imperceptibly," a space filled with displays of butterflies arranged "in neatly organized rows" in glass cabinets, which prompts the Chief Archivist to reflect that "I've often thought we must diagnose Nature as an omnipotent schizophrenic, whose every uncontrollable whim is, uncontrollably, possible." Surely this is either Dips's nightmare or his fondest hope. At least he is entranced by the splendid variety of the butterflies, "as though a miniature nation had turned out in its finest garments to watch us pass," but the uncontrollable possibility that lies beyond is another story.

Finally they come to "another dim room of uncertain proportions." Here Dips is again requested—and again refuses—to produce a sperm sample, and is told, by way of entreaty, that eggs are collected "from our women guests" as well, and that "we don't normally experience any difficulty of this nature." When he asks "What do you do with all this genetic booty?" he is told: "Nothing. Nothing at all. We merely catalogue it, as we catalogue everything" because "we want to understand how all change occurs. Social change, psychological change, genetic change, mythic change." His next question is "what is it that you want to change?" but for this no answer is forthcoming. Instead his attention is directed to "a complicated mass of machinery crowded around a big jug," and "In the jug [is] a human head."

Dips:

> To say I was not prepared for this vision is to present my reaction in a restrained manner. I screamed quite suddenly and very loudly, and succeeded in alarming myself, the Archivist, the Doctor, and the Head. I refer to this last personage impersonally because, although I was told his name I could by no means associate this entity with a merely human title. For me he must remain the first Head. There were more, many more. There were, apparently, corridors of them.

If this is Scotland, if there is in fact no way of getting back from this place to "the rest," then Dips is in trouble. These Heads are "voluntary sacrifices" and not, in fact, alive—a light switched on reveals nothing but skulls—but they are nevertheless "keen to keep in touch." Here is what happens when Dips is connected to one via electrodes:

> All at once I began thinking in disjointed blurts. Jagged colours and shapes came into my head involuntarily. It was very frightening, as though you were in a plane and the clouds suddenly cleared; I felt I was much closer to the ground than I had realized, and that the 'ground' consisted of a startlingly unknown territory.
>
> None of this was linguistic, and there were scarcely any "images", in the visual sense. It just seemed like great slabs of something 'other' were intruding into my consciousness . . .
>
> I knew that time had ceased to operate for the duration of this sensation, and that this reformation of the very principle of duration would sustain itself as long as we maintained contact.

"Most of us," he is told comfortingly when he returns "totally disorientated and somewhat ashamed," "cannae thole the way the Heids go on, but ye get used tae it." He is complimented on his "recovery time" ("very quick"), offered a job as Junior Archivist (which he apparently accepts, or succumbs to), is thanked for the sperm sample ("an invariable first reaction," and his "fine and vigorous"), and here "Horse Island" ends.

I tell this story at some length because most readers will be unfamiliar with it, and in order to establish that the inverted doublings of its vision—Scotland and not-Scotland, knowable and unknowable, past and not past, dead and not yet, living and not quite—are not merely schematic but imbue virtually every detail of the telling: what is most inescapable in "Horse Island" is the confusion of identity—historical, national, personal—and the sense that this confusion is at once (another doobling) desperately dreadful and exhilarating. I tell the story in the first place because these inverted doublings themselves speak of characteristically Scottish preoccupations with a national history felt to be both uniquely burdensome and uniquely pregnant with possibilities unrealized.

If it is problematic to speak in such terms—as if the literature of Scotland has no life other than as an emblem of the place, as if the whole corpus were wholly overdetermined, every signifier shackled to the same sign, all roads lead-

> A small nation's memory is not smaller than the memory of a large one and so can digest the existing material more thoroughly.
> —Kafka

ing to Caledonia—it is because this leaves no room for a life to be lived beyond the terms of some not particularly nourishing national identity. As Herbert himself protests elsewhere, in "Owre Mony Nemms" (from *Sharawaggi*, his collaborative collection with Robert Crawford):

> Thuv harpit oan at me aboot Britain,
> o Scoatlan and Englan;
> Eh huvnae a clue whut thur oan aboot.
> Eh ken anely thi peelreestie o thi yirth
> an thon's no gote a nemm.[10]

And "Horse Island" itself cautions us likewise with regard to the certainty of naming where we are when, smug as any vacationer, we cross the border (via a nonexistent causeway). Part of what "Horse Island" is up to is the affirmation of a possibility that is neither Scotland nor its anti-self but a place, rather—pick it off a map, call it what you will—not prematurely knowable by its name. In fact, "Horse Island"—in its relentless inversions and its destabilization of the knowable or nameable—seems designed to remind us that if we name this place "Scotland," or think that in naming it such we perform an act of meaning, we are quite wrong (or at least, not quite right). In this case, it seems, you *can't* get there from here.

But this vision of the nameless—of what's "no gote a nemm"—is framed for us here by a manic compulsion to name and to know by name, to identify. If it *is* the case that you can't get there from here (to Scotland from "Scotland"), the assertion of that fact would seem itself to be an inversion, an attempted negation, of the opposing claim—the endless harping on national, as opposed to nameless, identity—which Herbert's story pursues in equal measure. Osmond Dips, crossing to Horse Island, is both leaving Scotland and arriving there—no escape, no otherwhere imaginable—where the language is Scots, as opposed to his own English, and where even Archimedes is said (in jest, but nevertheless) to have spoken "the Doric."

And as Herbert writes in "The Hermitage" (again from *Sharawaggi*),

> Thae wha sing lyk this
>   ur exiles ivrywhaur.[11]

The trope evokes an eternal incomer's perspective, like a Flying Scotsman eternally cut off from and hankering for home, disembodied as the dreadful heads of "Horse Island" and just as keen to keep in touch. The problematic nature of Scottish cultural self-consciousness as the donnée, vortex, or prism of Scottish literature, in the context of cultural domination and the gaze of inanition, characteristically casts questions of national identity in the light of crisis—inducing fevers high-grade, low-grade, or denied—and sustains,

> Culloden
> where the sun shone
> on the feeding raven.
> Let it be forgotten!
> —I. C. Smith

when it does not expunge, an effort to keep the national culture alive. And this condition produces yet another doubling: what is lost becomes what is inescapable, precisely the circumstance elaborated in "Horse Island."

ﻼ   ﻼ   ﻼ

Questions of the past, and of cultural identity, domination, and anxiety, are all strongly identified with questions of language: the deid and the leid are aptly rhymed. Edwin Morgan, from *Nothing Not Giving Messages*:

> It's always very hard to define something like Scottishness . . .

> I think the tendency in the past has been for this to be felt strongly, that we must be Scottish, we must show this. Possibly this goes back to Scott and Burns or even further. It depends partly on the whole situation of Scotland with its unfinished political history, loose ends all over the place . . .

> It is perhaps a regional problem but it's more acute in Scotland which has a historical identity in any case and is a place where there are already traditions in existence, and these issues are not being served by the present situation. It is partly also the purely practical situation of having publishers almost entirely in London who perhaps can't be expected to be very interested in the exact expression of Scottish language or Scottish feeling . . .[12]

From "Registering the Reality of Scotland" (1971):

> There is undeniably something very attractive about the idea of a language expressing and preserving the "soul" of a people.

> Lowland Scots today may be only the shreds of a language, but they are remarkably tenacious and expressive threads which show no signs of disappearing.

But still:

The answer to the question, what do people speak in Scotland? cannot be given directly, since it depends to an unusual extent on social relations and social habits, and the instability, the mixture of Scots and English forms, which one can hear every day, is so thinly reflected in literature and journalism that the realities of the linguistic situation either seem to be poorly recognized, or are felt to be unproductive. On the whole, people seem not to *want* to recognize them. Newspapers, for example, reporting interviews with working-class citizens, never report what such speakers actually say—it is all tidied up and normalized into English, and yet quotation marks are used, even though no local reader of the newspaper, if he thought about it, would believe it was a direct quotation.[13]

> —We cantantabawr, tantingko backspetter now!
> —Edwin Morgan

"The Beatnik in the Kailyard" (1962):

No country which has once been independent, and is then overshadowed in union with a more powerful partner, can develop naturally and happily. Its political history is officially closed, but emotionally it remains unfinished. Its cultural traditions soon begin to show a lack of integration, and though this does not preclude fine work in a variety of styles it does mean that the steady nurturing and enriching of traditions which is characteristic of the greatest cultures is constantly frustrated, either by a sentimental native conservatism or by desperate attempts to imitate the modes of the dominating neighbor culture.

MacDiarmid . . . wanted the [Scottish Renascence] movement to be *modern*, in the sense that it would risk dealing with contemporary subjects and would experiment with new forms, but he also wanted it to be unmistakably *Scottish*, if possible by a revival and extension of the Scots vocabulary. MacDiarmid's own poetry is a good enough guarantee that this double aim can be realized; but looking at the movement as a whole, I think it is clear that the language problem, the problem of Scottishness, has proved something of an incubus, and the fact that it is a real and unavoidable incubus (shake it off, and you leave scars and puncture marks) makes it all the more difficult for the Scottish writer to develop integrally.[14]

"The Resources of Scotland" (1972):

The Scottish writer's dilemma today is that while he may want to keep helping a general literary Scots to develop, whether in the eclectic or

"Synthetic Scots" tradition of Hugh MacDiarmid or in some other way, he is on the other hand strongly urged . . . to write on the basis of the actual language of men.

But what guarantee have we got that what we are doing is distinctive and could not have been produced anywhere else?

The mature answer would be that there is no such guarantee and that it does not matter: Scottish writers must simply write as well as they can, and leave it to others to decide whether their provenance stands out, and what value it infuses into the work. Unfortunately Scotland is not in a mature state, and that mature answer would still be something of a luxury. So long as the political situation remains unhappy, the economic situation unhappier, and the language situation as complex and confused as it is, a Scottish writer will tend to be tugged, kicking against the pricks as hard as he likes, into at least the but if not the ben of involvement with the whole north-of-the-border ethos problem. Here, bad vibrations abound for many.

> If time is in the blink of an eye
>   there's not
> a ripple crossed our cornea
>   since
> the restoration of 1782, not a
>   lash fallen.
> Instead, our eyelids are
>   nailed to cheekbone
> and brow with the flags of
>   freedom
> to an infinity of dessications.
>   —Robert Mackenzie

Is history not the opium of the imagination?[15]

"Modern Makars Scots and English" (1954):

The poet in Scotland has some peculiar advantages, and some peculiar difficulties. Both stem from the fact that he has to make a deliberate choice as to what language he is going to write in—a choice between English and Lallans, or in some cases between English, Lallans and Gaelic. He might be envied for this kind of ambidexterity, for his ability to produce effects in one language which are not possible in another. "I am really sorry," said Lord Cockburn, "for the poor one-tongued Englishman." Yet . . . the "poor one-tongued Englishman" may well be thought to have the last laugh as far as poetry is concerned, for if a poet is to develop naturally and completely he wants to have a basic linguistic medium that he can take for granted . . .[16]

౩ఌ   ౩ఌ   ౩ఌ

> Yet the essence of a nation is that all individuals have many things in common, and also that they have forgotten many things.
>
> —Ernest Renan

Sharawaggi: Poems in Scots (1990) is concerned first, last and always—although not exclusively—with Scots itself, "the language problem, the problem of Scottishness." In examining this work I want to explore what this preoccupation means—that is, not only what it means, in the Scottish context, to be preoccupied with questions of cultural identity, but also what it means for those questions to be identified with questions of language. Here again the living and the dead (or thi livin an thi deid) stand in problematic relation to one another: language in *Sharawaggi*, Scots, is "the livin leid"— the living language—that speaks the body of itself, but does so in order "Tae wak a' Scoatlan's stour o deid."[17] These "bits o leid" I quote from Crawford's poem "Semiconductors" (the title a thrifty metaphor for the situation I'm describing, suggesting as it does both imperfect transmission and newfangled, previously unheard of, unimagined capabilities). "The livin leid" is a new inspiration, the breath of a new body, a new construction, an invention, but it is also quite wholly and inescapably bound up in—directed toward, drawn from, rhymed with—what life remains in the "stour o deid."[18] Although this is only to say what might be said of every language, every utterance, as it consumes, transforms, exalts, and ploughs under the flesh of its own living history, it is to say again that the case of Scots illuminates this general condition in the pointed context of cultural crisis and struggle.

The language itself represents a contradiction in terms: a womb and a tumulus, expressive and always in some measure, by definition, ineffective, a body of loss (only a semiconductor), a body of the dead that inspires the living who animate the body of the dead: a closed circle. To write in Scots as aggressively as Crawford and Herbert do is to embrace wholly the incubus of "the language problem, the problem of Scottishness"—not to shake the demon off, and not to succumb to it, but to embrace it (by means of electrodes

> I have seen words,
> Seen them with thanks too,
>   shivering, become
> Fragile and useless.
>
> —Burns Singer

if necessary): to master and direct its ways, to put it to use, at once to be transformed by it and to blast it (so to speak) out of the water.[19] (It is a protean enterprise, like Stephen Dedalus's in *Ulysses*, wrestling with his own incubi as he walks half-blind along Sandymount Strand, thinking to himself about language and history—a shout in the street: history and language, wisdom-concealing, shape-changing, enveloping, embraceable, and not the last word by a long shot.) The incubus as developmental stage: although both Crawford and Herbert explicitly and pervasively sustain their engagement with the problem and the resources of Scottishness, both explicitly insist as well on the horizon of this engagement—its limits, borders, constraints—and seek a radical transformation of its parameters, a way not so much beyond Scotland as through it and out the other side.

Sharawaggi[20] is constructed as an exercise in contradiction, in the dynamics of the dooble tongue: the first part of the book, "Sterts & Stobies" (published separately in pamphlet form in 1985) consists of thirteen poems by Crawford followed by "The Flyting of Crawford and Herbert" (a collaborative piece which is itself, in the tradition of flyting, an extravagance of contradiction) followed by thirteen poems by Herbert; the latter part of the book gives a longer sequence of pieces from each poet in turn, first Crawford, then Herbert. All of these *Poems in Scots* are concerned (on their face) with the linguistic problem of Scottishness, and in many this concern is explicitly thematized. Both Crawford's and Herbert's opening poems in "Sterts & Stobies"—Crawford's "Cock o' the North" and Herbert's "Bullseye," both titles emblems of aggressive thrust—are emblematic in this regard, and in their concern too to push beyond this obsessive territory toward what Morgan calls a "mature state" (if not toward some fantastical Horse Island).

Crawford's "Cock" is an address to a definitive type—the problem of Scottishness incarnate: "Auld Member / O' the Club o' Legless Scoatlan," "ya bloated big alumnus," "Big cocked-up Wallace" "Wi wet-luke sporrans an kail-nouveau art-humus / Fur poatit pines." This figure is at once a modern aberration and a dead letter from auld lang syne—"kail-nouveau"—committing the double crime of enslavement to and betrayal of Scotland's history, blending sentimentalism and a kind of brutal disregard: "Yir monumental 'Naw!'" (It is a prototypical figure of the Burns Club member in MacDiarmid's many flytings of same.) This Cock's art is a reduced article. A man whoring after his incubus, given over to "maister-baitin nyaff / O' hauf-biled airticles lik sheep's-heid broath / A' spilt an fozie oan a tartan cloath":[21] such a figure is the defining frame of reference, or at least the first point of departure, for Crawford's work in *Shara-waggi*—that, and Crawford's furious judgment upon it:

> Awa git changed
> Alutterlie, git stuffed, git high, git disestranged
> Fae a' yon world ya cannae see fur greetin
> An when yir Club togs up fur its big Meetin
> GIT TAE FUCK!

Herbert begins on similar footing with "Bullseye": "Thi Stotsman cometh wi a meteoaphoric expreshun." Herbert glosses "Stotsman" as "the Scottish eunuch," so a steer rather than a bull: though "Yince he wiz allutirly a bull," he is (like the "Auld Member / O' the Club o' Legless Scoatlan") something less now.[22] His "expreshun"—his face, primarily, but also his language—is metaphoric, something unexpressed, an indirection (a semiconductor: metaphor here is an intensive form of the condition of language generally—an embodiment of loss, a conjuring of the unexpressed). Herbert instructs us: "luke'um richt in thi fiss an discern / thi malegrugous girn o a bellit leid" ("malegrugous—grim, looking discontented; girn—complaint, a contorted expression; bellit—robbed of power; leid—language"). This is an analogous figure to Crawford's—"A soor, surly-gurly, tyauvit baist / wi a resemblance absurdos still til a bull"—defined by its relation to the problem of Scottishness in terms of some fruitless nostalgia, and with explicit reference in this case to the language problem: the specific site of loss and power.[23] And Herbert's response is a disguised variant of Crawford's anger: "Pity thi dool o thi Pair Auld Stot— / inna bull's ee'," he says, turning an object of pity into a target and in any case, again, quite fed up.

> This exclusive concern with language, like an excessive preoccupation with race, has its dangers and its drawbacks. Such exaggerations enclose one within a specific culture, considered as national; one limits oneself, one hems oneself in. One leaves the heady air that one breathes in the vast field of humanity in order to enclose oneself in a conventicle with one's compatriots. Nothing could be worse for the mind; nothing could be more disturbing for civilization.
>
> —Renan

For Herbert as for Crawford, then, the first object on the landscape of *Sharawaggi* is a cultural dead end, the very problem of Scottishness itself. Nothing in these opening poems suggests any alternative in thematic terms: only anger (a shout in the street) or mocking condescension, and darkly energetic, glossary-resistant language—states of negativity all. Scottishness here is an incubus that both Crawford and Herbert seek to leave behind but cannot afford to suppress. Both, for instance, offer Scots translations or versions of other poets' work—Crawford's "Fae the Vietnamese o Che-Lan-Vien," "Huy-Can," and "Do-Huy-Nhiem" ("Translatit wi Mai-Lan"), "Eftir thi German o Paul Celan," and "Eftir thi French o Michel Deguy"; Herbert's "After Neruda," "After the Italian of Mario Luzi," "from the Italian of Cavalcante," and "after the German of Hölderlin"—giving themselves (so to speak) a leg up and over the border, beyond the landscape of "Bullseye" and "Cock o' the North." (This is another gesture anticipated by MacDiarmid, whose *A Drunk Man Looks at the Thistle* incorporates Scots versions of poems from the Russian, French, Belgian French, and German, as well as a bit of Dante untranslated.) Herbert's "Owre Mony Nemms," quoted above, is his piece "After Neruda," and in itself perfectly represents the status of these efforts: the poem makes a plain rejection of what Morgan calls "the whole situation of Scotland with its unfinished political history," both in thematic terms and in its Chilean Spanish source, and instead of Scotland offers a vision of some mystic, if not universal, variety—"Whan Eh bidit wi thi roots" "an whan Eh habbilt wi a peebil."[24] This is a vision of what is nameless and thus unconquerable, ever-living, of what is only and always a marvel of the senses, roots which "gustit mair nor thi flooirs" and a pebble which "spangit lyk a chantir."[25] But at the same time, "Owre Mony Nemms" is clearly so far from its Neruda as to be in fact nowhere else *but* Scotland, a place not of the nameless but of over-many names, a place full up with its own history and no way to go further. (Herbert's mystic vision too is markedly one of reduction— "*anely* thi peelreestie o thi yirth," roots and a pebble—a coming down of circumstances and a seeking after redemption and power *there*.) In "Owre Mony Nemms" Herbert does make a border crossing, and does claim respite from the incubus, but only in some measure; he also finds himself at ground zero, crossing the border of Scotland as if walking backwards looking homeward.

"Owre Mony Nemms" follows immediately upon "Bullseye," and comes as a kind of alternative to the predicament delineated there, the indication of a way forward following upon the discovery of a dead end. This way forward is at once seriously constrained and driven by an aggressive sense of necessity, and by a sense that the current moment defines both the constraint and the necessity in new terms, representing a new range of possibilities and frustrations. As such, it is directly in line with the dominant tradition of Scottish resistance: both MacDiarmid and Burns see their own contemporary moments in the same way, as the historical embodiment of a threshold opening onto new possibilities, making new requirements, marked by new difficulties, posing new dangers.

The incubus is tenacious, recalcitrant: it defines a place in Herbert's "The laroch,"

> whaur a past can be graspd
> but nivir regaind
> an deid hopes keep
> lyk a fossil fruit.

Nevertheless, efforts persist. Crawford's "Eftir the Vampires" imagines the coming of "the Wulcat," which

> ript ther wallies aff,
> An drave a muckle stake thro puir mixt herts
> That squaached wi a mumpy soon o fartin chaff
> Deflatin doon tae gie us a' sic sterts—[26]

so it's not we ourselves who do the ghouls in and give ourselves a new beginning, but *deus ex machina*, the Wulcat, which gives it to us—

> Sic shoacks an new beginnins sae, nae doot,
> We'll gang roon, silver-buttont, cross the laund
> Afresh, eftir the vampires, strikin oot
> Fae the undeid shugbog tae yon path beyond.[27]

"Nae doot" is, no doubt, somewhat ironic, and suggests at least a bit of uncertainty. This is still a vision from the shugbog and not from the path beyond—still an utter absorption in the incubus—but it is also a vision, at least, of *some* beyond, "shoacks an new beginnins," and the (imminent or immanent) demise of the undead. *Eftir* has it both ways: coming after the vampires means both that they are already gone before and that they are not gone at all, that they are still the objects of our pursuit.

Herbert's "The Renaissance of Song," which imagines just that—or at least "*a renaissance o sang!*" (my emphasis)—suggests a similarly uncertain transcendence. The landscape here embodies a dark vision more domestic and immediate than a world of the un-

dead, but no less Scot-specific than the vampires, eunuchs, and
devotees of kail-nouveau we've already seen: a world in which
"auld mithir Lirklips / hoolocht owre thi land"—that is, "rolled like
a rockslide" over "a floor of a tenement, both the level and the area
between doors and stairs," in Herbert's gloss—"inna cauld sea's
grouse and grue ['shiver with fear, cold or repulsion'], / an doon
thi sealblack deeps, / the weelthrainit steps": a vision of a drown-
ing, and of the world ("thi land") reduced to the calculable floor-
space of a tenement, a reduction not mystical and natural like that
of "Owre Mony Nemms" but social and economic, "weelthrainit—
worn by constant use, like a familiar tune." A vision too of "aa'ur
weans" staring "aboot lyk hotties" ("those who have some message
pinned to their backs of which they are unaware"), a vision of a
world crashing and a people "dumbfounert" who nevertheless
"thirsty raise / a renaissance o sang!" Irony again holds this song
from rising further, but it does rise—like a barbaric yawp of
youth—and it does signify, or claim to signify, a rebirth.

Of what? Again and again it is a rebirth of language as much as
anything else, anything more (so to speak) substantive—a lan-
guage that establishes currency (or community) only in establish-
ing the uncertainties, illusions, and essentially combative politics of
any such function for language. It is this vision of a rebirth of lan-
guage in the spirit of radical rampant doobleness, of synthesis
without borders, that occupies the heart of *Sharawaggi*. Crawford's
"Fur Thi Muse o Synthesis" is a paean to the dooble tongue, to
synthesis as invention and intervention, not simply historical given
but political possibility. It begins:

> Interkat intercommuner, intercommunin
> At aw leid's interfaces, skeich
> Tae interpone a hooch that intermells
> An interverts auld jorrams tae reconduct
> Aureat thru lingua franca, intercommoun
> Thru joie-de-vivre-wurds, guttir thru dictionar, it's yirsel's
> Thi ane I T, thi richt wurdbank . . .

The passage reads, in the sluggishly precise English of Crawford's
facing-page translation, like so:

> Intricate negotiator between factions at variance, having intercourse at
> all language's interfaces, apt to startlingly interpose a cry of joy that
> intermingles and appropriates to a new, unfamiliar use old slow, mel-
> ancholy boatsongs to reconduct high diction through common speech,
> the language of conversation through exclamations of delight, gutter

through dictionary, it's you who are the only Information Technology, the true word-bank . . .

This is an English of glossary extended into narrative: it at once embodies an argument for the sleek power of Scots, comparatively speaking, and implies that any language put to hegemonic use—made to stand in for another, to speak another's meaning—is bound by its very powers to fall short. And in fact the poem argues for a kind of relentless coupling of languages, a multiplicitous, promiscuous linguaphilia. Crawford's synthetic alternative to language in its hegemonic mode is specifically Scottish, a synthesis of tongues and modes both historical and modern—"Intercepting delight, wildcat dotmatrixed forever from Jamieson's *Dictionary of the Scottish Language*" ("Interclosin delicht, / Wulcat dotmatrixed fur aye fae Jamieson")—but the Scottish, in this case, is a sign for a language without borders, a vision not of cultural or national but cosmic identity. It may "appear confused nonsense to fools" ("kythe hirdumdirdum / Tae gowks") but it has "an oblique look of beauty" with the power "to dislocate light from total ruin, and to consecrate people alive and lively again" ("a gledge o beauty," "tae ratch licht fae skau, an tae sacre / Fowk vivual an vieve again").

If the language of *Sharawaggi* is an embodiment of negativity, then, in relation to the English its glosses parry, it is also so in relation to the incubus of Scottishness, and thus an embodiment of affirmation beyond the anxiety of national identity: an affirmation of linguistic renaissance (in the general context of penury, inanition, and catastrophe) that subverts the very premise of identity as a national phenomenon. Scotland here is the place that is not a nation—precisely what it is—and this condition represents not, as we might expect, a loss of identity but a precarious breakthrough to some previously unimaginable, unspeakable conception.

Crawford's vision of a language defined by the crossing of linguistic borders, a language "that maks / Regenerate thi stolum o Scoatlan" ("which makes regenerate the large, broken off fragment of Scotland") is ambiguously either a current linguistic reality or an exhortation and anticipation: its "gledge o beauty" "*will* magnetize metal," its "pygmies of phonemes ['lusbirdans o phonemes'] *have leapt* to stand on the moon" (my emphases), its call coming (has it come?) "when the poets who came to the keyboard of the language as if they were the last folk to be invited to a party" ("lik piper's invites") discover and herald its coming. Crawford's synthesis, like Herbert's "renaissance o sang," is real, a conception not without substance, but it emerges tenuously in a landscape of reduced circumstances and last-ditch efforts, a landscape of "total ruin," and it ends (in these two poems) just when its appearance is announced.

The consecrated rebirth that Crawford and Herbert envision is to be mediated by language alone, but their thematic emphasis is less on the rebirth itself (and on the powers and virtues of border-lessness) than on vigorous persistence in negativity toward the forces of its obstruction: this is a renaissance against all odds, back to the wall. Crawford's "Thi Unbiggars" celebrates "Yon Scoats un-biggars o waas, wir Calgacusses o thi imaginashun" ("those Scottish unbuilders of walls, our Calgacusses of the imagination"), whose doing is all undoing, aimed at the border-building work of those—Roman or English—"still heapin stanes oan thi Hadrian's Waa o ther Culchur." The unbiggars—"Alexander Graham Bell, John Logie Baird, Thomson Lord Kelvin, and Hugh MacDiarmid"—"teach us our knowledge of our way out" ("learn us / Wir wayken-nin"); they represent "wir leid ayont back hauds" ("our language beyond barriers"). But again, the world in which such assertions are made is a world that has, for the most part, no use for them, a world that puffs up and trivializes them, feeds on and denies them—a world not "beyond barriers" but constituted *by* barriers: barriers of national and class identity that render any transgression neutralized.

> Auld Bell medd loats o Americans rich; an Kelvin
> Wiz Loarded an becam pairt o thi leid;
> But yous, Baird, makar o TV in Trinidad,
> An MacDiarmid thinkin o China in Milngavie—
> Whit did yous get? Yi fucked yirsels an wer deid.

Old Bell made lots of Americans rich; and Kelvin was Lorded and be-came part of the language; but you, Baird, inventor of television in Trinidad, and MacDiarmid thinking about China in Milngavie—what did you get? You screwed yourselves and were dead.

> If yi wur lucky they nemmd a schule eftir yi
> In Helensburgh; if yi wernae, they lukit
> A wee bit embarrassed and left ut tae nice-gabbit fowk
> Fae Oaxfurd tae polately imply yi wer a load o shite.

If you were lucky they named a school after you in Helensburgh; if you were not, they looked a little bit embarrassed and left it to people in Oxford with fussy tastes in food to imply politely that you were a load of crap.

"Eftir yous ther ar nae waas," Crawford asserts, "After you there are no walls"—the unbiggars represent a creative, destructive force—but their names are written "in the sleep of language" ("i thi leid's sleep"); although these "nemms" represent "wir wurld" (our world, a Scotticism that doesn't make it at all into Crawford's English gloss) and the "buzz-saa'd" demise of "Aa yon toapiaries o R P English" ("All those topiaries of Received Pronunciation English"), the unbuilders remain defined by the negation they seek to negate, like their prototype Calgacus named by Romans, his native name forever unknown.

Workers of the dooble world, the unbiggars preeminently are acolytes of nothingness where something (anything) means a wall, where the wall defines all. Each of the figures Crawford names represents negation—of distance in time and space, of the unthinkable barriers to communication, Absolute Zero, Synthetic Scots: unbiggars, great levellers. Each of these negations represents an affirmation as well, of course, an impulse toward some kind of common measure, a vision of radical commonality, of rampant borderlessness; but this impulse is compromised, neutralized, even in its realization. Each seeks a release from gravitational pull, from empire, an effort to establish a non-relation by obliterating borders and distance. There is little to say of this release, however, or of the condition it is to deliver us into, other than that its premise is (the hardest thing imaginable) the imagination of the absence of borders, and that it promises, in commonality, renewal. The Archival Heads of "Horse Island" are one figure for this premise and this renewal, and the poems in *Sharawaggi* are another. Their language is both a negation—of English and of earlier, more rural, and more traditionally grounded forms of synthetic Scots—and a glimpse of the pleasures and the powers that lie on the far side of this negation.

A glimpse, a gledge of beauty. Often enough there is scarcely even that, scarcely more than raw refusal: Herbert's "And Death Must Wait" comes down (quite literally, down the page) to a taunt that

> daith that canna salivate
> in breid-desirin
> deid-man's jaas
>
> maun wait, maun wait:
> *an daith himsel maun wait!*

And (or but) this taunt rises out of (or seeps from beneath) a world of

Gnipper an gnappir, pangin yir wame,
yi grist ma seed, ma load
shot,
ma luv-shank's marra
sookit oot
by daith's vacuum[28]

Herbert's landscape here is at once a matter of lovemaking and of
death, in either case of final expenditure: the language of the
poem, in dooble fashion, is such that we suspend our reading be-
tween metaphors of creation (or expression) and destruction (or
absorption), sex and death each the tenor and each the vehicle of
the other. In either case, although "daith retreats" ("vanquisht by
vagina's / generous saalt gape"), it remains "hungry," and its hun-
ger so pervasive, reaching even to the touch of love and hope of
generation, that simply saying *"No"* to it takes up all a man's (or
poem's) breath. "And Death Must Wait" speaks of staving off the
void, but staving it off to what end—toward what notion of Life
instead—remains obscure, ambiguous, conflicted: "luv-shank's
marra / sookit oot." A largely impersonal sexual possibility, a tem-
porary defeat of death, a dream of a desire for bread: even if there
is not much here—or if what is here is presented in the shadowy
terms of a last gasp—the poem celebrates the experience of coming
to know that no negation is absolute, that of "yi grist" no less than
"ma seed," of "daith" no less than "ma luv-shank's marra," of En-
glish no less than Scots: all hegemony less than final, no border
fully substantial.

Or Herbert's "The Shyster," which is composed again of re-
duced circumstances—"nae money fur thi metir, nae / claes that ur
spare," nothing at all to spare but the barest of bare subsistence,
the smell of "ma bluid and banes" when "Eh bile" them—and in
which Herbert hugs to himself these circumstances, this impover-
ished landscape, as the mark of his utterly intransigent resistance:
"Wheesht an awa, yi Christ, yi shystir; / yi canna come in here!" This cry,
like the taunt that ends "And Death Must Wait," is the reciprocal
response of a cornered man to the experience of being cornered,
and little else—but this is still plenty, is indeed everything, in
countering the "monumental 'Naw!' " of utter poverty, death, or
the "Club o' Legless Scoatlan" (in Crawford's "Cock o' the North").

Such poems rest upon negation ("GIT TAE FUCK!") as the sine
qua non of carrying on, of creation, and provide relatively little in
thematic terms to indicate what comes next. They say nevertheless,
nevertheless, nevertheless, *something*, and then they run out of

breath. It is language itself—that is, not the various thematic materials of the poems but their linguistic materiality—that primarily embodies the visionary in *Sharawaggi,* and this condition of the work is thematized as well. It is a vision, again, of radical borderlessness, a language "disestranged / Fae a' yon warld": a language, in Crawford's "The Grate Tradition," of "leamers fae thi imperium o thi daurk," "ripe nuts that separate easily from the husk of the imperium of the darkness"—a rejection of "thi Inglis smiddy" ("the English smithy") which has "smushed ur denied ma kulchur / Wi naw even a smudge" ("secretly devoured and denied my culture with not even a suppressed laugh"), and a promise to "grow / Fae a hazy goog tae an aigle wi satelite een / Speirin oot owre ma ain an ither fowks' launs" ("grow from a slightly crazed fledgling to an eagle with satellite eyes inquiring with concern out over my own and other people's lands"), "Laureatin thi slaewurms wha'll faa thi yird" ("conferring doctorates on the slow-worms who shall inherit the earth")—a language of power, beyond borders, Scottish, organic. A vision not distinguishing "amang thi Ersche, Scoats, Tibetans, oar Inglis," and a vision of Terra Scotia—"Ur thi Granzebenes" (the Grampians) "Naethin?": a refusal and an affirmation of locality, a language neither English nor Scots R P, a language that stands against empire (or is secreted, like a ripe nut, from it) not only in the thematic tropes it elaborates obsessively but in its linguistic politics as well, its linguistic body.

In Crawford's "Thi Whangie" it is "Deidleid, deidleid" that shines, its "muckle chainsaw o sang" that sounds against "thi subfuscit fowk wha smirk"[29]—and that emanates in pure negativity "Fae thi yirdmou, yon Delphi, thi Whangie," from "earth-mouth," "a geological feature in the Campsie Hills near Glasgow, taking the form of a sharp gash in the rock said to have been caused by a flick of the Devil's tail." In "Hoo This Wiz Medd" it's "A crunchy Scots Lorca, sum leid that's fit / Fur Homer an Vietnamese" that's wanting ("It wiz medd waantin"), like the "gledge o Scots-Greek" in "Thi Whangie," desired

> naw jist tae hamschakel
> Thi Puir Wees, but tae pluff wi a hammerflush
> Yon dry scran o Scoatlan, makkin a ew-gowan
> O bleezin lasers

and that targets the condition of "bein fushionless an seggin / In Cambuslang queezie wi sterns."[30] In "Deidspeak" it is something called Deadlanguage (Deadtalk?) that "acherspires i thi drucken

groon" (germinates in the drunken ground), is "Roused whan a
shakker passes" ("shakker—nervous tremour, fit"), has "A tabbit
luke" ("tabbit—opportunity of advantage occurring") and makes
Crawford's speaker "claucht ma fire / That's chitterin doon tae a
peak."[31] In each case language itself is not only the signifier but the
signified, the central figure, site of power, oppression, and libera-
tion, promise and embodiment of rebirth, of identity forged and
afloat on antisyzygy, free.

It's a heavy burden for any language to bear, to be not just the
repository and embodiment of culture but its inventor, makar, re-
deemer, Lord Dr. Frankenstein Graham Bell. It is the burden,
again, that all languages share—national languages, the languages
of dispossessed or embattled cultures, the discourses of smaller or
more scattered communities, of individuals, argot, slang, baby talk,
techno-neologism, ideological lingo, fresh metaphor—although
some more desperately self-conscious of powerlessness than oth-
ers. The point, again, is that Scots brings to bear upon these mat-
ters of linguistic identity and invention, power and dispossession,
the context of cultural crisis; and this context gives to Scottish lan-
guage a specifically dooble charge, a double frame of reference—
simultaneous vision of borderlessness and locality, of particularity
without identity, of this place (the text) not quite Scotland and un-
mistakably Scottish.

Scots embodies language, then, at Absolute Zero, a baseline for
all subsequent developments, all subsequent measurements of the
possibility of life. In Herbert's
"The Hermitage" there is *nothing*
but language, and a language
without substantiation: "Thi leid is
aa lies. Thi leid is aa." Not much
basis here for subsequent develop-
ments. "Cormundum" ("Confes-
sion") begins with an epigraph

> What there is now to cele-
> brate:
> The only art where failure is
> renowned.
> —Veronica Forrest-Thomson

from Psalms—"Create in me a clean heart, O God; and renew a
right spirit within me"—but ends with "Scoatlan's braith draggin
lyk a serpint owre / thi causie o ma spine," nowhere but "this Dis-
naeland, this / Brokendoon" land of our dead-end forebears.[32]
These are "ma birthin-lands," marked by language that does not
speak, "Pictland's buttirflehs o ridirs, z-rods, tunan / foarks," "thi
fush-bricht ignorance oan ivry fiss," "thi wurkir turnin oan / thi
wurkir lyk / a cannibal turbine, let alane merry Inglan (aye / lat
well alane)"—a landscape utterly without a future, and a landscape
defined as a language: "this / / is Scoatlan's braith." Here there is

no renewal, no creation, no clean heart, no right spirit, the confession only of "oor severt heid an erse o gless," and a promise that they "sall open til thir celsitudes o noth, thi stern." If language—confession, prayer, boast, *cri de coeur*—promises rebirth, it seems to do so against all odds: nothing *but* language contributes to the effort, no affirmation *but* language, the last and only disconnected hope.

"Scotland the Twit" is even more explicit. A tale of advent—"Thi furst o things that Eh did see / oan Christmas Dey i thi moarnin"—and a landscape defined again in terms of peculiarly modern inanition: the first thing "Eh did see" "wiz Iggy Poap oan Brekfist TV" in whom "Eh kent / ma brithir-eedjut." The image does function in fact as a kind of advent, the crossing of a threshold from which there is no return—a new beginning, advent of the mundane: "Ma dreams furgoat, Eh tuke thi doag / oot." And it is from this unlikely vantage that something more is called for:

> Eh went tae thi end o thi pier
> tae waatch fur seals, an sedd
> "Affoard me noo a vishun:
> a dauphin bairn cleavin thi reamin
> waves o thi Tay wu'll you
> *sit doon!*" (this tae thi doag),
> a flinty arraheid
> o burds went by, as gif ti sey
> "Wu'll hae nin o that noansinse."

The dog belongs to him, or he to the dog, but it is not *his*, just "thi" dog: nothing in "Scotland the Twit" speaks of the possibility of connection—with the exception of one brother idiot recognizing another (while the latter remains entirely unaware of the presence of the former)—and "vishun" is explicitly dismissed, preposterous, in fact a joke. Nothing remains of vision at all except language—a vision of language, of language as a vision of nothing but itself:

> An whan thi sun cemm up
> an Dundee cam alist in clementines
> an neuralgia wiz bestowit oan me,
> three swans Eh saw gae sailin by, twa siller,
> yin gray, oan Christmas Day . . .
> an rejecket them
> oot a haund; ut widnae dae
> tae seek ayont thi things
> Eh'd keekit thru, save fur this paitturn's sake.

It would not do to seek beyond—to read Scotland now for what might explain it, or what it might portend: no future and no past in the present, nothing but this pattern—of swans at sunrise, neuralgia in Dundee, but also of language, a textual pattern, that speaks itself (to please itself) while remaining essentially mute.

This pattern of language embodies a possible exception to (or deliverance from) the rule of necessity, both the necessity of slow death and the necessity of new vision: a radical refusal, polymorphously anarchic, comic, ironic, satiric, obscene, hermetic. It speaks both of profound cultural impoverishment—no value anywhere but in a language that speaks only to itself—and of an insistence on vision, on an Otherwise, if only in such reduced terms. In fact the reduction of vision in "Scotland the Twit"—the pure ornamentation of "this paitturn's sake"—in rejecting both the neuralgia of daybreak in Dundee and the demand for a new vision embodies a desire (or aspires to one) wholly unfettered: finding in no past and no imaginable future a way to be—a song to sing, a livin leid—in the present. Language is not merely utopian here but utopia itself.[33]

In "Sink the Discovery!" (Herbert), which comes entirely without gloss, "wir aa jist / savidgis, penntit Inglis" ("orriz Tonto'd sey, / Pictman speaks wi foarkit tung"), "a naishun o obliteraishuns": but "wi cheenge the hurehzin's shepp / / by waulkin alangside ut," where

> A wee dug that wid
> huvtae be crehd Benji loups i thi Tay
> an scrabbils at thi waatir's lettirs as tho tae
> haal an auld wurd hame, then gaes aff wi a
> soustir inniz mou.

The wee dog is a figure for the "wi" who change the horizon's shape by keeping on the move, and hauling old words home is certainly (along with forging new words) one way *Sharawaggi* has of imagining this power over the shape of the world: this *is* "licht's last stab," the dog is a character out of "this Disnaeland, this / Brokendoon" and in fact finds no words auld or new but something—which is not nothing—to carry in his mouth, an emblem, at least, of both language and sustenance. Similarly, "Epistle to the Bishop of Dunkeld," a prayer to "Gavin Douglas, *wlgar Virgill*, douchty gabbir," translator as national guardian ("Scoatlan in eterne // yi saw")—in which Herbert, disconnected from everything ("Syne aathin's o thi meenit" and "syne Eh'm sae selkith o ut"), makes this request:

gee me thi virr tae stap ut, e'en wi
havirs, clishmaclavirs, tint codices—

gee me thi verr tae lift fu lichtly
Ane ald crag stane huge, gret, and gray![34]

Language—even nonsense and lost to use—is again the last and
only (if disconnected) hope of changing the horizon's shape: lifting
one great huge grey crag stone. The material and the ethereal—
stone and breath—and negation and affirmation—"tae stap," "tae
lift"—meet here in one trope of impossible and undeniable (non-
sensical) hope.

So it is with all prayers: they turn words into bread and bread
into words, they live on the tongue in inspiration and expiration,
in metaphors of heart and head; they embody, if nothing else, the
contradiction of the impossible and the undeniable. Here (again)
it is language that bears the burden of this hope—language alone
that hears the prayer—and that would seem to be muted in the
face of it. In both "Sink the Discovery!" and the "Epistle" to Doug-
las, language is replaced by things ("a / soustir inniz mou," "*Ane ald
crag stane*," mute things) which simultaneously represent the loss of
language and a new linguistic possibility, a dead end and a live
hope. In Crawford's "Scots Architecture on Sauchiehall Street" it
is the street itself which becomes language: where a culture is gone
save for language alone, all cultural phenomena become language,
"that general assembly of shops and precincts suitable for a linguis-
tic atlas or a very deep structure grammar" ("Yon gallimaufray o
shoaps n precincts fit / Fura linguistic atlas, urra very deep /
Strukchur grammar").

Crawford goes on:

> Chomsky inna tweedy bunnit
> Widnae mind moochin aroon ootside
> M & S oar C & A douce as RP, an takkin notes
> Oan hoo thae gallus queues o gauberty-shells at 30s dance halls
> Still exist, reekin wi cit, jist as if
> Thae wur auld wurds—*huddroun, shug-shug*, oar *broasy airt*—
> Lyin aroon, rippled, yet vieve i thi big
> Goab o thi street that sprays oot *thermoplastic*
> An *neo-geo* wi *whirret*—thi Sauchiehall Street Centre
> Embedded doon i thi wan sentence . . .

Chomsky in a tweedy flat cap would not mind loitering like a spy out-
side Marks and Spencers or C & A respectable as Received Pronuncia-
tion, and taking notes on how those tremendous queues of goblin

people who make a noise like little barking dogs combined with the sound of shells striking against each other at thirties dance halls still exist, smelling strongly of civet, just as if they were old words—a word meaning "slovenly," a word meaning "to jog continuously," or a word meaning "inactive"—lying around, separated like seeds of flax from the stalk, yet alive in the big mouth of the street that sprays out the word "thermoplastic" and the word "neo-geo" with the word that means "a blow"—the Sauchiehall Street Centre embedded down in the one sentence . . .

Thae vennels' sentence-order's
Fae Middle Scoats—pit that in yir pipe, Noam!—
An yon yuppified Mackintosh tearoom's
A construction fae Gaelic. Fowk git flung oot rip-rap
Alang thi Buik o thi pavemint, a crood o Gavin
Douglasses,
Wee waffin Dunbars, a point-game, an yit
Therra team—ootlanders, bachles, computer analysts
Oan Hogmanay, each yin a wurd i thi leid,
Thi spang-new wi the auld cryin oot in houghmagandie,
Makkin bastards o speik tae beatify stammerals an jass
Ideas o purity. Toshy an Tom Leonard
Jimmer a soodie o Neil Gow's farts, bit it soons
Magic. Bill Herbert, a Citizens' Aladdin amang
sparklin Vimto,
Nips doon *ex machina* wi a lamp bricht wi crap-o-
thi-wattir
Tae toarch aa thi Lunnonry o thi TLS—Auld Blethirbags
Reekin lik a sookit pike.

The sentence-order of those alleys comes from Middle Scots—put that in your pipe, Noam!—and that yuppified Mackintosh tearoom's a construction from Gaelic. People get thrown out violently along the Bible of the pavement, a crowd of Gavin Douglasses, small Dunbars who excel at dancing, a game in which each player plays for himself at the various shots, and yet they are a team—foreigners, clumsy, unimportant people, computer analysts on Hogmanay, each one a word in the language, the brand-new with the old crying out in fornication, making illegitimates of language to beatify those who falter in speech, and to dash all ideas of purity. Charles Rennie Mackintosh and Tom Leonard create out of scrapings on the violin a hodge-podge of Neil Gow's farts, but it sounds wonderful. Bill Herbert, an Aladdin of the People among sparkling Vimto, pops down *ex machina* with a lamp shining with the luck-bringing water collected from a well just after midnight at the start of the new year to torch all the London-values of the *Times Literary Supplement*—Old Fluent, Stupid Talker stinking like a semi-putrescent scavenger fish.

He concludes:

> Thi haill leid pouts.
> C'moan, Sauchiehall Street, speik me!

The whole, healthy language starts up suddenly and noisily as if rising from underwater. Come on, Sauchiehall Street, speak me!

All of the issues of *Sharawaggi* I've been exploring here come together in Crawford's vision of Sauchiehall Street, as befits a vision of a great coming together. It is explicitly a sexual vision, "the brand-new with the old crying out in fornication," a vision of sexuality as radical, rampant heterology, comminglings of the disparate, border crossings, order smashings ("making illegitimates of language to beatify those who falter in speech, and to dash all ideas of purity"), of sexuality as a redemption of the outcast, redemption even of farts, and scourge of the English: a sexuality impervious to systematic study—put that in your pipe!—or domestication of any kind, a livin leid. "A point-game, an yit / Therra team": a reconstitution of identity neither singular nor common but continually, dynamically synthetic, a reconstitution of language that knows no borders.

> A conversation between a wellington and a herring.
> —I. C. Smith

Sharawaggi: a landscape of the dead and gone and the living dead, a world of lost hope, in which all resistance takes the form of negation, in which negation preeminently takes the form of language, in which language takes the form of sexual metaphor—both thematically and linguistically—and in which sexualization is utopian; this is the landscape I've constructed so far. In "Horse Island," which is a different sort of utopia, sexuality represents an obsessive-compulsive nightmare of "genetic booty": it has nothing to do with connections between living people but goes entirely to sustain the information technologies of the local (all too local) government—what we might call, with Lawrence, sex in the head. *Sharawaggi*'s sexuality is manifestly of the body, and represents a situation even more complex, bewildering, and unpredictable than the basement of the Archive itself—if not, finally, a defeat of the incubus of Scottishness, an utter transformation of the terms in which it manifests itself.

In Herbert's "The Socialist Manifesto for East Balgillo," it is so

peculiar a sexuality that it is hardly recognizable as such—perhaps
pre-sexuality is more like it. Again the landscape is language
("Sandy Hole Gaelic's pirn's / unspoolan i thi prisk un-guschet / o
aa thocht's birth's biforrows"),[35] and it is in language ("therr,
whaur garrons o thi speak / ur growein back lyk a lizard's tail")[36]
that the come together come together, in a vision of "scarts an
jenny- / wullocks," where "aathin's lyk pellack, / thi peltin-pyock o
aa 'feel'osophy":[37] a vision of wondrous flesh and sexual wholeness
available only to the imagination (porpoise flesh, hermaphrodit-
ism), and a vision of the union of philosophy, feeling, and work.
East Balgillo, like Crawford's Sauchiehall Street, embodies a poly-
morphous pleasure zone that Herbert's and Crawford's language
itself is meant to herald: conceived under the sign of the postmod-
ern, of juxtaposition and interchange, of militant marginality
against the center, of Eros, of brain and heart and hand rejoined.

In Herbert's "Pictish Music Perhaps," nature and lost history are
rejoined as well, as a boy and his grandfather "inna rowboat" move
"undir thi cleuchs and intae / thi caves":

> Eh dinna ken whaur Kilchattan
> Cave is, save inna buik, but Eh ken o
>
> thi piper that mairchit in, and pleyd,
> mairchin in, an thi lugs o thi locals werr
> lissnin til thi tintin lilt, a timidinnitus that
> peeried an wearied until ut cam
>
> fae titans' cloisters lyk thi whuspir fae
> a bed o oystirs i thi Tay o shells shuttan
> lyk applause, feet drappin lyk a tap that
> wauks yi, fingirs flappan lyk ribbuns oan
>
> an extractir, drooly slavirs o sand aroond
> toyts' jaas haufrisin lyk a cobra-coarnfield til
> sum whifflan o thi mune's pu . . .[38]

The identification here of the natural world with the living leid of
Pictish ghosts is itself an identification in its own way of head,
heart, and hand, thinking, feeling, and doing:

> Eh pit meh fingir oan a wurd
> i thi dickshunary that precedit whit Eh yaize
> an feel ut trummil.

In the end, then, *Sharawaggi*'s encounter with the incubus of the
language problem moves from a seemingly reductionist posi-

tion—in which language represents the sole site of cultural identity and regeneration, and in which this identity is bound to the notion of the national—to a sweeping vision of something more than regeneration, and beyond identity: a wholly new configuration of categories, nature, history, thought, feeling, action all at once released from alienation. What Gramsci hopefully calls "the working out at a higher level of one's own conception of reality" emerges "through the struggle of political 'hegemonies' and of opposing directions":[39] alienation produces its own dialectical antithesis. It is an ambitious, essentially utopian vision hemmed in all round—and in the end not so much realized as recognized, a possibility only newly recognizable, the gift, in the end, of the incubus—a bordered vision without borders.

The essentially eroticized conception of language that mediates this vision represents a particularly male vantage. Herbert's "Penis Envoi," appended to (or depending from) "Cock of the South," begins with the poet "—Scrievan this in pitmirk, / awaukent frae deep sleep," and moves into a vision of

> thi sornin sun
> that lyk a kraken rose,
> wuntellan uts jeely shanks
> frae whaur ut restit i thi starn—[40]

(The landscape here again is the familiar one: "thi mauchy frozen mornin," the blue of the sky figured in terms of "pirrin—seeping like blood from a wound," the sun like a beast from the deep signalling a final end.) Here the poet asks:

> whit phallic shapes went by
> lyk whales, thi scales
> o whilk owrebalancin ma fears
> an makan minutes o thi years
> that lig atween us i thi daurk?

This is a reconfiguration of categories to be sure. Why phallic? Herbert is speaking here of the years that lie between him and MacDiarmid—"(On reading *To Circumjack Cencrastus* 'in difficult days')" is the poem's epigraph—and of MacDiarmid's Drunk Man, like Tam O'Shanter a paradigmatic emblem of the male adrift (like clouds). In this case the sexual metaphor is onanistic, a matter of touching minds alone:

Eh felt thon makar's still joy
an went hame drucken wi life:
sae yi maun gang, ma sang; up
fae thi murdirt depths,
and anerly touch thae minds
that dinna crine at licht—
thi lave belang i thi nicht![41]

"Thi lave belang i thi nicht!": this closing line of "Penis Envoi,"
like the various shouts and curses that end a considerable number
of these poems, speaks a kind of erection of borders at odds with
the work's otherwise relentless assault on such erections; the phal-
lologos too is a dooble tongue. But the category of the phallic is
perhaps not to be regarded too schematically, as a matter merely
of (choose your metaphor) thrust, aggression, creation, priapic ob-
session, castration anxiety, the sword, the cigar, the pen; for Craw-
ford and Herbert, perhaps, the dominant mode of the phallic is
irony, or self-mockery, or gratuitousness, silliness, uselessness, the
unaccounted for, the non-Calvinist—which is to say, the still possi-
ble although unimagined and, no doubt, unlikely.

In this light the phallic bias of *Sharawaggi* takes on a kind of femi-
nist aspect—or becomes a drag performance, another mode of
cross-dressing the border: it bears testimony to an experience of
marginalization (and inanition) which has less to do with questions
of nationality than with questions of other borders, and which
seeks not so much identity as release from identity, not essence but
synthesis.

I'll close this preliminary movement with Crawford's "The Herr-
Knit Bunnet" as a fitting emblem of the whole: an attempt "tae
shak us free / an hair butter a naishun" ("to shake us free and
cleanse a nation of impurities"), driven by a form of language, a
world of signs, evanescent inscriptions—"pronyeand scuddin-
stanes" ("piercing stones skimming the surface of the water")—
framed in terms of a massive sexual reorientation. To begin with,
Crawford presents a figure, if not sexual, certainly phallic: "Ah
glaum . . . , turnin thi dwang / O Scoatlan" ("I grope in the dark
. . . trying to raise the heavy caber of Scotland")—and goes on to
imagine "a kind of sudden throw to pluck the land out of being
blown over by sad winds in midsummer, and to take it down laugh-
ing through the snow with a knowledge of satisfaction so that you
would see its beautiful small hills clear again, the vagina of the
earth":

a kinna haich tae raise thi laun oot
O bein swiffed in midsimmer an tae tak it doon
Laughin thru thi snaa wi a sairin sae yi'd ken aa its nocks
Vieve again, thi cunt o thi yird.

This is a vision of Highland games as fornication, and it culminates in "thi herr-knit bunnet" itself, "the hair-knit beret," "a het teuchter's bunnet purled fae human herr" ("a hot unsophisticated Highlander's beret stocking-stitched from human hair"): this beret is "skaab-dark," "moosewob atwen thi bens' shanks / Electric wi threids o herr" ("dark as the bottom of the sea, . . . spiderweb between the legs of the mountains electric with threads of hair"). To knit a hat of human hair is to turn to use the part of us that is dead, and to find it here in a genital site and electric with life: vieve in its weave. The whole of Scotland becomes an erotic (or pornographic) landscape here ("Ah've seen yi, Scoatlan!"), a national transformation effected essentially by language (in this case the semiotics of fashion and folklore): this is the unlikely imagination of *Sharawaggi*, a caber tossed.

2

Subjunctive Scotland: Hugh MacDiarmid

The metaphysics of nationalism speak of the entry into full self-realization of a unitary subject known as the people.
—Terry Eagleton

Thus contrar thingis evir-mar
Discoveryngis off the tothir ar.
—John Barbour

Norman MacCaig: All that your poetry proved was that great poetry can be written in Scots. It doesn't prove that Scots is not a dying language, it doesn't prove that Scots can be resuscitated, it only proves that you wrote great poems in Scots and it proves nothing else but that.
Hugh MacDiarmid: But that's adequate to constitute a modern Scots literature.
MacCaig: You've written a lot, but not a literature.
—BBC Radio 1964

THE WORK OF HUGH MACDIARMID, LIKE THE INCUBUS ITSELF, IS A monster that simply will not be denied, that must be engaged: the encounter, as with the incubus, presents particular challenges at once enabling and discomfiting.

Who's Who has long given my hobby as "Anglophobia." But it is a great deal more than a mere hobby. It is my very life.

There is a consensus of opinion that I have achieved a miracle—inventing a new language out of the dialects into which Scots has disintegrated; and, along with that, reviving large elements of vocabulary obsolete since the sixteenth century, and writing indisputably great poetry in this unlikely, if not impossible, medium.

I always like to feel—and generally succeed in securing an adequate basis for feeling—that my principal personal characteristics exhibit clearly the great historical directives of my people and dream, of course, always of such a moment in relation to Scotland as, when St.

Paul wrote to the Galatians, "universal" history stood over him and dictated his words.[1]

> It is quite unimportant whether we call
> Our ultimate reality matter, electric charge,
> ψ-waves, mind-stuff, neural stuff, or what not,
> Provided it obeys laws which can, in principle,
> Be formulated mathematically.

> something utterly unlike
> All that is commonly meant by loving One's country.[2]

Bombast, pedantry, monumental egotism, polemical didacticism, reductionism and wildly expansive, shifting, contradictory eclecticism, heroism, arcana, violence, and reason, some vision of rapture—"something utterly unlike"—of the corpse of the tongue and of the world resuscitated: these are MacDiarmid's characteristic modes of negotiating "Scotland," his Beatrice, the object of his love, ruler of his soul, and anointer of his prophecy (as distinct from, if not opposed to, Scotland, where Christopher Murray Grieve lived and did the work of Hugh MacDiarmid for most of the twentieth century). By these means he produces a challenging poetry, often powerfully delightful and often powerfully (and in the course of his career progressively) maddening.

In a sense, MacDiarmid aims not so much to engage or overcome the incubus as to *become* it, to show Scotland to itself (raising the flag of the phantasmal state to see who will see themselves in it) in the form of (under the standard or sign of) recalcitrant obsession, resistance, and the nevertheless possible although highly unlikely. He embodies the voice of this sublime

> So Scotland darts into the
>   towering wall of my heart
> And finds refuge now.
>   —MacDiarmid

alienation in the form of a multifarious, much fragmented plenitude, a voice that through all its changes speaks the condition alone of utter extremity. His many aliases (from Christopher Murray Grieve to Hugh MacDiarmid to C. M. Grieve, C. M. G., H. M'D., and Hugh M'Diarmid, to Isobel Guthrie, Gillechriosd Mac a'Ghreidhir, Gillechriosd Moraidh Mac a'Greidhir, James Maclaren, Stentor, A. L., A. K. L., A. K. Laidlaw, and possibly Arthur Leslie and Anon)[3] and his many poetic and political (or poeticopolitical)[4] maneuvers over the course of a long career, a wild divergence of modes of discourse—lyric Scots, mini-epic Scots, polemical Scots and English, geologists' English, Marxism, Anglophobia, world language—all are gathered into the service of this metaphysical nation of the (ever untamed) "unitary subject known as the people."

MacDiarmid's project seeks not so much Scotland as we do or do not know it, but the signs of Scotland, the abstraction of its identity (as I noted at the start with reference to my own project here): a subjunctive Scotland akin to that of *Sharawaggi* in its projection of an inescapable absence as totalizing common ground. (This is a very definition of the incubus—and part of any definition of that problematic and multifarious category, the postmodern.) Crawford and Herbert engage this absence with an orthographically and often semantically neologized (and urban-inflected) Scots, and pursue by this means an essentially erotic conception of the matter of borders and borderlessness; MacDiarmid's Scots, what he calls either Braid or Synthetic Scots, attempts a new language in the integration of (largely rural) old dialects, positing a putatively preexisting or phantasmal whole, and the conception of borders and borderlessness that derives from (or engenders) this attempt is cast in nationalist terms—or internationalist, Marxist terms, or the cosmic terms of lithogenesis or molecular mathematics.

It is in this profound tropism toward the monological that MacDiarmid's work embodies its relation to the incubus of Scottish identity (which itself knows only one word, *Scotland . . . Scotland*), and in this sense that it serves as a kind of counter-example to the work of Crawford and Herbert (which is nevertheless inconceivable without MacDiarmid). The polymorphousness that *Sharawaggi* takes as both a point of departure and a utopian revelation/ destination—the most transcendental of its signifiers—functions in MacDiarmid more narrowly, as strategy or instrumental condition: not, that is, so much an eroticized possibility as an undeniable fact in the service of Truth. This difference in his treatment of the polymorphous (and in his attraction to the monological) may in fact date MacDiarmid (may mod as opposed to postmod him), although by the same token it helps to deconstruct the hierarchy of signifiers in the imagination of *Sharawaggi*. One could say, for instance, that if both MacDiarmid and Crawford/Herbert conceive some notion of a People metaphysically, and if for Crawford and Herbert in *Sharawaggi* this is a sexualized and for MacDiarmid a nationalized conception, that these different frames of metaphysical reference merely establish different sets of problems and possibilities, variant contradictions and illusions. (The tongue of the People is dooble here, its Scottish *parole* both sexual and national.)

The tension between these two impulses in MacDiarmid's

work—between the monological and the rampant, the synthetic, the dooble—is related in metaphorical terms (if not more directly) to the tension between the Scottish and the English as signifying categories at this late date in the long history of their political engagements of one another: a poetic embodiment of the voice of the one and the voice of the other locked in eternal struggle. The dooble tongue, Synthetic Scots, the Caledonian antisyzygy—all visions of borderlessness, of transcendence of borders—discover themselves under the transcendental ultimacy of an *idée fixe*, a border, the monologos of the one true word (Scots, Marx, epanadiplosis, math): and it is MacDiarmid's negotiation of this dynamic process that I want to examine here.

> The Twentieth Century at
>   Eternity
> Gapes—and the clock strikes:
>   Tea!
> —MacDiarmid

Yeats may provide a more familiar frame of reference. Tom Paulin, *Minotaur: Poetry and the Nation State* (1992):

Yeats denied that he was a nationalist, "except in Ireland for passing reasons," and he dismissed "State and Nation" as merely "the work of the intellect . . . not worth the blade of grass God gives for the nest of the linnet". His rejection of the nation state is a strategy which aims to identify poetry with an elemental simplicity:

> I never bade you go
> To Moscow or to Rome.
> Renounce that drudgery,
> Call the Muses home.
>
> Seek those images
> That constitute the wild,
> The lion and the virgin,
> The harlot and the child.

The primitive is offered as an alternative to political commitment in "Those Images", but Yeats's rejection of the ideology of Soviet communism and Italian fascism is disingenuous: he was a dedicated nation-builder, the shadow of the gunmen who founded the Irish Free State. His writing is entangled with the ideology of romantic nationalism, even though he wants to identify his poems with the prehistorical, with myth and transcendence. He therefore dismisses the state by denying that it has any imaginative qualities: it is simply mechanical.[5]

What Paulin calls "the primitive" or "prehistorical" or "elemental simplicity" or "myth and transcendence," Yeats calls here "the wild," and its emblems—lion, virgin, harlot, child—evoke both an emotional landscape and a moral one: in either case a landscape beyond the sway (or syzygy) of Reason, moving to the measure of messy heart and spinning gyre. This site of "the wild" is a kind of dooble tongue itself—speaking both transcendence and enmirement, nature and culture, heart and heartlessness, innocence and experience (these doublets not wholly congruent with one another, a proliferating and shifting of doublets); and it stands, in dooble fashion, against the "mechanical" monologic of nationalist ideology, the other one true word, not worth a linnet's grassblade but not, apparently, to be denied entirely either.

MacDiarmid's work fits a similar equation, although the values shift somewhat. Like Yeats, MacDiarmid pursues a course both vigorously nationalist (rather more relentlessly or less reluctantly than Yeats) as well as another course, variously conceived, toward some otherwise imagined possibility. Yeats names this latter—"the wild," above—by means of his symbols and images and systems of soul and heart and gyres, and from that vantage he looks down upon the ideologies of nations as from a great height (or tries to). When MacDiarmid names what stands beyond Nation he does so as well in cosmic terms—the sound that is left when the incubus is silenced—or naturalized terms, such as "kandym in the Waste Land," or political, internationalist terms (Marxist, for MacDiarmid, but also a projection of Scottish cultural antisyzygy), or scientific terms (naming Shetland rocks). But each of these other worlds of discourse beyond borders, beyond nationalist ideology, begins and ends in the naming of Scotland, the discourse of the incubus from which these others claim transcendence: MacDiarmid's work is thus structured like a massive epanadiplosis, dooble tongue twisted like a snake with its tail in its mouth, a perfectly closed circle.

> To write the histories with
> any accuracy is to write backwards,
> true to the falsity of experience.
>
> —Bob Perelman

> When shall Jerusalem return & overspread all the Nations?
> —Blake

Nation as inescapable illusion, the border beyond which it is impossible to think or go: nations in combination, in commonality
with other nations, but always a nation, a "unitary subject" smaller
than the whole. As Edwin Morgan notes, the incubus is a real
one—in its nationalist guise as in any other—not to be displaced
without severe cost to the body; MacDiarmid's vast closed circle is
a challenge to all who would follow in the attempt, and imagine
the maneuver to be readily accomplished. (This point underscores,
too, both the tentative and the violent gestures of *Sharawaggi*, and
the precarious dialectical negativities by which Crawford and Herbert engage the incubus anew.)

The modern National incubus is an essentially Romantic construction. (So is the postmodern sharawaggi of polymorphousness
and eros, the putative move beyond nationalist ideology in Crawford and Herbert, and the gothic fantasy of "Horse Island"—
different metaphysics, but metaphysics still, visions driven by
Romantic categories, romances of the occult in everyday life.)
Terry Eagleton, writing primarily about Ireland but with reference
beyond (he opens his essay by quoting "an African character" in a
Raymond Williams novel), emphasizes the totalizing tenaciousness
of this Romantic entity:

> The metaphysics of nationalism speak of the entry into full self-realiza
> tion of a unitary subject known as the people. As with all such philoso
> phies of the subject from Hegel to the present, this monadic subject
> must somehow curiously preexist its own process of materialization—
> must be equipped, even now, with certain highly determinate needs
> and desires, on the model of the autonomous human personality. The
> problem is not so much one of discriminating among this subject's
> needs and desires—of determining, for example, which of them fore
> shadow a desirable future and which are merely the reflexes of an op
> pressive present—but rather the sheer fact that these desires are
> repressed. The model, in other words, is an expression/blockage one,
> of a familiar Romantic kind; and as with any model of such historical
> tenacity there is undoubtedly much to be said for it. Subjects, national
> or otherwise, do indeed experience needs that are repressed but de
> mand realization; it is just that one ironic effect of such repression is to
> render us radically uncertain of what our needs really are. The very
> repressive conditions that make it necessary for the subject to express
> itself freely also tend to render it partially opaque to itself. If subjects
> have needs, then we already know what one at least of these needs
> must be, namely, the need to know what one's needs are. The meta
> physics of nationalism tend to obscure this point, by assuming a subject
> somehow intuitively present to itself; in privileging the concept of self-
> realization, it elevates a subject-object relation over a subject-subject

one, forgetting that the expression and formulation of needs are always a dialogical affair, that needs and desires are always in some sense received back from an "other." On the other hand, those contemporary thinkers, like Jürgen Habermas, who recall us to this truth tend to forget in their turn about the political necessities of lifting the repression, so that such dialogism can actually take place.[6]

Eagleton's point is that to consider the Romanticism of Nationalism as in some way flawed is beside the point: nationalist metaphysics is both the reflex of an oppressive present and the foreshadowing (agent?) of a desirable future. (We might say that Romantic metaphysics is a condition rather than a flaw—and a condition from which we still suffer.) The incubus, the Nation, the transcendental yearning metaphysics of Romanticism: each is a figure of the dialectic between blockage and expression, each a portal through complicity to freedom. As the character from Williams remarks:

> Was it Pound
> who said, *The way out is via the door*—
> —Robert Creeley

> Nationalism . . . is in this sense like class. To have it, and to feel it, is the only way to end it. If you fail to claim it, or give it up too soon, you will merely be cheated, by other classes and other nations.[7]

Eagleton elaborates:

> Nationalism, like class, would thus seem to involve an impossible irony. It is sometimes forgotten that social class, for Karl Marx at least, is itself a form of alienation, canceling the particularity of an individual life into collective anonymity. Where Marx differs from the commonplace liberal view of such matters is in his belief that to undo this alienation you had to go, not around class, but somehow all the way through it and out the other side. To wish class or nation away, to seek to live sheer irreducible difference *now* in the manner of some contemporary post-structuralist theory, is to play straight into the hands of the oppressor. In a similar way, the philosopher Julia Kristeva has argued that the whole concept of gender is "metaphysical"—a violent stabilizing of the sheer precariousness and ambiguity of sexual identity to some spuriously self-identical essence. The goal of a feminist politics would therefore be not an affirmation of some "female identity," but a troubling and subverting of all such sexual straitjacketing. Yet the grim truth remains that women are oppressed as *women*—that such sexual categories, ontologically empty though they may be, continue to exert an implacable political force. It would thus be the worst form of prema-

ture utopianism for women to strive now merely to circumvent their sexual identities, celebrating only the particular and polymorphous, rather than—once again—try somehow to go right through those estranging definitions to emerge somewhere on the other side. Women are not so much fighting for the freedom to be women—as though we all understood exactly what that meant—as for the freedom to be fully human; but that inevitably abstract humanity can be articulated in the here and now only through their womanhood, since this is the place where their humanity is wounded and refused. Sexual politics, like class or nationalist struggle, will thus necessarily be caught up in the very metaphysical categories it hopes finally to abolish; and any such movement will demand a difficult, perhaps ultimately impossible double optic, at once fighting on a terrain already mapped out by its antagonists and seeking even now to prefigure within that mundane strategy styles of being and identity for which we have as yet no proper names.[8]

In other words: "the impasse of any transformative politics is that it can unravel what Marx and Stephen Dedalus call the nightmare of history only with the poor, contaminated instruments which that history has handed it." Or as Seamus Deane puts it: "Eagleton's analysis of nationalism identifies the radical contradictions that necessarily beset it. The oppositional terms it deploys are the very terms it must ultimately abolish."[9]

Eagleton views nationalism, then, like ideologies of class and gender, as a form of self-contradicted consciousness, at once a self-defeating illusion (with spiritual and potentially horrible material consequences) and a form of radical praxis—a lesser (perhaps because necessary) evil than its mirror twin imperialism. For MacDiarmid, certainly, the shoe fits. He is, throughout his career, virulently nationalist and something other than that—"particular and polymorphous," drunk flat on his back by the side of the road, lost in the stars, a worker of worldwide britherhood, or a student of stones; the tension between the nationalist impulse and the cosmic or internationalist is never resolved, and is indeed sustained as the very project of that career. (The Sign of Scotland represents this tension.)

Virulently nationalist: the phrase has an axiomatic ring, like something out of Flaubert's Dictionary of Received Ideas (Nationalism: often virulent). I take license for the plaguey metaphor from MacDiarmid's own early poem "Ex vermibus" (a title which might be rendered in English as "By the Agency of Worms," from his first collection in Scots, Sangschaw [1925]):

Gape, gape, gorlin',
For I ha'e a worm
That'll gi'e ye a slee and sliggy sang
Wi' mony a whuram.

Syne i' the lift
Byous spatrils you'll mak',
For a gorlin' wi' worms like this in its wame
Nae airels sall lack.

But owre the tree-taps
Maun flee like a sperk,
Till it hes the haill o' the Heavens alunt
Frae dawin' to derk.[10]

This dark ditty, a virtual image of the self-contradicted, is a forebear of Herbert's poem "And Death Must Wait," a familiar conflation of the sexual, linguistic, and national in one lyric space. MacDiarmid's poem is manifestly a proud (or owre proud) sexual and romantic boast, and equally so a linguistic (Scots) manifesto; the worm that comes (inside) to move the body and breath of the fledgling is the tongue of the Scots nation as well as the tongue "o' the Heavens alunt" and the tongue as well that licks at the ear in blunt seduction—a worm in any case, ex vermibus, negation from beyond. (In Herbert's poem, it is the "hungry-wurm" of "daith" "rummellan inniz / crop" that poses the lyric's chief danger, and that sex, however alienated, is celebrated for defeating.) MacDiarmid's embrace of the nationalist worm (incubus by another name) is not an innocent one, but, to use Blake's terms, a gesture toward experience. It can't be helped, it has everything to do with loss, and—deus ex vermibus—it moves the action along (it is hoped) toward a reversal of fortune.

If the first point to be made, then, about the struggle between monologos and polymorphousness is that for MacDiarmid the monologos is inescapable—itself an absolute precondition of polymorphousness—the second point to be made is that the monologos is itself, for MacDiarmid, polymorphous: a worm, a wall, a Received Pronunciation, a protean mutability. Or, to put it another way, MacDiarmid's nationalist worm in fact is both transcendental and a negation of the transcendental (it both occupies "the haill o' the Heavens" and displaces—replaces—that place), the monologos itself a dooble tongue.

(Wrang-heidit? Mm. *But heidit! That's the thing.*)

—MacDiarmid

Do I really want
to invoke Lukacs's "antinomies of bourgeois
thought"

                                        —Perelman

This kind of confusion of categories—the monological polymor-
phous, the polymorphous monological—establishes the problem-
atic nature of either/or thought. (*Finnegans Wake* is perhaps the
definitive [if not the master] text of this sermon.) Either/or and/or
both/and, the confusion of oppositional categories is monolithic: a
corollary to the problem of Scottish cultural self-consciousness, of
self and other, with which we began. The condition suggested
would seem then not so much a holding of power as a continual
negotiation of power held always together (often a pitifully un-
equal negotiation, true): an alienated because oppositionally con-
ceived process that conceives (oppositionally), in negation a form
of doobling, the possibility of a different process, different relation
to power—conceived but neither born nor named.

It's in this connection—the destabilization from within of either/
or, by means of metaphor—that the sexual vehicle of *Sharawaggi*
would appear to promise deliverance more readily than MacDiar-
mid's nationalist vehicle (the tenor being metaphysically unitary
and Scottish). But this would be something of a fond hope, as
Crawford's and Herbert's work in this vein draws directly upon
MacDiarmid's. The latter (which is to say, the earlier) establishes
the sexual dimension of the polymorphous monological (as it had
been established for Grieve by those previous, Burns most nota-
bly), and demonstrates the difficulties under which this sexuality
struggles.

If Crawford and Herbert, in other words, celebrate the sexual
metaphor in a spirit of rampant assent, MacDiarmid is obliged to
take a more vexed approach: the
metaphor is celebrated, as in "Ex
vermibus" above, rising like a re-
naissance o sang, but as much
a threat as a promise—and
throughout his work it remains a
seriously constrained, anxious cat-
egory, a worm or serpent, a supine drunk, an ecstasy of the Ro-
mantic sublime. In Herbert's "Cock of the South," with its
epigraph "On reading *To Circumjack Cencrastus* 'in difficult days,' "
it is precisely a vision of this anxious category, of MacDiarmid's
"phallic shapes" ("owrebalancin ma fears") that saves the poet
("Scrievan this in pitmirk, / awaukent frae deep sleep") from

among these mysteries
We poets sit ceraunic as a
  chalumeau
                    —MacDiarmid

thi fizzog o wir naishun
surfacin thru aa wir creaishun
lyk a melonchalany Bloab
fae Fufty Thoosan Fathums. . . .

MacDiarmid's "phallic shapes" represent a vision not of some "hideous replica / o aa thi Georgians stud fur / (which wad be aboot thi Nashunal Anthum's / equivalent in verse gin therr's ony)," but a vision that evokes for Herbert instead

. . . thi disremembert banes
o a Scoatlan that merely
disna hail thi coanquerin goargan in
these sel-same Salamandrake deys . . .[11]

If MacDiarmid's sexual metaphor, then, is problematic—less, shall we say, liberated than Crawford/Herbert's—it remains nevertheless a potent form of alienation.

Without Contraries is no progression.

—Blake

The dooble play that bigs and braks
In endless victory and defeat
Is in your spikes and roses shown,
And a' my soul is hagger'd wi't.

—MacDiarmid

MacDiarmid's signature work, *A Drunk Man Looks at the Thistle* (1926), moves under the sign of dialectic: in fact, the thistle (whose spikes and roses he addresses above) represents for him the condition of nothing imaginable beyond dialectic—dialectic as monologos, or as an attempt to think within the structure of oppositionality, of monologic's either/or, in the spirit of undoing that structure. This is a deeply, maddeningly forlorn condition, even driven to distraction, though not entirely a hopeless one. Failure is renowned.

Blake's famous dictum (in the context of his own meditations on imperial politics, nationalist emanations, sexuality, and the materiality of literary production) identifies this conception of dialectic with what *we* have come to identify as Romanticism—the sign beyond the sign of dialectic beyond the sign of the thistle. The dialectic of Romanticism, a condition without horizon (and a tool as well), posits power and alienation (here the thistle's spikes and roses, respectively and vice versa) as inalienable, contrair emanations, polymorphous and monological turn and turn about. The mono and the poly masquerade as transcendentals in this system, but represent (finally) mainly only each other and the system itself, and seem to function merely as counters, markers in a kind of literary play. By this I mean a serious play, conceived in terms like Hans-Georg Gadamer's:

> When do we speak of play and what is implied when we do? Surely the first thing is the to and fro of constantly repeated movement—we only have to think of certain expressions like "the play of light" and "the play of the waves" where we have such a constant coming and going, back and forth, a movement that is not tied down to any goal . . . movement *as* movement, exhibiting so to speak a phenomenon of excess, of living self-representation.[12]

It is this "dooble play that bigs and braks / In endless victory and defeat," and that haggers the Drunk Man's soul.

Power, monologic/duality/polymorphousness, alienation: the Drunk Man's condition is a kind of hangover of great, indeed inescapable, Romantic metaphors—not transcendental but embodying the limits of the conceivably possible, the One and/or the Other (and the—nameless—one other than the One and/or the Other) as provisional bedrock. (Milton, Shakespeare, Spenser, and Chaucer, like Blake, are poets of an imperial England, with their own complicated conceptions of language in relation to the mono and the poly, and their own treatment of sexuality as a function of this relation. These convergences of cultural materials—sexuality, nationalism, modes of discourse—are older than Romanticism, in some connections as old as Plato and no doubt older. I call the great metaphors Romantic because the period we have come to call Romantic—under which I would subsume the modern and postmodern as well—is defined in part by a characteristic attitude toward these matters: an attitude more explicitly, self-consciously, anxiously obsessive.) If *A Drunk Man Looks at the Thistle* is in part concerned to establish the timeless, cosmic pedigree of this terrible tangle, it is also concerned to demonstrate the particular form of its feverish modern emanation.

I want to trace (and embellish) here, then, the lines of the Drunk Man's spiel, in order to establish its relation both to the imagination of *Sharawaggi* and to the Romantic enterprise of Burns's work—the root, I would argue, of this particular Scottish tradition.

The Drunk Man's dance with the dialectic is, to begin with, a formal matter, and the history of the poem's form is by now familiar enough: MacDiarmid wrote a great deal of disparate material in a short space of time, conceived as a whole but without particular order—the piece growing and shrinking dramatically from "over a thousand lines" on 17 December 1925 to "over 600 lines" on 12 February 1926 ("when the poet offered it to his publishers . . . for publication in the autumn, saying that he was anxious to keep it by him 'for a little yet, at any rate, for final revision' ") to 2600 lines on 22 June, to something considerably larger ("at least six times as big . . . as 'Sangschaw' ") on 6 August, to 2685 upon publication in November. At some point in this process (versions of the story differ) MacDiarmid and his friend, the composer F. G. Scott, spent a long evening arranging and rearranging pieces of the poem, cutting some and adding some as well (the last two lines of the poem, by at least one account, belong to Scott); when the poem was reprinted by Macmillan in the *Collected Poems* of 1962, it was divided into fifty-nine separately titled sections, an alteration so definitive that the poem "could no longer take its chronological place in the corpus of his poems but would require to be relegated to the back of the volume, where the 'Hitherto Uncollected' items were to appear"—titles which (or versions of which) nevertheless may have attached to these pieces, or other pieces, thirty-five or -six years earlier, when MacDiarmid first wrote the poem; and it is now known both in the form of anthologized, de- and recontextualized sections—poems (as it were) in themselves—and as an "original" single continuous text in more recent editions such as Weston's and Buthlay's (Buthlay's with facing page annotation providing the again absent section-titles, doobling the doobling once more).[13]

All of which is to say, first, that the *Drunk Man* is of a piece with all of MacDiarmid's large-scale work, in its identity crisis and formal instability, in its resistance to and aspiration toward the condition of monologos. The writing of *To Circumjack Cencrastus*, which follows in 1930 and is conceived by MacDiarmid as a kind of antidote to the *Drunk Man* ("positive where it is negative, optimistic where it is pessimistic, and constructive where it is destructive"),[14] has a similar form and a similar history of pieces coalescing and dispersing, extracted and recirculated (many of them bearing titles, in the late *More Collected Poems* [1970] with no reference to their original setting). In its fullest assembly, it appears under the familiar title, somewhat more of an obvious collage than the *Drunk Man*, incorporating section titles at irregular intervals, some numbered sections as well, some both numbered and titled, and "notes on some of my more obscure allusions" at the end;[15] these various gestures are, in effect, challenges to the monological dimension of the poem's own discourse, and suggest that whatever forces allow *A Drunk Man Looks at the Thistle* at least to appear to be one whole have, with *Cencrastus*, begun to give way.

With the later works (works predominantly in English) this process accelerates, though the terms of monologic and its disarray remain. *In Memoriam James Joyce* appears in 1955 as a piece "From *A Vision of World Language*" (a larger work which never appears), made up of six titled sections (the first of which is also called by the title of the whole) which also appear separately, unattributed to the whole,

> And all this here, everything I write, of course,
> Is an extended metaphor for something I never mention
> —MacDiarmid

elsewhere (as in *More Collected Poems*). Others of the long poems disintegrate entirely, as Herbert notes in his helpfully concise archaeology of the matter. In April 1937 the poet speaks of "my monumental *A Cornish Heroic Song*, which is now I think about five times as long as *Circumjack* and not yet completed" (Herbert notes that this would make the poem over sixteen thousand lines long); by the next February, Herbert tells us, he is writing to T. S. Eliot about " 'an important long poem' he'd like Faber to consider, of 'between 4,000 and 5,000 lines—entitled *Mature Art*' "—which he claims in a letter to William Soutar is "really a separable section of the 'Cornish Heroic Song' " (also known by its "full title . . . 'Cornish Heroic Song for Valda Trevlyn'," which is itself said to be—in the letter to Eliot—circularly, an "appendix" to *Mature Art*) of which the *Joyce* is also said to be "a small portion . . . complete in itself"; there is also a "vast poem" in three volumes consisting of the *Joyce*, a piece called *The Kind of Poetry I Want* (which appears separately under that title in 1961, although the same title heads a chapter of *Lucky Poet* in 1943, which includes passages of the same material as well as something—later, in the *Complete Poems* of 1978—called "Further Passages from 'The Kind of Poetry I Want'," plus a good deal of prose), and a piece called *Impavidi Progediamur*[16] (which never appears—as MacDiarmid himself notes in the *Complete Poems*, "There is no proper sequence in which poems I attributed to *Impavidi Progediamur* can be presented, but the interested reader will find in the Index of Titles a list of those poems that at one time or another I thought of including in that work"; he also notes that "Other large-scale projects, such as 'Clann Albann' [with its parts 'The Muckle Toon' and 'Fier comme un Ecossais'] and the complete 'Cornish Heroic Song for Valda Trevlyn', were either abandoned or subsumed in other works, and are not recorded here").[17] There is also what Herbert calls "the enormous diatribe *The Battle Continues*" (1957) and "the three poems known collectively as *Direadh*" (1974), the former containing "sections from *In Memoriam* and the first *Direadh* poem, as well as from the mid-thirties Scots poem 'Ode to All Rebels' and a poem later absorbed into the *Impavidi Progediamur* project" (this latter "also called *Haud Forrit* for one part of its development"). And MacDiarmid's list of titles which " 'at one time or another I thought of including in that work' . . . contains poems like 'The Glen of Silence', and 'Once in a Cornish Garden', which were earlier claimed as part of the *Cornish Heroic Song*" conceived almost forty years earlier, and not simply never finished but found in the end to have disappeared, scattered and missing like the limbs of Osiris.[18]

"What can be done with such an inchoate mass?" Herbert reasonably asks, and argues that "a complete poem can nonetheless be perceived, and that practically all of his late work can be seen to fit into its structure." This "complete poem" is of a peculiar kind, however (or perhaps not peculiar at all, only extreme in the scale and energy of its self-consciousness with regard to this condition). Herbert calls it "an unclosable text," and (in both its thematic and formal concerns) "a hymn to potentialities rather than accepted notions."[19] The poem exists, that is, in no determinable form—beyond even the possibility of determinable form, somewhere, in other words, out of this world, beyond the determinations of Romantic dialectic (since in this world, that poem does not exist). The indeterminable form of the poem is a constellation of abortions that nevertheless do not die: they continue to lay claim even in (or because of) their disappearance.

It is MacDiarmid's burden and genius, his pound of flesh to the incubus, to embody this condition as a critical negation, to envision the form of disappearance as a heroic mode: a formal representation of confusion and interchangeability, of both the flux and the sway of identity, of the monologos at bay, of borders and the illusions of borders. The "unclosable text" stands for Scotland, and represents both the unfinishable *agon* of cultural identity and Scotland's characteristic form of resistance to that *agon* (resistance to closing the text of Scotland)—and represents as well, in this resistance, a promise of the (always prob-

THE FLESH I SELL
MYSELF
. . . .
FOR A CONTROLLING
INTEREST IN THE SIGN
                —Perelman

lematic) polymorphous, a gift to the history that proceeds, in Walter Benjamin's terms, from the side of the victim.[20]

(This is the promise that in *Sharawaggi* is perhaps ultimately sexual, and that in MacDiarmid is perhaps more hopeless; MacDiarmid's grand project in this connection both looks forward to *Sharawaggi* [like MacDiarmid's work a mirror and undoing of the Scottish *agon*, and a vision of escape into polymorphousness—Herbert notes the "post-Modernist" nature of MacDiarmid's "modes of execution, and the resulting inconclusive fruition"],[21] and looks back to Burns, whose project in Song [a kind of non- or anti-narrative national epic] is similarly unclosable, textually polymorphous and unstable, shifting pieces among shifting wholes, a gesture, in the end, against empire.)

Against this background, the *Drunk Man* appears as a text of startling unity—even, as I will argue below, a text of one multiform poem written again and again, fifty-nine or however many times. The *Drunk Man* shares with *Cencrastus* and the others a condition of collage, and in its explicit thematization and formalization of duality, antisyzygy, it embodies the sign of radical uncertainty; unlike the others, the *Drunk Man* speaks as if whole—an illusion more hopeful, or more unwitting.

The language of the poem, MacDiarmid's first (and most continuously extended) large-scale work in Scots, is a formal matter too, of course, bearing particular freight; and relative to the structural circumstances of the *Drunk Man* and the other long poems, the language has the virtue of more immediate presence. MacDiarmid's language is again a fairly familiar story: a collage Scots, vocabulary and usage synthesized (braided, although Braid Scots means Broad Scots) from diverse regional dialects, diverse centuries, and John Jamieson's *Etymological Dictionary of the Scottish Language*. While a modern Prometheus, this language is in another respect plainly traditional—casting the "unitary subject" of the people's tongue in the light of preexistence.

This Scots, for readers of Scots as for readers of English, foregrounds (whatever its other concerns may be) the materiality of language, and in this way too resists the monologic of the transcendental: as Jerome McGann argues, in the more general context of Modernist Romanticism, "the textual move is the opposite of transcendental because we are not borne away with these pages, we are borne down by them."[22] McGann goes on, with reference to Susan Howe, and to "a world held in being by its faith in the referential structure of signs": "As this world disappears we glimpse language turning toward a more elemental condition, toward an Adamic language of performative utterances ('her cry') and scripts that function purely as sonic and visible forms."[23] This is (of course) not a new argument, nor one specific to Scotland (obviously) or to modern times: the sonic and the visible, the material emanations of language (the sensuous polymorph) stand against the abstractions of sense—in its dual nature, language both tool and body part. Making sense in one sense stands against making sense in another, and this general condition of language represents itself in various forms, is put to various purposes, in various places and times—as for Blake, Morris, MacDiarmid, Crawford and Herbert, Howe, or Burns.

In "Gairmscoile" (from *Penny Wheep*, 1926—with its epigraph "Oor tree's no' daised wud yet / But's routh o' fruit to yield"), it is "a' Scotland's destiny," " 'yont a' desire and will," that is linked to this material face and vibration of language, "the rouch dirl o' an auld Scots strain"—material Scots the voice of a beastliness, a senselessness, an unintelligibility that nevertheless (or for that reason) transcends the foolishness of certainty: these are "beasts rowtin' " that "Life . . . deemed extinct." Language here is a sonic, visual, and not entirely decipherable matter of matter alone (though I make my point here, as MacDiarmid does, partly in thematic terms, bearing the message away from the page, blowing breath into its clay): language a materiality claimed to transcend (or at least resist) transcendence, a dooble tongue polymorphing the monologos.[24]

The materiality of language is also, in "Gairmscoile," a sexualized metaphor: what is heard as the sound of all Scotland's destiny is "the beasts' wild matin'-call," "nameless lo'enotes"—and a politicized metaphor as well, since these notes hold us "in a thrall." The beast of this poets' school—the voice beyond sense—is what "Brides sometimes catch," "Beekin' abune the herts they thocht to lo'e / And horror-stricken ken that i' themselves / A like beast stan's," and with which they couple and "brak / The bubbles o' twa souls and the haill warld gangs black." This is an image of mutually orgasmic consummation, of moving through sense to senselessness, of a totalizing reorientation:

> —Wull Gabriel in Esperanto cry
> Or a' the warld's undeemis jargons try?
> *It's soon, no' sense, that faddoms the herts o' men,*
> *And by my sangs the rouch auld Scots I ken*
> *E'en herts that ha'e nae Scots 'll dirl richt thro'*

As nocht else could—for here's a language rings
Wi' datchie sesames, and names for nameless things.[25]

Needless, perhaps, to say, this sexualized materiality is a thwarted language: unheard by "thowless fules" and "Crouse sumphs that hate nane 'bies wha'd wauken them," MacDiarmid's poet is rudely reoriented in another direction entirely ("Whummelt I tak' a bobquaw for the lift. / Instead o' sangs my mou' drites eerned phlegm")—though this is still, monologically, a material tongue clotted with phlegm. The Scots move, in other words, is not so much the opposite of transcendental (the here-or-anywhere-out-of-this-world duality of the monologos) as a way of moving within that economy, of embodying its illusions and brushing it, in Benjamin's terms again, against the grain.[26]

As John Weston notes, "orthographically [MacDiarmid's] old Scots poetry bows to England but his politics is fiercely nationalist."[27] But it might rather be said that in its nationalism too this "old Scots poetry bows to England," if a strutting provocation can be construed as a kind of bow. Still, within this tightened space—the materiality of language shrunk to a cipher, beyond the pale—there is room for a kind of movement. Donald Wesling, "Mikhaïl Bakhtin and the Social Poetics of Dialect":

> The theory of dialect is also a theory of glossolalia, at least in the sense that the partial bafflement of the standard speaker-reader is intended. The uncanniness of the sounds and syntax will violate and restructure the table of values, coming as these effects do from another site within the same language . . .

> Socially and dialogically, to bring in terms from Bakhtin, the crucial thing about dialect poetry is that we inhabit the others' speech, *chuzhaja rech'*, but beyond that we inhabit—in the sense of *sobytie*, being with or identifying with—the actual rebarbative sounds.[28]

by opening themselves to such radical self-alienation, imaginative work escapes the happy valley of production and consumption.
—Jerome McGann

Language can, in its marginalized materiality, at least baffle. And this is certainly one of the more prominent features of Scots for readers of English. Many words in Scots are orthographically identical to words in English; others differ slightly—contractions like *a'* for *all*, anachronisms (in English) like *aye* for *ever*, and words like *tae* for *to* or *too*; others differ further, but within the bounds of fairly simple substitution, like *gin* for *if*; still others permit such direct substitution while suggesting some loss in the translation, such as *harns* for *brains*, *thowless* for *lethargic* or *impotent*, or *heich-skeich* for *irresponsible*; and some, such as *yow-trummle* or *houghmagandie*, simply submit to no single English word.[29] And this is to say nothing of the requirements and signifying possibilities of pronunciation, or of the rebarbative sounds' embodiment beyond signification. The materially baffling nature of this discourse—its resistance to the presumption of being understood, its insistence on the unassimilated—marks it as a subversive (if, again, deeply constrained) force: a position that Crawford and Herbert, and other contemporary poets like Tom Leonard and Robert Alan Jamieson, claim with even more aggressive neologism.

Wesling's argument for the power of bafflement depends largely upon his distinction between *dialect* and *language*, a vexed issue wherever linguistic politics meets a nationalist incubus:

> Some Scots writers claim they are writing another language entirely, because Scots itself exists as a grouping of dialectical sub-sets; aside from linguistic reasons for doubting this, the socio-political case for taking Scots and other discourses as dialects of English is well worth making.[30]

Wesling's point is that, while the classification of dialect is a kind of demotion from that of language (in terms of independent identity, a compromised position), still it is upon dialect that the possibilities for bafflement, violation, and restructuring depend; the closeness and permeability of the border between two modes of discourse make the distance between them subversive, and embody the destabilization of all discourse.

(Wesling draws here on the "Glasgow-Scots" of Tom Leonard and the "London-Caribbean" of Linton Kwesi Johnson, as well as on Bakhtin, and on Gilles Deleuze & Felix Guattari in their work on Kafka. He argues that dialect, because it is spoken in the consciousness of its otherness, its shifting relation to normativity, is a gesture beyond national culture [or "monoculture"] to "interculture"[31]—which is one way of explaining the link between MacDiarmid's traditional linguistic nationalism and Modernist or Socialist internationalism. Pushing

> bad buzz man
> dead seen
>
> goahty learn new langwij
> sumhm ihnturnashnl
> Noah Glasgow hangup
> —Tom Leonard

further, from Deleuze & Guattari, or from Kafka, Wesling derives the sense of dialect as a condition of all language, each mode of discourse [even the monological] a language-within-a-language. Deleuze & Guattari call this condition "minor literature" and ascribe to it "three characteristics": "the deterritorialization of language, the connection of the individual to a political immediacy, and the collective assemblage of enunciation. We might as well say that minor no longer designates specific literatures but the revolutionary conditions for every literature within the heart of what is called great (or established) literature."[32] If MacDiarmid's Scots, then, is subversive in its materiality—subversive of production and consumption, of English, of understanding—it is held at once within the imagination of nationalism and as a rebuke to that imagination, a tongue doobled once again.)[33]

MacDiarmid refers to the "dooble tongue" explicitly in two contexts from *Cencrastus*. The oft-quoted couplet "Curse on my dooble life and dooble tongue, / —Guid Scots wi' English a' hamstrung," comes over a thousand lines into the poem, at one of the climaxes of the section "Frae Anither Window in Thrums," followed by this functionally parenthetical but italicized quatrain of explanation:

> *Speakin' o' Scotland in English words*
> *As it were Beethoven chirpt by birds;*
> *Or as if a Board school teacher*
> *Tried to teach Rimbaud and Nietzsche.*[34]

This model represents the oppositional emanation of the dooble tongue, its simplest mirroring of negativities, its self and other. Within this conceptual oppositionality, however, something else moves—kin and mockery of the beasts of "Gairmscoile," or Tennyson's Kraken, or Blake's Leviathan—at the heart of the poem, from the start, something oppositional even to oppositionality, something outside or beyond (or such, at any rate, is the helpless hope). This is the voice of Cencrastus itself, *The Curly Snake* its subtitle,[35] in the poem's opening section (untitled, but appearing in *More Collected Poems* as "There Is No Movement in the World Like Yours"):

> The dooble tongue has spoken and been heard.
> What poet has repeated ocht it said?
> There is nae movement in the warld like yours.[36]

The serpentine creature this dooble tongue belongs to is defined without being named—the first clue that this voice speaks beyond even duality, speaks other than the other of the other:

> You are as different frae a'thing else
> As water frae a book, fear frae the stars . . .
> The licht that History sheds on onything
> Is naething to the licht you shed on it.

This is in effect the condition that the language of the poet here, as the language of the *Drunk Man* four years earlier, aspires to—the serpent and the thistle in the end (and from the beginning) endlessly analogical twins of the monologos. The serpent's unspeakable and mighty word (the dooble tongue, Scots, its incarnation here) is despised, feared, admired, irresistable in the end, and obscure:

> The simple explanations that you gi'e
> O' age-lang mysteries are little liked
> Even by them wha best appreciate
> The soond advice you gied to Mither Eve,
>   Or think they dae.

It is a totalizing tongue, in its fractious way, a mirror of monologic: "There is nae movement in the warld like yours / Save faith's." It is enamored of poets, who

> . . . in throes o' composition whiles
> See you as fishermen in favourite pools
> May see a muckle fish they canna catch
> Clood-like beneath the glitterin' fry they can

—the one that gets away. It is a tongue identified ambiguously, either the muckle fish or the glitterin' fry

> *Contra nando incrementum* lyin'
> Under the roarin' cataracts o' Life,
> Like the catalysis that underlies
> A' the illusions o' romantic love.[37]

Swimming against the stream, or flying (underwater) against the production of offspring, a tongue speaking waste, representing the limits of romantic love—as do the beasts of "Gairmscoile" in their appearance before brides, and their transformation of bridal illusions. An undomesticated sexual tongue.

This is a considerably more complexly dualistic conception of the dooble tongue than that of Scots hamstrung with English, although for MacDiarmid these are all of a piece. The dooble tongue as agent of linguistic nationalism, and the dooble tongue as the forked sensorium of the "great green spot-bellied snake,"[38] speaking versions of radical multivalence within its own totalizing otherness, come together in *Cencrastus* as in *A Drunk Man*. Cencrastus is the voice "O' Unnatural thocht at work," and "The poet's hame is in the serpent's mooth"—but home is always, in this context, the place of exile, the voice of the dooble tongue a voice of the unnatural (and the historical), a definitive condition that eludes naming, not so much a language-within-a-language as a language beyond language. (The snake is, again, an aspiration: "Freedom is *inconceivable*. The word / Betrays the cause—" "till it seems / This is Thocht's fixed unalterable mode.")[39]

> poetry as dissent, including formal dissent; poetry that makes sounds possible to be heard that are not otherwise articulated
> —Charles Bernstein

It is the voice of nothing but change (unspeakable change): "A'thing on earth repeats itsel' but you / And a'thing langs to pit an end to change"—

> There is nae movement in the warld like yours
> Save sic divergences as dinna leave
> Things a' the mair the same the mair they change
> But alter them forever in a way
> Unheralded and unbelievable . . .

It is the voice as well of changelessness, of the One that is left when the Many depart:

> There is nae movement in the warld like yours,
> Save his, wha, ere he writes, ken's he'll no' fail
> To recognize his dear ev'n tho' her hair
> (A'e threid o' which, pu'd through his nails, 'ud frizz
> In coontless kinks like Scotland's craziest burn
> —Aye, yon bright water even wi' the sky
> That if, when we were bairns, we threw corks on't
> We panted to keep up wi' them in vain)
> Whiles loosened owre him like the sun at noon
> That insubstantializes a' the warld
> Is syne bound, coil on coil in smaller space
>   To show the smoothness o' her brow . . .

It is the voice, in other words, of everything ("a' the warld is manifest in you / —Religion, Art, Commerce and Industry, / Social and Sexual Relationships") and still at the same time the voice that denies the world, and still at the same time the voice of Scotland, kinked like a crazy burn ("Shairly the process should be clear to Scots"):

> What is Cencrastus but the wriggle
> O' Man's divided vertebrae?
> —Gin that were a' I wadna jiggle
> For my pairt wi't anither day
>
> For human unity needna mean
> Ocht to the problems I'm concerned wi',
> Nae anaconda but a green
> Kailworm is a' that seems to me.[40]

The task of the wielder of this tongue—the challenge of the material—is to "scrawl a phrase frae Scotland yet / On the palimpsest o' th' Infinite," and this is, again, a matter associated with a thwarted, compelling, illusion-ridden sexuality:

> Nae wumman ever had a tongue like this,
> No' even the twinklin' aphrodisiac tip
> O' Helen's slidin' through her roondit lips
> Or Saint Sophia's whisperin' in God's lug
> Or subtler members in the warld the day
> I aiblins ken owre muckle o', or wull,
> Or wad!—[41]

Finally for MacDiarmid the dooble tongue is the tongue that will not be pinned down and spoken for—a nationalist flag of Scotland and a more radically destabilizing manifesto of the uncertainty that moves in the body of language, that denies all nations, all identities, all human rational and signifying illusions.

It is a tall order for any language to fill (Sharawaggi derives a similarly vast and embattled conception of the function of language), but it begins humbly enough in the pleasure of the body, even the pleasure of picking a scab. (The pleasure of the body, the material experience of language, is essential to the distinction drawn in Burns's work between Poetry and Song as well.) And it never strays in its materiality, for MacDiarmid and for those who read him, from the relation of Scots to English. Glossaries provided at the end of the volume, or at the bottoms of pages, or in the margins, or not at all, or in the form of facing-page translations (this last something MacDiarmid never produced as such, although he did attempt a rendering in English of the *Drunk Man*)—

> a new language
> is a kind of scar
> and heals after a while
> into a passable imitation
> of what went before
> —Eavan Boland

each of these approaches to the baffling materiality of Scots embodies a slightly different conception of the relation between Scots and English (from Scots as an English with some curious vocabulary and orthography, to Scots as a language requiring facing-page [and always, to an extent, garbling] translation), and each identifies the materiality of Scots as its specific lever in this relation.

The serpent slithers across the ground. The materiality of the dooble tongue undermines all conceptual certainty—or aims to. As formally and linguistically, so thematically: in *A Drunk Man* the Ane and the endlessly Ither engage dialectically, all identity shifting continuously. The Drunk Man signifies the utter instability of all signification (he is in fact flat on his back, which is a kind of stability though identified with dizziness): all of his signs are sliding signs. The thistle, the moon, the serpent, the whiskey, the soul, the mind, Scotland, the creation—all come to represent or to be represented by countless other things or notions in the course of the poem, and all slide among themselves back and forth, all in duality interchangeable, standing *for* one another and for everything. Turn and turn about: the closed circle of epanadiplosis.

This interchangeability of signs (not sings) is in effect the subject of the poem—the resistance it offers to the One True Word (of English, of sobriety, of civilization) and the demon it bears in subjection: the means by which the poem becomes one poem, "Sic Transit Gloria Scotiae" and "A Vision of Myself" and "Poet's Pub" and "The Unknown Goddess" and "The Gothic Thistle" and "Our Educational System" and "Man and the Infinite" and "The Psycho-Somatic Quandary" and "Love" and "Repetition Complex" and "The Feminine Principle" and "Yank Oot Your Orra Boughs" and "The Form and Purpose of the Thistle" and "Ballad of the Crucified Rose" and "A Stick-Nest in Ygdrasil" and "The Goal of Scottish History" and "Metaphysical Pictures of the Thistle" and "The Thistle as a Spider's Web" and "Creation's Whirligig" and "My Quarrel with England," among others, moving unstably in their own directions, and telling over and over the same tale of themselves, the instability of all concept, name, identity, language.

The *Drunk Man* has a dialogue with its own dead-end monologic, his dooble tongue the tongue of rampant slippage. The poem is structurally a retelling of "Tam O'Shanter": the wife waiting at home, imagined to be cross and indulgent, in her own totalizing wisdom excluded from the husband's drinking world (the ramifications of which fill up the space of the poem)—or anti-husband, spendthrift's world, oot an aboot an unco fou. The hero is both victim or thrall of a normative economy and exile from that economy, the embodiment of a *felix* (nevertheless terrifying) *culpa*. Like Tam, and like the voice of Herbert's "Penis Envoi," the Drunk Man represents an essentially onanistic or voyeuristic sexuality, a restriction of the senses. In Tam's case, the cry of sexual (or voyeuristic) excitement, his claim beyond himself and the psychodrama of his pickled brain (beyond the abstraction of the gaze), is what gets him in trouble, setting the demons on his tail (and costing his mare Meg hers). For the Drunk Man the sexual impulse, alienated from sensible Jean and adrift in the moonlight, finds no galvanic "Weel done, Cutty-sark!" but remains objectless. Like the thistle (and like Scots) it is both ineradicable and baffled, inconceivable and undeniable.

As the *Drunk Man* begins, the question of sexuality is explicitly situated in eclipse, or on the dark side of a constellation that includes the Scots Nation, whiskey, and questions of economy. Lamenting the rising cost and lesser worth of the whiskey ("And a' that's Scotch aboot it is the name, / Like a' thing else ca'd Scottish nooadays"), and lamenting as well his own aging body—

> The elbuck fankles in the coorse o' time,
> The sheckle's no' sae souple, and the thrapple
> Grows deef and dour . . .[42]

—the Drunk Man figures "the wife" as a kind of useless antithesis. Husband and wife function as a constrained sexual economy (an essentially rationalist and productive economy), and anti-husband and his "thieveless cronies" (83) function, such as they can, in a wilderness without meaning "—A' destitute o' speerit juist the same" (20).

> Yin canna thow the cockles o' yin's hert
> Wi'oot ha'en cauld feet noo, jalousin' what
> The wife'll say (I dinna blame her fur't).
>
> (14–16)[43]

It is the figure of Burns in these opening passages of the *Drunk Man* that embodies MacDiarmid's vision of a voice speaking the unspeakable Other, beyond Nation, beyond the incubus, drunkenness, the thistle, onanism, beyond the destitution of spirit. This figure is both sexualized in a wholly obscure way and a figure of indeterminate identity (these two conditions at once congruent and discordant):

> I'se warrant you'd shy clear o' a' the hunner
>
> Odd Burns Clubs tae, or ninety-nine o' them,
> And haud your birthday in a different kip
> Whaur your name isna ta'en in vain—as Christ
> Gied a' Jerusalem's Pharisees the slip
>
> —Christ wha'd ha'e been Chief Rabbi gin he'd lik't!—
> Wi' publicans and sinners to forgether,
> But, losh! the publicans noo are Pharisees,
> And I'm no' shair o' maist the sinners either.
>
> (84–92)[44]

A different kip: Burns is not to be found in this world but, God bless him, pursues his sexual pleasure elsewhere (we might say that he pursues it in the glossary—or that we do, if *kip* is unknown to us); and he escapes us as well here slipping into Christ—who slips (giving us the slip) for a moment into Chief Rabbi—and from there to "a' the names in History" (113).

The Sign of Burns, like the Sign of Sexuality, is the Sign That Won't Stay Put, and it makes its entrance here under the Sign of Radical Dissociation—the Drunk Man is nothing if not stationary, stays nothing if not put, lost in his own slippage ("It isna me that's fou at a', / But the fu' mune, the doited jade" [97–98]).[45] He imagines himself, far from all these thoughts, these transcendental kips, "safe in my ain bed" (100), the site of his dislocation. (Until he remembers "*Jean! Jean!* Gin *she's* no' here it's no' *oor* bed" [101]—"the wife" again, here first named, at once Reality Principle and Missing Piece, both Totalizing Other and Anti-Other.) But the blurry vision of the Drunk Man is a vision nonetheless, and Burns his first extended name for it: a vision informed by sexual truancy and marked by unarticulated longings, which embodies and affirms the polymorphous other, and to which the Drunk Man has no connection. (As in Kafka, "there is an infinite amount of hope, but not for us.")[46]

This is where "Sic Transit Gloria Scotiae" becomes "A Vision of Myself." The transition is formally unmarked, the one continuing the quatrains of the other, but it turns resignation ("I maun feed

frae the common trough ana' / Whaur a' the lees o' hope are jum-
bled up" [121–22]) into resolve—

> In wi' your gruntle then, puir wheengin' saul,
> Lap up the ugsome aidle wi' the lave,
> What gin it's your ain vomit that you swill
>
> (125–27)[47]

—and thence into recommencement, the same poem over again.
The Drunk Man declares himself again to be, as with Cruivie and
Gilsanquhar, beyond the pale of civilized concourse ("As the
haill's / Mair than the pairt sae I than reason yet" [131–32]),[48]
sworn enemy of all human normativity:

> I'll ha'e nae hauf-way hoose, but aye be whaur
> Extremes meet—it's the only way I ken
> To dodge the curst conceit o' bein' richt
> That damns the vast majority o' men.
>
> (141–44)

And he declares himself again, in the end, helpless, disconnected,
in thrall to blind drive:

> I ha'e nae doot some foreign philosopher
> Has wrocht a system oot to justify
> A' this: but I'm a Scot wha blin'ly follows
> Auld Scottish instincts, and I winna try.
>
> For I've nae faith in ocht I can explain,
> And stert whaur the philosophers leave aff,
> Content to glimpse its loops I dinna ettle
> To land the sea-serpent's sel' wi' ony gaff.
>
> (149–56)[49]

Here the Nation and the Curly-Snake, the polymorphous mono-
logical and the monological polymorphous, turn into one another,
the Sign, again, that won't stay put: again the condition is madden-
ing and the site of an unco (or *outré*) power, and here even Jean
falls under the same sign, the (watered-down) water of life, whiskey
conjuring "the sea-serpent's sel' " under fou mune:

> Water! Water! There was owre muckle o't
> In yonder whisky, sae I'm in deep water
> (And gin I could wun hame I'd be in het,
> For even Jean maun natter, natter, natter)
>
> (161–64)[50]

(Although the water of Jean is hot, dissociated even in its identifica-
tion.)

And so the poem proceeds, as Joyce puts it, "the seim anew."[51]
Christ appears again, as if to herald a new beginning, again in the
context of utter inanition—

> And in the toon that I belang tae
> —What tho'ts Montrose or Nazareth?—
> Helplessly the folk continue
> To lead their livin' death! . . .
>
> (165–68)

and then the first formal break in the poem, the same quatrains
only consistently (rather than irregularly) in *abab* rhyme, and itali-
cized and indented: a rendering (in MacDiarmid's note) "From the
Russian of Alexander Blok" (in the English translation MacDiar-
mid worked from, called "The Lady Unknown"), called by Mac-
Diarmid "Poet's Pub."

Here again the material, however far afield it may appear (*"I ken
nae Russian"* [2224]), is yoked to the same signifying field: as the
Drunk Man notes earlier, in his first reference to the thistle, "A
blin' bird's nest / Is aiblins biggin' in the thistle" (34–35)—careful
discriminations are not the order of the day.[52] The poem begins
again as a vision of "Elfland" ("an enchanted distance" in the En-
glish crib from Blok)[53] discovered in the *veritas in vino*, a vision
again sexualized and baffled in its access to sexuality (like the fig-
ure of Burns earlier). The Drunk Man waxes nostalgic for sexual
hope:

> *The hauflins 'yont the burgh boonds*
> *Gang ilka nicht, and a' the same,*
> *Their bonnets cocked; their bluid that stounds*
> *Is playin' at a fine auld game.*
>
> (177–80)[54]

But he lives, in the burgh, at a less than enchanted distance even
from this hope, 'yont its boonds, as he inserts Jean (no part of
Blok's vision) to indicate: *"(Jean ettles nocht o' this, puir lass)"* (186).[55]
And he lives even further from the Unknown Lady who comes in
the midst of men drinking alone (*"rough / And reid-een'd fules that . . .
droon"* [192])[56] nevertheless holding herself apart from them—like
Burns, or like the sea-serpent: her sexualized and disorienting
promise (*"Frae'r robes, . . . / A rooky dwamin' perfume"* [200])[57] is at
once plainly made and unavailable, *"wealth unspent"* (217).

The second reference to the thistle, the first since its appearance as the blind bird's nest site, occurs here over two hundred lines into the poem: "The munelicht's like a lookin'-glass, / The thistle's like mysel' " (221–22). The Drunk Man is again figured, in another piece "Freely adapted" from Blok (in two six-line stanzas), dissociated from "*The features lang fore-kent*" and "*unforecast*" (248), this time of "The Unknown Goddess" (in MacDiarmid's here and gone again section title, "The Unknown Woman" in his English crib).[58] To be split in two (by two by two, a braid of interlocking couplets),

> This is a poetic act,
> the poem being formed from the scission
> of the self where its imaginary total
> shatters in real time as it meets
> its alienated social material
> and sits ejected from eternity viewing
> the narrative of its salvation
> —Perelman

adrift on the radical slipperiness of signification, and to hold nevertheless (or as a result) a vision—of Burns, of the Unknown Goddess/Woman/Lady, of the phallus, of the thistle: this is the Drunk Man's condition.

With "My Nation's Soul," for example, the Drunk Man shifts back into quatrains, longer and more irregular (generally *abcb* pentameters) as if to embody the capaciousness and stress of his subject, and begins, weirdly Elizabethan, yet again:

> Or dost thou mak' a thistle o' me, wumman? But for thee
> I were as happy as the munelicht, withoot care,
> But thocht o' thee—o' thy contempt and ire—
> Turns hauf the warld into the youky thistle there.
>
> (253–56)[59]

This wumman is unavoidably both the Unknown one and Jean as well, her opposite number as it were. Thistle, self, moonlight, whiskey ("This munelicht's fell like whiskey noo I see't" [281]), "wumman," serpent, Reason ("the knowledge o' Guid and Ill," "this Frankenstein that nae man can escape" [261, 268]), "the Throne o' God," "Man torn in twa" (274–75) come and go and change their partners in a web of interchangeable identities, nonentities, deceptions and dislocations. And through the misty promiscuous interchange of inebriation, too, each of these counters, these ciphers of otherness, comes to embody (momentarily, in a trick of munelicht) something beyond this web—here in "My Nation's Soul" it is drink which is "the apter, aiblins, to be true" (280).[60]

The Drunk Man's limitations, as he begins yet again with "The Gothic Thistle," are explicitly linked to the limitations of the nation:

> To meddle wi' the thistle and to pluck
> The figs frae't is *my* metier, I think.
> Awak', my muse, and gin you're in puir fettle,
> We aye can blame it on th' inferior drink.
>
> (341–44)

It is a condition of utter paralysis, in "The Octopus" ("Adapted from the Russian of Zinaida Hippius," called "Psyche" in MacDiarmid's crib: Buthlay notes that the "insertion of a 'poulp' in line 5" belongs to Deutsch and Yarmolinsky's English, that "there is no octopus in the original, the title of which is 'Ona' ['She']"): "*A shaggy poulp, embracin' me and stingin', / And as a serpent cauld agen my hert*" (357–58).[61] But the muse does wake and wake and wake:

> *But ilka windin' has its coonter-pairt*
> *—The opposite 'thoot which it couldna be—*
> *In some wild kink or queer perversity*
> *O' this great thistle, green wi' jealousy,*
> *That breenges 'twixt the munelicht and my hert. . . .*
>
> Plant, what are you then? Your leafs
> Mind me o' the pipes' lood drone . . .
>
> (406–12)[62]

The thistle reminds him as well of "alligators / That ha'e gobbled owre a haill / Company o' Heilant sodgers" (416–18), and of "Mephistopheles in Heaven" (427), and of a man who landed on one once, with "naething on ava aneth his kilt. / Schönberg has nae notation for his whistle" (433–34).[63] In short, Scotland and the thistle stand both for and against one another, and stand both for and against the Drunk Man, who declares (in "Our Educational System"):

> Guid sakes, I'm in a dreidfu' state.
> I'll hae nae inklin' sune
> Gin I'm the drinker or the drink,
> The thistle or the mune.
> I'm geylies feart I couldna tell
> Gin I s'ud lay me doon
> The difference betwixt the warld
> And my ain heid gaen' roon'! . . .
>
> (446–53)[64]

The Man's condition, in other words, is not conducive to vision—or is so promiscuously conducive that it's all the same: there is no way out of where he is, no auld brig or rules about witches or bogles and running water, no passage elsewhere. His thwarted vision-quest has many emanations—nationalist ("My Nation's Soul"), personal ("A Vision of Myself"), cosmic ("Man and Infinity"), scientific ("The Psycho-Somatic Quandary"), organic ("The Barren Fig"), gendered ("The Feminine Principle"), erotic ("Love Often Wuns Free"), mythic ("A Stick-Nest in Ygdrasil")—and is a type of the Romantic vision-quest, the standard Romantic alienated imagination. (Again, the matter is as old no doubt as prehistory, assuming different forms in dialectical relation to changing cultural arrangements: what we have come to identify as the Romantic form of this alienation—subsuming again what we have come to call the Modern or Modernist and what we squabble over calling the postmodern—is distinguished in part by the sense of the endemic, an alienation culturally pervasive, the ineradicable fruit of sociopolitical development: distinguished, in short, by its back against the wall.)

Passing candidates arise for the mantle of vision, claim the capacity to stand outside inanition, and break down in one way or another, or stagger off, winded, like Atalanta's suitors. Another Romantic favorite, childhood:

> Drums in the Walligate, pipes in the air,
> Come and hear the cryin' o' the Fair.
>
> A' as it used to be, when I was a loon
> On Common-Ridin' Day in the Muckle Toon.
>
> . . . .
> Devil the star! It's Jean I'll ha'e
> Again as she was on her weddin' day . . .

(455–58, 475–76)[65]

"The aucht-fit thistle wallops on hie" (461) over the proceedings, and "Drums in the Walligate, pipes in the air, / The wallopin' thistle is ill to bear" (469–70)—with Buthlay's gloss on *ill* being *difficult.* For the Drunk Man as for Yeats, this center does not hold, as for Pound it does not cohere. "The Crying of the Fair" butts right up against "Man and the Infinite," which reaches a crescendo of "Nerves in stounds o' delight," "Swippert and swith wi' virr / In the howes o' man's hert" (477, 483–84),

> Like a Leviathan astert,
> Till'ts coils like a thistle's leafs
> Sweep space wi' levin sheafs.
>
> (486–88)[66]

The thistle "rises in flight upon flight," "Frae laichest deeps o' the ocean" (489–90), but these "Fountains" "o' my hert," "ootloupin' the starns" (501–2), turn abruptly into their opposites, turn out to be figments, simply, of their own negation:

> —The howes o' Man's hert are bare,
> The Dragon's left them for good,
> There's nocht but naethingness there,
> The hole whaur the Thistle stood
>
> (507–10)[67]

All is lost, in the sign of the wallopin thistle, or if gained, nevertheless—as before—unavailable. The figure of the Poet, another candidate, in "The Challenge of the Arts" belongs to a community of "artists" who "live for oor antrin lichtnin's / In the haingles atweenwhiles" (539–40),[68] and who "breenge in unkennable shapes" of deepest gloss Scots: "—*Crockats up, hair kaimed to the lift, / And no' to cree legs wi'!* . . ." (Buthlays's gloss: "crockats up—on one's dignity [MacD—but J{amieson} has 'to set up one's crockats': to show ill-humour, or give an indiscreet answer]; kaimed—combed; no' to cree legs wi'—not safe to meddle with [an aberrant form of 'no' (gude) to creel eggs wi', not safe to deal with"). This poet's lichtnin's are kin to the thistle's levin sheafs, and antrin indeed, more rare perhaps, in 1926, than "the practice of Cadgers or Egglers, who collect eggs through the country, and pack them in their hampers" from which MacDiarmid's "dubious . . . Scots" expression "to cree legs" derives.[69] The bizarrely hermetic nature of the vision here is at once its chief claim and diminution: and the poet too, like the poem, moves only "frae inklin' to inklin' " (538).

A Drunk Man is a "vegetable cat's melody" or "*Concert Miaulant*," "A triumph o' discord shairly" (565–67) which means both triumph over and veneration of.[70] This is the vertebra of the curly-snake called "The Ineducable," where the Challenge of the Arts meets its Waterloo. The poem is also a vision of Christianity as a sailors' song:

> We're ootward boond frae Scotland.
> Guid-bye, fare-ye-weel; guid-bye, fare-ye-weel.
> The cross-tap is a monkey-tree
> That nane o' us can spiel.

> We've never seen the Captain,
> But the first mate is a Jew
>
> (549–54)[71]

—a vision mad with helpless energy and blind faith. Sandwiched between two pieces "constructed around unusual Scots expressions found in Jamieson's Dictionary," "Outward Bound" identifies Scotland yet again as a condition of internal exile.[72]

Or sexuality, again. In "The Psycho-Somatic Quandary" and "Love," the Drunk Man experiences a phallo-thistle erection ("I'se warrant Jean 'ud no' be lang / In findin' whence this thistle sprang") which he envisions as a world apart ("Mebbe it's juist because I'm no' / Beddit wi' her that gars it grow!" [591–94]). This is a sexuality, again, of alienation—not a bodily wumman but a light that reveals a bodily man, a reflection of an abstraction:

> A luvin' wumman is a licht
> That shows a man his waefu' plicht,
> Bleezin' steady on ilka bane,
> Wrigglin' sinnen an' twinin' vein . . .
>
> (595–98)[73]

A luvin' wumman, like the woman, lady, or goddess Unknown, like the thistle phallus, like the "courage-bag confined" (580), is emblem both transcendental and thoroughly compromised—identified, for the Drunk Man, with "a' the miseries o' his flesh . . ." (603).[74]

"Millions o' wimmen" (636) offer no escape from "The Repetition Complex." In this section, Mary—prototype and anomaly of women—is figured as myth ("in jizzen / As it were claith o' gowd" [644–45]) and as myth debunked (by the "orra duds" of "Ilka ither bairntime" [646–47]), and the product of sexuality as a matter of "bellythraw, ripples, and worm-i'-the-cheek" (650): "—yet, gi'en a mither's love, / —Hee, hee!—wha kens hoo't micht improve" (665–66). This last is an embittered faith, to say the least. It is at this point (with the hopefully helpful title to the section "To Be Yourselves and Make That Worth Being") that Burns reenters the poem—"Puir Burns, wha's bouquet like a shot kail blaws" (723). He reenters overripe, ambiguously identified with

> The vandal Scot! Frae Brankstone's deidly barrow
> I struggle yet to free a'e winsome marrow,
> To show what Scotland micht ha'e hed instead
> O' this preposterous Presbyterian breed.
>
> (735–38)[75]

This is the Burns again of the different kip, of the vision sustained although missing and unaccounted for—joined here by Dunbar: neither of them in the end (and from the start) much help against the "drumlie clood o' crudity and cant, / Obliteratin' " (771–72), but still the (missing) sign of inanition's Other.[76]

"*Yank Oot Your Orra Boughs*" is still ahead, but it speaks to this moment in the poem as well as the moment speaks for itself (or better)—as each passage in the poem speaks to each interchangeably, a nightmare of hyper/insignificance: "Mebbe we're in a vicious circle cast, / Mebbe there's limits we can ne'er get past" (1026–27). There is, again, it seems (or would seem), no way out beyond the border of monologos. For the moment there is instead "My Quarrel with the Rose" and a return to the nationalist-political emanation:

> I micht ha'e been contentit wi' the Rose
> Gin I'd had ony reason to suppose
> That what the English dae can e'er mak' guid
> For what Scots dinna—and first and foremost should.
>
> I micht ha'e been contentit—gin the feck
> O' my ain folk had grovelled wi' less respec',
> But their obsequious devotion
> Made it for me a criminal emotion.
>
> (751–58)[77]

(In Herbert's "Cock of the South" the poet's vision is of "thi disremembirt banes / o a Scoatlan that merely / disna hail thi coanquerin goargan.")[78] The vision here is of Scotland as the mark of absence; and in the criminality—the border violation—of this absence, a vision of a place beyond the Rose ("fields on which it couldna draw," "Elements like mine that in a rose ne'er grew" [760, 766]) nevertheless "Happit for centuries in an alien gloom" (778).[79]

The *Drunk Man* is a successive demonstration of this condition in the theoretically endless panoply of its forms: the possibilities for (in Perelman's terms) the "narrative of salvation" are scant, unseizable, illusory, thwarted, or otherwise absurd, and obsessively-compulsively sought, insisted upon, and abandoned.[80] Conceptual possibilities that exist for Burns, or for Crawford and Herbert, are ruthlessly, lugubriously, splenetically, madly, energetically demolished by the Drunk Man, sucked into the hopeless vortex of monologic, its endless dualities and interchanges; and this represents, again, both MacDiarmid's relative limitations and his warning power. Everything, for the Drunk Man, becomes (again) everything else—the Rose of England the thistle's own unlikely bloom here—and nothing, for him, in itself, can possibly matter.

And so the poem begins again, "*Eneuch! For noo I'm in the mood, / Scotland*"—and immediately stops again:

> What's ocht to the people o' Scotland?
> Speak—and Cruivie'll goam at you,
> Gilsanquhar jalouse you're dottlin!"
>
> (779, 784–86)[81]

And then begins again—"Clear keltie aff an' fill again" (811)[82]— this time, again, on the note of sexuality happit in an alien gloom. Another break from the prevalent quatrains into couplets, a poem within a poem in quotation marks, is addressed " 'To Luna at the Craidle-and-Coffin,' " otherwise called " 'Auld bag o' tricks' " (819, 821)—the moon, the imagination, the condition of wax and wane and ebb and flow, addressed and spurned as an entirely mechanical sexual opportunity: " 'You pay nae heed but plop me in, / Syne shove me oot'," (827–28). What the Drunk Man tells Luna, in quite so many words, is that he will not fuck her.

But the quotation closes and another abruptly begins, a second set of five couplets, depicting this (or another) sexual opportunity as nevertheless inescapable: "I canna ride awa' like Tam, / But e'en maun bide juist whaur I am" (833–34). Then the quatrains return and with them another summation of sorts (the Drunk Man summing up as often as he recommences)—ejaculation, urination, and the waste of beer all figured together in one trope:

> My belly on the gantrees there,
> The spigot frae my cullage,
> And wow but how the fizzin' yill
> In spilth increased the ullage!
>
> (845–48)[83]

It is a tapsal-teerie (although perfectly normal) world in which spilth increases ullage, in which overabundance and deficiency represent one another. The sexual here, through all its forms— Luna, Cutty Sark, the enactment of "true love" (954), the propagation of the species and of cosmic vertigo—is linked repeatedly to a conception of production (of bairns, of self—"I'll no' be born again / In ony brat you can produce" [824–25], of fizz and ullage) with no capacity for ending, a metastasis, "Cratur withoot climacteric!" (830).[84] All of MacDiarmid's visionary illusions—Burns in the kip, the unknown females, the Scots tongue—point to the Sign (signs of the sign) that moves apart from Production, and all fall under its sway: antisyzygy as manifesto of a lost cause.

At this point the Drunk Man's condition brings him, with "The Mortal Flaw," back to materiality as to a rock, an orienting perspective outside his own head (like the Jewish First Mate Jesus, a promise of navigational certainty)—but where materiality means the thistle in the moonlight, and whiskey a bottomless transcendental thirst, to come back to one's senses is to leave them entirely, and both to inhabit and lose one's mind:

> What forest worn to the back-hauf's this,
> What Eden brocht doon to a bean-swaup?
> The thistle's to the earth as the man
> In the mune's to the mune, puir chap.
>
> . . . .
>
> What forest worn to the back-hauf's this,
> What Eden brocht doon to a bean-swaup?
> —A' the ferlies o' natur' spring frae the earth,
> And into't again maun drap.
>
> (861–64, 909–12)[85]

One of these ferlies is Scotland—or, more precisely, the materialization of Scots:

> A spook o' soond that frae the unkent grave
> In which oor nation lies loups up to wave
> Sic leprous chuns as tatties have
> That cellar-boond send spindles gropin'
> Towards ony hole that's open,
>
> Like waesome fingers in the dark that think
> They still may widen the ane and only chink
> That e'er has gi'en mankind a blink
> O' Hope—tho' ev'n in that puir licht
> They s'ud ha'e seen their hopeless plicht.
>
> (1010–19)[86]

The materiality of language and the sexuality of hope meet here in the form of the potato—"—For naething's seen or kent that's near a thing itsel'!" (1088)—and it is here (amang the hert's orra boughs) that the Drunk Man raises the possibility that "Mebbe we're in a vicious circle cast."

One asks with admiration how this poem can possibly continue: flat on his back, the Drunk Man can't fall over, but he can fall asleep and he doesn't, and in this he claims too to be verily Scotland. Efforts to "brak' the habit o' my life / A worthier to devise" persist (1145–46) in "Ballad of the Crucified Rose": " 'My nobler instincts sall nae mair / This contrair shape be gi'en' " (1148–49). The Drunk Man here is quoting "the thocht that hid ahint / The thistle's ugsome guise" (1143–44), quoting himself, that is, at a remove; though "The dream o' beauty's dernin' yet / Ahint the ugsome shape," it is a

> —Vain dream that in a pinheid here
> And there can e'er escape!
>
> The vices that defeat the dream
> Are in the plant itsel',
> And till they're purged its virtues maun
> In pain and misery dwell.
>
> Let Deils rejoice to see the waste,
> The fond hope brocht to nocht.
> The thistle in their een is as
> A favourite lust they've wrocht.
>
> (1187–98)[87]

The poem goes on (because the tongue is well-watered, although like "a' the seas" of "A Red, Red Rose" it begins to grow dry in lines 1379–80) because of its own impossibility of continuing, *because* it is "brocht to nocht": "The bitter taste is on my tongue, / I chowl my chafts, and pray" (1215–16), "The language that but sparely flooers / And maistly gangs to weed" (1219–20).[88]

> These are the thistle's characters,
> To argie there's nae need.
> Hoo weel my verse embodies
> The thistle you can read!
> —But will a Scotsman never
> Frae this vile growth be freed? . . .
>
> (1225–30)[89]

The *Drunk Man* creates and re-creates itself *ex nihilo*. He chowls his chafts at—provokes and mourns—the thistle, emblem of his impossible and unstoppable continuation (in part, again, a sexual curse):

> O stranglin' rictus, sterile spasm,
> Thou stricture in the groins o' licht,
> Thou ootrie gangrel frae the wilds

> O' chaos fenced frae Eden yet
> By the unsplinterable wa'
> O' munebeams like a bleeze o' swords!
>
> (1292–97)[90]

And the vision—the Drunk Man's look at the thistle—continues, if not for us:

> The thistle like a snawstorm drives,
> Or like a flicht o' swallows lifts,
> Or like a swarm o' midges hings,
> A plague o' moths, a starry sky,
> But's naething but a thistle yet,
> And still the puzzle stands unsolved.
>
> (1338–43)[91]

Indistinguishably polymorphous and monological, the thistle here stands for a defeat that will not end (like Culloden, say—or Bannockburn for that matter). Here "a' a people's genius" is only

> A rumple-fyke in Heaven's doup,
> While Calvinism uses her
> To breed a minister or twa!
>
> (1330–33)[92]

That Calvinism should figure in terms of a displaced, productive sexuality is only one of the Drunk Man's more obvious contrair shapes (his mouth *is* getting dry). Opposition is privileged in the thistle's conceptual economy (because when you're One you know what the Other is about, but when you're *that* one you know nothing: "Gin I was sober I micht think / It was like something drunk men see!" [1351–52]), and sexual vexation is the type of oppositional transaction claimed, in "The Thistle's Characteristics" again, to be essential or transcendental:

> —My mither's womb that reins me still
> Until I tae can prick the witch
> And "Wumman" cry wi' Christ at last,
> "Then what hast thou to do wi' me?"
>
> The tug-o'-war is in me still . . .
>
> (1357–61)

To speak then not the mither tongue but to "speak in tongues / We dinna ken and never wull" (1408–9), to "feel like souls set free /

Frae mortal coils" (1407–8—*to feel* being ambiguously self-contra-
dicted, a doobling within a doobling): this is, to put it yet another
way, the Drunk Man's project. And sexuality, whatever claims are
made for it (and however close to the heart of the problematic),
offers no more access to the pursuit of this feeling tongue than any
other oppositionally conceived enterprise:

> My sinnens and my veins are but
> As muckle o' a single shoot
> Wha's fibre I can ne'er unwaft
> O' my wife's flesh and mither's flesh
> And a' the flesh o' humankind . . .
>
> (1493–97)[93]

The shoot of the thistle represents in this connection both sexuality
itself and (again) the very helplessness that sexuality is claimed
(persistently and unsuccessfully) to overcome or move beyond: the
thistle, at the heart of sexuality the void.

As the Drunk Man's signs and endless dualities continue to slide
amongst themselves in perpetual motion, he finds his comfort
nonetheless, lying in that very dizziness—and so the poem contin-
ues, immune to all logic, in spite of every reasonable (and unrea-
sonable) expectation. Its very continuance, at this point, is its *point*,
it seems, and the more in disarray the better: a sustainable nega-
tion of monologos.

> It may be nocht but cussedness,
> But I'm content gin a' my thocht
> Can dae nae mair than let me see,
> Free frae desire o' happiness,
> The foolish faiths o' ither men
> In breedin', industry, and War,
> Religion, Science, or ocht else
> Gang smash—when I ha'e nane mysel',
> Or better gin I share them tae,
> Or mind at least a time I did!
>
> (1615–24)

Free from desire of happiness, in the context of the hegemony of
the Military Industrial Sexual Production Complex, the Drunk
Man represents a desire, at least, to smash (himself as well)—or, at
least, to watch all smash, since he is powerless himself, prostrate,
addled and smashed himself, to effect it.

Powerlessness and the foolishness of all certainty materialize
here in the abrupt image of a birth that has no other reference in
the poem, and that is certainly not occurring now—Jean's labor,
apparently like the Drunk Man's, without issue or end: *"Jean has
stuck sic a fork in the wa' / That I row in agonie"* (1634–35).[94] At least
one foolish faith—faith in the definition of gender—gangs smash
here, and the End seems to be drawing near ("Baith bairns and
Gods'll be obsolete soon / [The twaesome gang thegither]" [1648–
49]), but the poem has over a thousand lines to go, and it begins
again here in the hope of its own helplessness, even, it "may be,"
as "the stane the builders rejec' / Becomes the corner stane" (1651–
52), "In workin' oot mankind's great synthesis . . ." (1658).

The process of this continuance is of "thocht-preventin' thocht
concealed" (1688) revealed again and again, a revelation that as-
pires to the "certainty that nocht can be, / And hoo that certainty
to gain" (1719–20). In refusing, under the conditions it discovers
for itself, to stop, the *Drunk Man* is both an act of defiance against
foolish (or all) faith, against the certainties that structure our disso-
nant concourse, against monologos, and an act in thrall to mono-
logos, to certainty, to no other possibility. The poem defies
certainty by describing it, embodying the madness that certainty—
Death, England, Mother, Thistle—both is heir to and engenders.
It aims to escape even itself.

For the border between Life and Thought—"Whaur Life begins,
Thocht ends" (1762)—is definitive, like the certainty of uncer-
tainty, and to the extent that this poem is Thought, its very contin-
uation impedes it. And this condition represents perhaps the most
deeply self-contradicted form of the dooble tongue: not a matter
of English and Scots so much as Speech and Silence. Arriving at
this point in its staggering development, the poem claims language
itself—the materiality rather than the meaning of language, the
purely sonic in opposition to silence—as its transcendental opposi-
tional transaction. Language is of no more use in the end—in the
effort to escape the vicious circularity and self-reflexivity of
"thocht-preventin' thocht," of sober reason—than any other can-
didate for transcendentality the poem evokes: indeed, it bears this
inescapable condition within it, but it bears, at least, again, as well,
the virtue of presence. The poem's form, its virtually endless obei-
sance to and refusal of silence, its vision of language as celebration
and as blot, is the Drunk Man's only discovery in the end—
although it too proves impossible to hold.

The visionary capacity is inextinguishable in spite of the most incessant unravelling, dead-ending, mutation, and abortion, a Frankenstein indeed:

> But there are flegsome deeps
> Whaur the soul o' Scotland sleeps
> That I to bottom need
> To wauk Guid kens what deid,
> Play at stertle-a-stobie,
> Wi' nation's dust for hobby,
> Or wi' God's sel' commerce
> For the makin' o' a verse.
>
> (1779–86)[95]

The national, again, like the sexual and the cosmic, like the materiality of language, is both definitive and useless, a negation of itself, a gruesome game. If the poem continues, then (as it does), it does so witlessly, as a gesture beyond nation, beyond sex, beyond God, beyond all the dualities of monologos; its continuance through these intense inanities—the repeated inadequacy of its discourse to solve the puzzle, and the persistent recognition of this inadequacy, the constantly inconstant identification and re-identification—is the Drunk Man's only way to speak for if not find a tongue "we dinna ken and never wull" (1409). ("*A miracle's / Oor only chance*" [719–20].)

This passage of "nation's dust," of scaled-down Scots nationalism, comes from "Letter to Dostoevski" (as earlier "The Goal of Scottish History" begins with "*Narodbogonosets*" [1640], "God-bearers" in Dostoevski's tongue [in MacDiarmid's note]). Melville, who had appeared earlier, returns, bringing Leviathan with him (the one that won't go rather than the one that got away); "the senseless strife / In which alane is life" (1809–10) returns (having never left, senseless strife the body of the poem itself); and Burns again, who

> . . . in Edinburgh
> Breenged arse-owre-heid thoro'
> A' *it* could be the spur o'
> To pleuch his sauted furrow,
> And turned frae men o' honour
> To what could only scunner
> What thinks that common-sense
> Can e'er be but a fence
> To keep a soul worth ha'en
> Frae what it s'ud be daein' . . .
>
> (1811–20)[96]

Another rumor of a different kip, Burns again escapes into his publically private uncivil place, and for the here and now of the Drunk Man there is no escape: "—Aye, open wide my hert / To a' the thistle's smert" (1827–28).

Whatever their possibilities may be elsewhere, for the Drunk Man Burns, Melville, Dostoevski, sex, Scots, and the others, offer, finally, none. Not one can break the endless chain of the self-reflexive dance of the signifiers, not one can offer a sustainable narrative of salvation (which is to say, escape). What the Drunk Man offers instead is a sustained narrative of damnation, and a sustained narrative of salvation in the form of its own impossibility. Thus, forever, the condition continues ("And yet this essence frae the clay / In dooble form aye braks away" [1938–39]), the aspiration born of and opposed to it continues ("To pit in a concrete abstraction / My country's contrair qualities" [2017–18]), and the poem begins again.

A paradigm among Romantic paradigms, the Drunk Man represents the monad adrift: to pursue his "coorse"—to attempt to "wun free" of this impossible condition—is to "leave the lave to dree / Their weirdless destiny" (1880–81).[97]

Again the condition and the aspiration are both restated and debunked, and again the rose-topped thistle and thorny England are raised as opposite signs endlessly self-contradicted.

The aspiration here takes the form, "In the Peculiar Light of Love," of an appeal to Jean:

> O Jean, in whom my spirit sees
> Clearer than through whisky or disease,
> Its dernin' nature, wad the searching licht
> Oor union raises poor'd owre me the nicht.
>
> (2024–27)[98]

Jean is asked to "*Clear my lourd flesh, and let me move / In the peculiar licht of love,*" to

> Be thou the licht in which I stand
> Entire, in thistle-shape, as planned,
> And no hauf-hidden and hauf-seen as here
> In munelicht, whisky, and in fleshly fear . . .
>
> (2032–33, 2036–39)[99]

But Jean would appear to be clearly of the flesh herself, by this point, "Wha's fibre I can ne'er unwaft / O' my wife's flesh and mither's flesh" (1493–95) entangling his own sinews and veins—or, alternately, oppositionally, so abstracted from the flesh, so much the voice of conscience, of second thought, of foolish certainty, as to have no inkling of the flesh, powerless even to address its terrors, *"The grisly form in which I'm caught"* (2041). And although "Metaphysical Pictures of the Thistle" imagines that

> Like leafs aboot a thistle-shank, my bluid
> Could still thraw roses up
>   —And up!
>
> (2076–78)

—this erection in the *"hope o' bein' released"* (2055) quickly becomes "the force in me that hauds / Me raxed and rigid and ridiculous," and his "roses drap" (2178–80).[100] The Drunk Man *is* the thistle ("my grisly leafs," "my endless spikes" [2176–77]), and to "Move coonter" (2178) to this condition is beyond him.

Instead, he runs into a parody of Eliot's Sweeney, called "The Thistle as a Spider's Web," in which he restates the condition, against and within which this futile aspiration (futile coontermove) expires and inspires, in no uncertain terms: "The circles of our hungry thought / Swing savagely from pole to pole" (2188–89):

> What's in a name? From pole to pole
> Our interlinked mentality spins.
> I know that you are Deosil, and suppose
> That therefore I am Widdershins.
>
> Do you reverse? Shall us? Then let's.
> Cyclone and Anti?—how absurd!
>
> (2196–201)[101]

Mr. Eliot in the Drunk Man's condition *is* no doubt perhaps absurd, but this is no solution to the puzzle: another embodiment of it, rather. The Drunk Man cannot "Move coonter," cannot begin again, without turning into his opposite, and knowing himself by that turn.

The thistle as the Curly-Snake, in "Creation's Whirligig," runs counter to itself, and reaches ever to begin again:

> Grugous thistle, to my een
> Your widdifow ramel evince
> Sibness to snakes wha's coils
> Rin coonter airts at yince,

> And fain I'd follow each
> Gin you the trick'll teach.
>
> (2348–54)[102]

But there are new beginnings and there are new beginnings, and the next one, again, is an old one, "My Quarrel with England":

> For I stand still for forces which
> Were subjugated to mak' way
> For England's poo'er, and to enrich
> The kinds o' English, and o' Scots,
> The least congenial to my thoughts.
>
> Hauf his soul a Scot maun use
> Indulgin' in illusions,
> And hauf in gettin' rid o' them
> And comin' to conclusions
> Wi' the demoralisin' dearth
> O' onything worth while on Earth. . . .
>
> I'm weary o' the rose as o' my brain,
> And for a deeper knowledge I am fain
> Than frae this noddin' object I can gain.
>
> (2384–97)

And thus begins—the beginning, it may be said, of the end—"The Great Wheel," the Drunk Man's last long run before ending in silence.

The two short sections remaining after this—"The Stars Like Thistle's Roses Flower" and "Yet Ha'e I Silence Left"—would seem to come by way of coda, if the formal logic of the poem permitted of such substantive distinctions; at any rate silence at least, deeper knowledge or deeper sleep, is upon us shortly:

> It maitters not my mind the day,
> Nocht maitters that I strive to dae
> —For the wheel moves on in its ain way.
>
> (2422–24)

The vision continues inextinguishable and unexpectable:

> The Phoenix guise't'll rise in syne
> Is mair than Euclid or Einstein
> Can dream o' or's in dreams o' mine.
>
> .   .   .   .

> Yet I exult oor sang has yet
> To grow wings that'll cairry it
> Ayont its native speck o' grit,
>
> And I exult to find in me
> The thocht that this can ever be,
> A hope still for humanity.
>
> (2455–57, 2491–96)

Through the incubus and out the other side, beyond nation, beyond monologos, perhaps, although

> Nae verse is worth a ha'et until
> It can join issue wi' the Will
> That raised the Wheel and spins it still
> . . . .
> And we may aiblins swing content
> Upon the wheel in which we're pent
> In adequate enlightenment.
>
> Nae ither thocht can mitigate
> The horror o' the endless Fate
> A'thing's whirled in predestinate.
>
> (2482–84, 2509–14)

In the end no escape but restatement.

  In the end

> The function, as it seems to me,
> O' poetry is to bring to be
> At lang, lang last that unity . . .
>
> (2584–86)

a unity that the entire poem slaves to deconstruct. The self-contradiction of the Drunk Man's dooble tongue, its unity and disarray, speaks to both the part and the whole, the fragment and the one, in terms alone of the relation between them:

> Whatever Scotland is to me,
> Be it aye pairt o' a' men see
> O' Earth and o' Eternity
>
> Wha winna hide their heids in't till
> It seems the haill o' Space to fill,
> As 'twere an unsurmounted hill.

He canna Scotland see wha yet
Canna see the Infinite,
And Scotland in true scale to it.

(2521–29)[103]

Nothing exists beyond this relation, no whole, no part beyond the relation of negativities we call by these names.

At this point, like the cavalry from a different national narrative, a voice arrives from beyond—in the Drunk Man's tongue of a Calvinist preacher: " *'Wheesht! It's for the guid o' your soul' "* (2616). The voice says that Scotland alone resists the monologos of the Wheel, but only in the monologic of its own ignorance: " *'The wheel can whummle a' but them' "* who " *'deem their ignorance their glory,' "* and who " *'ca' their obstinacy "Hame" ' "* (2625, 2627–28). It is an ambiguous message at best. And worse:

> *"A Scottish poet maun assume*
> *The burden o' his people's doom,*
> *And dee to brak' their livin' tomb.*
>
> *Mony ha'e tried, but a' ha'e failed.*
> *Their sacrifice has nocht availed.*
> *Upon the thistle they're impaled.*
>
> *You maun choose but gin ye'd see*
> *Anither category ye*
> *Maun tine your nationality."*

(2638–46)[104]

The Drunk Man's reply is "Auch, to Hell, / I'll tak' it to avizandum," as if to begin again later and to end at once, to escape and not to.[105] "O wae's me on the weary wheel" "And blessin' on the weary wheel" (2651, 2653), and nothing exists beyond this relation, in speech and in silence and in ending, none.

Silence and ending are what he claims next (and last, until the claims he makes on us, reading him). He says, "Yet ha'e I silence left, the croon of a' " (2671),[106] and goes on about it for a few lines—a quick catalog of female apparitions ("No her," "No her," "No her" [2672, 2674, 2676], langsyne seen, improbably kything, "withooten shape" [2676]) who escape him, and one "unkennable" male apparition, "God whom, gin e'er He saw a man, 'ud be / E'en mair dumfooner'd at the sicht than he" (2677–79). Then he names Silence again as the last thing to his own name—names it without naming it, personifying and gendering it as an alternative male apparition:

. . . Him, whom nocht in man or Deity
Or Daith or Dreid or Laneliness can touch,
Wha's deed owre often and has seen owre much.

(2680–82)

This is to say, he names without naming Scotland, the thistle, the moon, himself, as well as Silence, which he then names again: "O I ha'e Silence left" (2683). And then Jean is imagined to say, in effect, "Aye, let's hear it then," and then we do.

> Black and white bodies on the melting icefloes beneath the ozone holes invisible behind the fog—if the theatrical climate could be kept cold enough, the political narratives could be felt with the clarity of a test pattern.
>
> —Perelman

Improvisations: Robert Burns

I wander thro' each charter'd street,
Near where the charter'd Thames does flow

—Blake

for it is not so much a question now of feeling satisfaction at the infinite elasticity and receptivity of our own cultural outlook, but rather of locating the ultimate structural limits of that outlook and coming to terms with its negation, with what it cannot absorb without losing its own identity and wholly transforming itself. . . . Not interest or fascination, therefore, but rather that sense of dreariness with which we come to the end of our own world and observe with a certain self-protective lassitude that there is nothing for us on the other side of the boundary . . .

—Fredric Jameson

Far from me the Island
and every loved image in Scotland,
there is a foreign sand in History
spoiling the machines of the mind.

—Sorley MacLean

3

Recitativo

1
MY LIFE WITH BURNS

ACTUALLY BURNS IS ONE OF MY EARLIEST LITERARY MEMORIES. WHEN I was fifteen or so (the age at which Burns is said to have begun doing "the work of a man"), my brother was a college student and read to me in a mad voice—especially the opening lines, repeatedly—from "To a Mouse" and "To a Louse," particularly "To a Louse": "Ha! whare ye gaun, ye crowlan ferlie! / Your impudence protects you sairly. / Ye ugly, creepan, blastet wonner, / Detested, shunn'd, by saunt an' sinner." They never became quite tag lines, but almost—we both recite them from memory still, over twenty-five years later.

It was around the same time that my high school English teacher presented the class with a mimeographed sheet of Blake's songs, copied out in Mr. K.'s own pedantic hand and arranged cheek by jowl (innocence by experience) over the whole page, with irregular wavy lines drawn to mark the borders between them; Blake was apparently not available in the textbook—(im)probably called *Adventures in Literature*—distributed by my school district. I remember this teacher saying, with regard to "The Sick Rose," that "nobody knows what this poem means"—and then going on to suggest his own hypothetical possibilities: my first memory of thinking that poetry was an extraordinary thing.

Burns was no more available than Blake. Holden Caulfield led me to "Comin thro' the rye" (which seemed a slight thing, when I looked at it), and a friend on a bicycle riding home from school one day told me that "the best laid plans of mice and men oft go astray" was in fact "the best laid schemes o' *Mice* an' *Men*, / Gang aft agley"—with particularly gleeful emphasis on *gang aft agley*—which led me back to the poems my brother'd given me. But otherwise, through the course of my schooling, through college and graduate school too, I might not have read another Scots word.

Somewhere along the way I picked up that "Auld lang syne" was Burns's, and his name must have come up in class somewhere or in my reading—a vague association with the titles "Tam O'Shanter" and "Death and Doctor Hornbook," with the line "My love is like a red, red rose," with some business about fornication, with early stirrings of Romanticism—but I can't say that we ever read or discussed Burns in school.

(Perhaps "A man's a man for a' that"—I can picture it on the page in *Adventures in Literature*. I remember being excited and amused by the elision of *a'* and by the sonic and graphic syncopations of the line, the odd torque it puts on the most meager linguistic materials. I remember reading "Why dois your brand sae drap wi bluid, / Edward, Edward" [another text for bicycling recitation] and "Sir Patrick Spens," too—so a *few* Scots words, cast in the dreamtime of the ballads, but certainly nothing much in the way of curriculum, and nothing at all after [the dreamtime of] high school.)

> Oh, enviable, early days,
> When dancing thoughtless Pleasure's maze,
>   To Care, to Guilt unknown!
>
>   —Burns

2

In the summer of 1991 (six years past the terminal degree, twelve into teaching full-time) I had the thought to read Burns, and opened the Kinsley one-volume edition (which I'd bought some months previous when I'd had *half* a thought that, at some point, reading Burns might be a thing to do: the summer before, from a pay phone, I'd been told by an angel "now *there's* a story that hasn't been told" and that I'd find The Jolly Beggars particularly appealing)—and found that I couldn't read him, didn't know how, somehow, didn't know what to make of it.

I had become interested—writing a dissertation on William Morris—in marginalized figures of the Romantic tradition, once more than popular and now largely unread, in questions of canon formation and the assimilation (the repressive desublimation, as I learned to call it) of oppositional thought. The gods of my schooling had been modernist, mostly, and (pedagogically) practical-critical, and by the time I came to read Morris late in the game I was beginning to sense that Literature was not Everything—that for-

mal values were not absolute but profoundly conditional upon
place and time, that taste was (delicious) illusion, that in reading
literature I was reading history and, through history, politics per-
sonal and cultural: that literature was not so much a thing as an
act, and that the subject was endless. I was interested in textual
material that we no longer seemed to know how to read.

The process of coming to be able to read such material may be a
model for all reading, or for some dimension (the erotics) of all
reading—some recognition of the dialectic between self and other,
reader and text, that informs all literary study, an act of construc-
tion (making love) or praxis more than transmission or identifica-
tion. But more specifically, the process of coming to be able to read
material that is in the process of becoming unreadable to us is a
matter of registering a precise, historical loss. Such texts represent
visions of a way (or a place) beyond—inaccessible to—the currently
customary (or hegemonic, politically encoded) ways of reading, of
being or thought: specific visions in themselves, but also, collec-
tively, the very possibility of such visions. Coming to Burns out of
Morris, my assumption is that the customary (hegemonic, etc.) is
problematic (to say the least), in part for political reasons having to
do with global capitalism and industrialized culture, and in part
for reasons that—like the poor of the proverb—shall always be
with us, no matter our political or economic arrangements: the
simple problem of imagining otherwise, the shaping and reshap-
ing of limits.

Burns was a particularly striking case, programmatically un-
readable in any number of ways. The most obvious problem, per-
haps, is the business of glossary—Scots rendered marginal, a
footnote, an appendix; one may come not to need the gloss largely,
but there is no escaping it. Problematically too, a great bulk of the
poems are plainly bound to specific recipients and occasions—if
not exclusively so bound, definitively so. They are designed ex-
pressly not for us but for someone else. More problematic still,
even more plainly resistant to textual consumption, a greater bulk
of the material is in the form not of poems but of songs. (Are we
supposed to sing? How do you write about that?) Burns's politics,
further—"A fig for those by law protected!"—his radical democ-
racy and vulgarity vigorously and persistently claim an antithetical
site of value, or valuelessness: Scottish as opposed to English, or
British as opposed to Scottish, or something always other than
something else, a radical denial of valuation itself, of the making of
equivalences. Not Edinburgh but Ayrshire, not Ayrshire but
Mauchline, not Mauchline but the The Court of Equity (a club of

three members, Fornicators By Profession): the politics of Burns's work is local rather than otherwise, performative rather than textual, programmatically resistant to the ministrations of whatever critical strategem.

Courts for Cowards are erected, Churches built to please the priest, and Literary Criticism federally funded. My angel—a friend, who writes back—put the matter like this:

> the basic problem: how to treat in a high cultural form (litcrit ie) a subject whose "value" lies in his valuelessness? culture has always found ways to commodify "Burns"—witness the 19th c—but "Burns" has no value, any more than Scotland does, or "scots" or "life" or "energy."
>
> but litcrit is fundamentally a discourse of (cultural) values—valuable to the person who performs it (tenure, fame, cultural priesthoodness, etc) and to the society that integrates it.
>
> but surely we don't value or want to value burns, did he "value" his lovers? we "love" him, and care less whether anyone else does, and care less whether he is (or isn't) worthy of it. he's a man, for a that. and "a that" isn't necessarily adorable or good at all.

3

None of this, however, was obvious to me at the time, a decade ago now, when I made my first deliberate acquaintance with Burns. All that was obvious was that when I looked at him, he seemed to disappear. I mentioned this to a friend—an early teacher who, years ago, first gave me Wordsworth and Rousseau and Henry Miller—and he said "Did he write anything? I always thought Burns was someone who was just *around*, you know, like Leadbelly, and he heard all this great stuff and he wrote it down."

So I backed up and read through the Jack and Noble 1982 collection of essays—one each on the song lyrics, the satires, the poetry, music and love, the bawdry, the epistles, Romantic Revolt, and "Robert Burns: Superscot"—looking for ways to talk. I was struck by Iain Crichton Smith's comment that

> In a sense nothing much can be said of a Burns lyric except that it is there. No resources of modern scholarship can be brought to bear on it.[1]

(Leadbelly might have agreed.) But otherwise the essays bore a curious affect, to my mind—reading them left an odd sensation—as if Burns were indeed quite a familiar object: these good people, at least, had no trouble reading him. Plenty of useful stuff, as we say, gathered here—lots of information, hermeneutics, and historical reflection—but no sense of Burns unread or unreadable, nothing that addressed the problem I was having. How to read Burns when you *don't* assume that you can?

I read excellent Daiches, Donald Low, Raymond Bentman, others: the question remained. Although Daiches, for instance, notes that Burns's "work represented the last brilliant flare-up of a Scottish literary tradition that had been developing for centuries and that in the eighteenth century was in its final, disintegrating phase," his readings of the Kilmarnock poems do not quite register the sense of loss that this remark suggests; he proceeds, that is, as if we still read Burns, when of course as a rule (even in Scotland) we don't. We don't read Scots in general, period—and Daiches knows this too. He grows up in Edinburgh, the son of a rabbi whose "native language was Yiddish," and mentions hearing as a child a form of Scots-Yiddish spoken among the "trebblers" of the Fife coast ("It must have been one of the most short-lived languages in the world"); he is aware that dialect is problematic, but treats it—a subject for litcrit—as if it were not.[2]

The distance of the object is blurred thus—accounted for, as if the value of any such distance could be spelled out in so many words, boiled down, understood: and the oppositional character of the object, its resistance to assimilation, its patent valuelessness, its waste element, its potential for provocative boredom (Fredric Jameson: "Boredom . . . is a powerful hermeneutic instrument: it marks the spot where something painful is buried")—all this is lost.[3] The "lostness" of the object is lost, the site of its identity and power: Burns canters across the stage a kind of centaur, four-footing down the road to oblivion with the head of an Immortal Memory—like something out of "Horse Island."

So I backed up again to read some MacDiarmid, with whom I was even less familiar than I was with our Bardie, not having read a single poem, not knowing a single title, for all my honors courses and advanced degrees—a name I'd heard, and found quoted in Jack and Noble:

of genuine Burns criticism . . . there is scarcely a vestige. Burns, as a poet, has long ceased to be taken seriously by anyone really interested in literature . . . It is high time the Burns legend was destroyed and the man himself, "in the round," a credible human figure, rescued from the eponymous proliferation of moralitarian excrescences under which he is buried . . .[4]

I read *At the Sign of the Thistle* and the *Drunk Man*, I read Duncan Glen on the Scottish Renaissance, I found *The Oxford Book of Scottish Verse* and *The Faber Book of Twentieth-Century Scottish Poetry*, I laid in some theory: doing my job. I began reading in the tradition, reading names entirely new to me—Barbour, Henryson, Dunbar, Douglas, Ramsay, Fergusson—and more contemporary figures like Soutar, Garioch, Morgan (the Mayakovsky translations), the Smiths S. G. and I. C., Leonard, Crawford, Herbert. I put aside reading Burns, for the most part, and listened a great deal to Ewan MacColl's Smithsonian Folkways recordings of the songs, teaching them to myself, singing them driving to work or on walks around town with my daughter in her stroller. I hae a wife o' my ain. Green grow the rashes, O. Is there for honest poverty. I learned about twenty.

My taxman gave me an old LP of The Merry Muses (more Ewan MacColl) and I learned a dozen more washing the dishes with a Walkman. (I listened to Jean Redpath's Burns, Andy Stewart's Burns, Greg Brown's Songs of Blake, Bob Dylan's *World Gone Wrong*, Woody Guthrie, Leadbelly.)

I went to Scotland in the summer of 1993, to Alloway, the National Library in Edinburgh, the Mitchell in Glasgow, the Hebrides. Musty texts and fresh academic studies, fleshing out the lay of the land. I was looking for material on Burns which might be unavailable to me in the States, of which I found some, and for twentieth-century Scots poetry, of which I found a great deal. Oxford and Faber had not prepared me for the breadth and depth and vitality of a living Scots tradition—but there it is, and it seemed to offer a way of approaching the problem of reading (and writing) Burns. When I read "Horse Island," Osmond Dips's problem seemed a version of my own; I came home and began. I was 37, Burns's age when he died.

> The King's poor blackguard slave am I,
> And scarce dow spare a minute;
> But I'll be with you by and bye,
> Or else the devil's in it!

R. B.[5]

4
MAKE IT NEW

Burns's marginality to the canon gives to his work the aura of the contemporary—something (not to be found on Horse Island) that hasn't been entirely and before-the-fact incorporated, covered (as teachers say), embraced; or to put it the other way round, in order for Burns to *be* contemporary, he must be read in his obsolescence. Thus, however accidentally, the notion of working backwards to his Bardship. But working backwards—to embody the distances, historical and conceptual, across which we approach Burns—is only part of the problem: the other part, my angel, is what to say once we do circle back, how to speak, how further still to embody those distances, denials, refusals, negations—and why we should want to, what it means to engage the recuperation of losses, to take their measure.

How do Herbert, Crawford, Morgan, and MacDiarmid prepare us to read the unreadable?

Each attempts self-consciously to write the unwritable—"Horse Island," *Sharawaggi*, Morgan's concrete and madly schema-driven pieces, the *Drunk Man*—each reaches for the language of a disembodied head, each seeks to imagine a body not already accounted for, each depicts the condition of being trapped, stuck, lost in a place where no one (but the incubus, maybe) will hear you scream. Each screams.

The incubus of Scottish cultural self-consciousness for these figures is nationalist or neurotic or otherwise but in every case epanadiplotic, locked in self-reference, in the endless dooblings of monologic, crazed and angry about being crazed, unrestful, subjected. Each too imagines a way out, an impossible border crossing, a romantic escape trail, conceived in terms of some sexual condition—a different kip, a phallo-thistle, a caber-toss at thi cunt o thi yird—like Kafka's hope, which exists (although not for us), thwarted.

Sexuality (fraught and ungainly, hidden, rude, coarse, unsocialized) emerges as the imagination of some different order—one *not* locked in epanadiplosis, in monologos, not nationalist or neurotic, not self-conscious—an imagination of paradise (as modernity knows it), of breakthrough, of connection, of social and spiritual troth, of polymorphous, perverse material pleasure, of presence. The utopian end, even, to alienation, to anxiety and the denial of anxiety, the antithesis to modern psycho-cultural domination by global structures of capitalist industry, an effort toward anither story than the story of triumphant civilization, of the progressive march of sociopolitical perfection—the vulgar/the vulgate as radical politics, an old story. Angel, bear with me.

These figures represent modern and postmodern variations on the position of a chiefly Scottish dialect: MacDiarmid goes mad and holes up in the Shetlands, recuperates and rants (in English) for another quarter-century; Morgan moves back and forth between Glasgow and Saturn; Crawford and Herbert mine Jamieson and make it up as they go along; and a collectivity of Osmond Dips is all their readership—who knows *where* they are? Stuck to electrodes, ejaculating unawares, in the basement of the Archive.

If Burns then is conjured to appear readable—as in the critical literature, as in the *Norton Anthology* of Englit—these later figures remind us that the problem he worked at remains as mystifying as ever, and quite as thoroughly beyond the pale. (*Sharawaggi* is born obsolescent, as is the life of Horse Island: the futuristic obsolete.) Dooblings upon dooblings, negations upon negations: the linguistic politics of the Scots tongue and the politics of Scottish cultural/ social constructions remain, in our century, a circle closed upon itself and closed to the imagination of Norton Oxford Faber—a wee free circle, off the map.

5

The incubus of the Scottish modern and postmodern bears a Scottish romantic address, and when we knock at the door, Rab answers. Burns, that is, grapples with the incubus of the marginal—of the Scottish, of the vulgate, of the vulgar—at the point when it is first coming to assume the form we recognize it in now. He speaks to the moment of the new world order's birth, the King's slave prophesying at the cradle. The omens are ill.

The Romantic Revolt, read through Burns, is a revolt of slaves. The Bard's own slavery is manifold. The land he farmed was not his own but managed, "factored," in the context of a landholding system just then first infused "with wealth from the West Indies or India," the booty of colonialist power.[6] (The revolt of the slaves of San Domingo [Hispaniola today] led by Toussaint L'Ouverture in 1791 overthrows white rule; in 1994 [the newspaper tells me] the Haitian crowd assembled sarcastically sings "Auld Lang Syne," in Creole, to General Raoul Cedras, up on the State balcony announcing his departure under military pressure from the United States and with the understanding of certain financial arrangements, the end of his de facto rule.) If not quite Rimbaud a century later, suspected of trafficking in slaves, Burns himself was on the point of a passage to Jamaica early in 1786—the Kilmarnock volume, apparently, intended to raise funds for the excursion, (and/ or) to be "just the last foolish action I intend to do; and then turn

a wise man as fast as possible."[7] The new world order then was co-
lonial, and there would be no getting out.[8]

Later, Burns served as an officer of the Excise, the King's own
immediate blackguard, by appointment to the belly of the beast. In
between, he served up Scottish
ploughman spice (or shepherd's
pie) to the Edinburgh literati for
the self-reflection of their cul-
ture—and refused to serve, as
well, declining or neglecting to
offer a second book after the
splash of the first, turning instead

> But the ae best dance e'er
> cam to the Land
> Was, the deil's awa wi' th'
> Exciseman.
> —Burns

gratis and for the most part anonymously to the (re)construction of
a vast body of Scots folksong. "As to any remuneration, you may
think my Songs either *above*, or *below* price; for they shall absolutely
be the one or the other.—In the honest enthusiasm with which I
embark in your undertaking, to talk of money, wages, fee, hire,
&c. would be downright Sodomy of Soul!"[9]

He was called for public denunciation and contrition in the
kirk—for fornication—but not called to the repentance stool,
standing for the occasion in his own pew instead. He was enslaved
to the elements, to the scarcity farming of Scotland, to ill health:
powerless, more or less constantly on the edge of material ruin.
His life is defined by powerlessness, and by the possibilities atten-
dant upon defeat: a Scottish trope from way back, a Romantic
trope coming down the pike, the trope of our own time coming
down the information superhighway.

6

He is a slave, as they say, to love as well—or something like it—to
passion, to sexual impulse, to the low pleasures of the body.

Max Beerbohm sketches him in *The Poets' Corner* (1904), a print
with the caption: "Robert Burns, having set his hand to the
plough, looks back at Highland Mary."[10] On a field, ploughed, two
figures all in olive drab with touches of faint red wash: Burns in
white sark, trousers shredded below the knee, and what appear to
be wooden shoes—his paunch slack and ample, his arms and his
whole frame chunky—looking less like Burns as we think of him
than like some Robinson Crusoe gone to seed, or a burgher gone
slumming, with both hands set firmly to a plough moving off be-
yond the frame of the picture; casting his eyes in the opposite di-

rection with a face of infinite resignation and infinite regret (and fear, and desire), at the sight of Mary in all-tartan toga, belt, scarf, and ribbon, barefoot dancing lightsome in the furrows—leaning back but moving forward, one big toe pointing the way, off opposite the plough—a figure from some Greco-Scottish urn. The slave to passion meets a stronger master. The rest of the landscape is bare.

Two letters from a single day, 20th Feb. 1793, Dumfries:[11]

What are you doing, what hurry have you got on your hands, my dear Cunningham, that I have not heard from you? Are you deeply engaged in the mazes of Law, the mysteries of Love, or in the profound wisdom of modern politics?—Curse on the word which ended the period!

Quere, What is Politics?

Answer, Politics is a science wherewith, by means of nefarious cunning, & hypocritical pretence, we govern civil Polities for the emolument of ourselves & our adherents.—

Quere, What is a Minister?

Answer, A Minister is an unprincipled fellow, who by the influence of hereditary, or acquired wealth; by superiour abilities; or by a lucky conjuncture of circumstances, obtains a principal place in the administration of the affairs of government.—

Q. What is a Patriot?

A. An individual exactly of the same description as a Minister, only, out of place.—

I have been interrupted in my Catechism, & am returned at a late hour, just to subscribe my name; to put you in mind that there is a forgotten friend of yours of that name, still in the land of the living, though I can hardly say, in the place of hope.—

I made the following Sonnet the other day, which has been so lucky as to obtain the approbation of no ordinary judge—our friend Syme.—

Sonnet on hearing a thrush in a morning walk in January—

> [see Kinsley, poem no. 400]
> Adieu!
> Rob{t} Burns

O thou, wisest among the Wise, meridian blaze of Prudence, full moon of Discretion, & Chief of many Counsellors!—How infinitely is thy puddle-headed, rattle-headed, wrong-headed, round-headed slave indebted to thy supereminent goodness, that from the luminous path of thy own right-lined rectitude, thou lookest benignly down on an erring Wretch, of whom the zig-zag wanderings defy all the powers of Calculation, from the simple copulation of Units up to the hidden mystery of Fluxions! May one feeble ray of that light of wisdom which darts

from thy sensorium, straight as the arrow of Heaven against the head
of the Unrighteous, & bright as the meteor of inspiration descending
on the holy & undefiled Priesthood—may it be my portion; so that I
may be less unworthy of the face & favour of that father of Proverbs &
master of Maxims, that antipode of Folly & magnet among the Sages,
the wise & witty Willie Nicol! Amen! Amen! Yea, so be it!!!

For me, I am a beast, a reptile, & know nothing.—From the cave of
my ignorance, amid the fogs of my dulness & pestilential fumes of my
Political heresies, I look up to thee, as doth a toad through the iron-
barred lucarne of a pestiferous dungeon to the cloudless glory of a
summer sun!—Sorely sighing in bitterness of soul, I say, when shall my
name be the quotation of the Wise, & my countenance be the delight
of the Godly, like the illustrious lord of Laggan's many hills?—As for
him, his works are perfect: never did the pen of Calumny blur the fair
page of his reputation, nor the bolt of Hatred fly at his dwelling. At his
approach is the standing up of men, even the Chief & the Ruler; &
before his presence the frail form of lovely Woman, humbly awaiting
his pleasure, is extended on the dust.—Thou mirror of purity, when
shall the elfine lamp of my glimmerous understanding, purged from
sensual appetites & gross desires, shine like the constellation of thy in-
tellectual powers? As for thee, thy thoughts are pure, & thy lips are
holy.—Never did the unhallowed breath of the Powers of darkness &
the pleasures of darkness, pollute the sacred flame of thy sky-de-
scended & heavenward-bound desires: never did the vapours of impu-
rity stain the unclouded serene of thy cerulean imagination.—O, that
like thine were the tenor of my life, like thine the tenor of my conversa-
tion! Then should no friend fear for my strength, no enemy rejoice in
my weakness! Then should I lie down, & rise up, & none to make me
afraid!—

May thy pity & thy prayer be exercised for,—
O thou lamp of Wisdom & mirror of Morality!

Thy devoted slave—
RB

7
ANITHER STORY

This letter to Willie Nicol is a triumphant piece of satire—if sat-
ire can ever be said to be triumphant: a (self-)portrait of the
wretched of the earth looking up to the lords of the earth as the
lords would have themselves looked upon. Amen! Amen! Yea, so
be it!!! The joke is Willie Nicol as the object of this gaze: the same
"Kind, honest-hearted Willie" for whom Burns names one of his
bairnies (one "ill-deedie, damn'd, wee, rumble gairie hurchin of

mine, whom, from that propensity to witty wickedness & manfu'
mischief, which even at twa days auld I foresaw would form the
striking features of his disposition, I named Willie Nicol")[12]—here,
rather, the Chief of many Counsellors, of supereminent goodness
and right-lined rectitude, with wisdom darting from his senso-
rium, the antipode of Folly, superior even to the puissant, cushy
lord of Laggan's many hills (a landowner with whom Nicol had
some dealings). The punch line is the purity of Willie's thoughts
and the holiness of his lips—the prayer for purgation of sensual
appetites and gross desires. The laugh is that the slave RB does
indeed embrace the Powers & pleasures of darkness, does pollute
the sacred flame of transcendent desire and the unclouded serene
of cerulean imagination—and so does Nicol, and so (for that mat-
ter) does the laird of Laggan and every other damned human
body.

In the dooble tongue of this letter, the Masters expect devotion
and—by jingo—that's what they get (or something like it): a ven-
triloquist's dummy. Burns, while serving up this baited schmaltz in
heaping helpings, reserves one thing for himself: the power to defy
all the powers of Calculation, from the simple copulation of Units
up to the hidden mystery of Fluxions. The claim to this power, and
the assumption that the presumptive object of such wacky venera-
tion as a devoted slave can provide is no better or worse (no other)
than Willie Nicol—this is Burns's chief Political heresy.

Hatred does fly at Burns's dwelling and Calumny blur the page
of his reputation, his friends do fear for his strength and his ene-
mies rejoice in his weakness, there is much to make him afraid: he
is an object of nothing but pity and prayer. That's the joke too.

8

In the discourse of the devoted slave, the pretense of social order
is punctured, mocked twice over—copied and, by virtue of being
copied, ridiculed: not, that is, social order itself, but only all pre-
tense of social order, only all false (troth-breaking) claims of social
order, claims of the powerful against the powerless. Chief among
these is the claim that this particular social order—the order of the
Lord of Laggan, say—*is* Social Order, period.

Burns, himself valueless, a beast, a reptile, mocks the contempo-
rary world of (unequal) value, mocks the making of equivalences
and inequalities, mocks the King, the Kirk, and all the lordly.
Claiming himself—"Thy devoted slave"—to be rendered in such

grotesque terms, Burns claims himself to be unrenderable, or beyond the reach of rendering in any but such terms. Thus his claim to the power to defy all powers of Calculation, of equivalence and inequality, of identification, appropriation, commodification, absorption, comprehension: he mocks the very limits of knowledge, yea, of knowledge as power, the presumptions of knowledge. It goes without saying that he mocks literary criticism too, refuses to be made a simulacrum of himself, for to be recuperated is to serve another's purpose: he walks away, laughing this time, and says "No thanks."

But making Willie Nicol laugh is one thing. For a slave to speak freely in public—the land of the living, if not the place of hope—is another.

> As for this world I despair of ever making a figure in it—I am not formed for the bustle of the busy nor the flutter of the Gay I shall never again be capable of it.—Indeed, I am altogether unconcern'd at the thoughts of it. I foresee that very probably Poverty & Obscurity await me & I am, in some measure prepared & daily preparing to meet & welcome them.
>   —Burns, to his father, 27 Dec 1781

> I never, My friend, thought Mankind very capable of any thing generous; but the stateliness of the Patricians in Edin{r}, and the damn'd servility of my plebeian brethren, who perhaps formerly eyed me askance, since I returned home, have nearly put me out of conceit altogether with my species.—I have bought a pocket Milton, which I carry perpetually about with me, in order to study the sentiments—the dauntless magnanimity; the intrepid unyielding independance; the desperate daring, and noble defiance of hardship, in that great Personage, Satan. 'Tis true, I have just now a little cash . . .
>   —Burns, to William Nicol, 18 June 1787

When "he appears in the public character of an Author" (himself in the third person) in 1786, Burns is obliged to establish himself more delicately. Still, the Preface to *Poems, Chiefly in the Scottish Dialect*, though hard to picture playing in Poosie Nansie's (with a straight face anyway)—perhaps in the right spirit, with much bitter mirth and mock-sober asseveration among the assembled—may be a text not unlike the letter to Willie after all.[13]

> The following trifles are not the productions of the Poet, who, with all the advantages of learned art, and perhaps amid the elegancies and idlenesses of upper life, looks down for a rural theme, with an eye to Theocrites or Virgil. To the Author of this, these and other celebrated

names their countrymen are, in their original languages, "A fountain shut up, and a book sealed." Unacquainted with the necessary requisites for commencing Poet by rule, he sings the sentiments and manners, he felt and saw in himself and his rustic compeers around him, in his and their native language.

Burns here sets out the terms of his own public recuperation, and if it is only a short hop from this sort of self-representation to the "Heaven-taught ploughman" of Henry Mackenzie's famous conceit (and its subsequent commodification and obsolescence), it's a hop nonetheless—one's feet lose contact with the ground. This opening of the Preface just as clearly refutes any such reading, and points us in another direction entirely, much as RB that devoted slave both lavishly fulfills and radically debunks the assumptions and expectations of his own imaginary audience. If he is to be recuperated at all here, in other words, it is only as that which cannot be recuperated.

For one thing, although he speaks here in plain English, Burns claims as his own an unco tongue (presumably defying all powers of Calculation): "his and their"—i.e. not your, not our—"native language." Glossary or no, Scottish dialect and rural experience will not be spoken for or comprehended in terms alien to itself— the terms of "learned art" (which provide the standard, of course, for Mackenzie's notion of a natural art), "perhaps amid the elegancies and idlenesses of upper life," the terms of a comfortable distance. Burns's first claim for these poems is that they are to be regarded as in a crucial sense unreadable for this audience—or at least that they are likely to be misread. With an eye to Theocrites and Virgil indeed!

Not that Burns hasn't read his Greeks and Latins: the sly disclaimer of "their original languages" pulls the rug out from any such presumption. Rather, he knows precisely to whom he speaks, and precisely what passes for lingua franca—and badge of membership—among such parties (indeed, among us), and he claims, instead, another community altogether. As in the letter to Nicol, his pose signifies at once submission (literally here, to the press) and inviolable independence (although hardly in this context conceivable)—the Satanic model of impossible existence, Scotia division, the contradiction of power.

At any rate, "none of the following works were ever composed with a view to the press," in which context, apparently, they can only be consumed as "trifles":

To amuse himself with the little creations of his own fancy, amid the toil and fatigues of a laborious life; to transcribe the various feelings, the loves, the griefs, the hopes, the fears, in his own breast; to find some kind of counterpoise to the struggles of a world, always an alien scene, a task uncouth to the poetical mind; these were his motives for courting the Muses, and in these he found Poetry to be it's own reward.

If the third-person grammar here is entirely conventional, a kind of hedge against immodesty, it serves to emphasize that Burns appears in the present company not as himself, quite, or rather appears here (again) to a company unprepared, by experience and disposition, to recognize him properly—a company to whom he cannot speak directly. Not at all unlettered (he has read his Theocrites and Virgil, presumably, in translation, as well as the English poets, and has had "the genius of a Ramsay, or the glorious dawnings of the poor, unfortunate Fergusson . . . often . . . in his eye"), he nevertheless enters here a world, always an alien scene, himself uncouth.

A dooble tongue, then: these Poems chiefly in the Scottish Dialect are an embodiment of self-amusement, self-representation, self-sustenance, self-protection, and of the authority of compeers, and—also—here, now, under the imprint of John Wilson, Kilmarnock (with an eye to Edinburgh), an object cast upon the vagaries of institutional taste, brought before an authority of broader reach. The embodiment of a contradiction: the difference between compeers and presumed peers—or more so, Peers—is definitive.

Of course to say as much is to describe the condition of Poetry itself (or Poetics), not just Scots poems, not just Burns's—but Burns understands the matter in particular terms. The contradiction between what my angel calls "the kingly privilege of simple beingness" and the marketplace of values is a recognition, for Caledonia's Bard, not to be taken (as we take it) for granted. He writes at a moment when that marketplace is gathering for an extraordinary push, for the grand imperial orgasm of the nineteenth and twentieth centuries—at a moment when "the system's claim to totality, which would suffer nothing to remain outside it" (in Theodor Adorno's lugubrious phrase), was not yet to be assumed, not yet a transparency, before life became lifestyle and complicity a foregone conclusion—when it was still possible to imagine (if only to imagine) a person without a master.[14]

He insists upon this imagination, if only in the form of its denial:

Now that he appears in the public character of an Author, he does it
with fear and trembling. So dear is fame to the rhyming tribe, that even
he, an obscure, nameless Bard, shrinks aghast, at the thought of being
branded as "An impertinent blockhead, obtruding his nonsense on the
world; and because he can make shift to jingle a few doggerel, Scotch
rhymes together, looks upon himself as a Poet of no small consequence
forsooth."

Fame is no doubt the spur—"he certainly looks upon himself as
possest of some poetic abilities, otherwise his publishing in the
manner he has done, would be a manoeuvre below the worst char-
acter, which, he hopes, his worst enemy will ever give him"—and
the price of fame is clear as well: whatever it is, Impertinent Block-
head or Heaven-taught Ploughman, a judgment always alien. Elvis
could tell you all about it.

Robert Burns, in effect, disappears into "the public character of
an Author," "the Author of this," a "nameless Bard"—no wonder
he seemed to vanish every time I looked. (The Preface itself is un-
signed, unattributed, as if not by Burns himself but by someone
closely interested, a press agent perhaps, a noted literatus, a Rever-
end Hugh Blair or Doctor Moore.) And in this way, mediating his
mediation at the hands of critical industry and in the eye of the
public, Burns preserves (as in the letter to Willie Nicol) an imagina-
tion of a self far otherwise: a negative image, unreadable unless
you reverse everything, embodied fully here but not for us, an un-
speakable self that nevertheless speaks itself. A few doggerel Scotch
rhymes, a whole person. A kind of miracle. Or gone to Jamaica,
perhaps, after all—a different kip, anither story. Unrecovered.

Not for us: the writer of the Preface employs the first person
only once, in the plural, marking "an observation of that cele-
brated Poet, whose divine Elegies do honor to our language"—
with a note identifying the poet as Shenstone, and thus "our"
language as English.

To his Subscribers, the Author returns his most sincere thanks. Not
the mercenary bow over a counter, but the heart-throbbing gratitude
of the Bard, conscious how much he is indebted to Benevolence and
Friendship, for gratifying him, if he deserves it, in that dearest wish of
every poetic bosom—to be distinguished. He begs his readers, particu-
larly the Learned and the Polite, who may honor him with a perusal,
that they will make every allowance for Education and Circumstances
of Life: but, if after a fair, candid, and impartial criticism, he shall stand
convicted of Dulness and Nonsense, let him be done by, as he would
in that case do by others—let him be condemned, without mercy, to
contempt and oblivion.

Is fairness, candor, and impartiality too much to hope for in the context of the making of allowances—a context of social inequality? The relationship (the distance) between the Author and his Subscribers is precisely the issue. And if it's easy enough to gather the sap of obsequiousness that drips from this prose—decorous to a fault, Burns begs every allowance—nevertheless there is nothing humble about it: the decorum of the obsequious unhumble—that old Satanic metaphor again. More baited schmaltz.

To be distinguished, which is to say, to be recognized in a kind of sovereignty—"a King in exile," Carlyle calls him—is to make a claim of radical equality.[15] A dooble tongue: for all the begging, the preface ends here in a curse which cuts both ways. Who judges whom?

9

The Kilmarnock Preface is a kind of preemptive strike against literary criticism, as a preface is wont to be. Slyly manipulative, apparently utterly politely content to be put in his place and determined, nonetheless, to claim his place himself, the nameless Bard here makes his stand (in English) against English itself—against all worlds of impinging discrimination, against all presumptions of judgment, against the fetish of production and consumption, the fetish of manufactured worth. He claims (instead of English) a waste space of pleasure, self-knowledge, and counterpoise—a claim of the private against the public(ation) to which he (nevertheless) submits. The Ayrshire of Burns's book is a world quite apart, incommensurable and sufficient unto itself. Mauchline graffiti: Stately Patricians Go Home—This Means You.

Just as, within that Ayrshire, the Court of Equity is anither story althegither, incommensurable and quite intirely self-authorized—or the Tarbolton Bachelors' Club, or (for that matter) the Masons—and within these disattached little worlds, Burns himself incommensurable, a rantin dog his own lane self til the rocks melt wi' the sun.

THE TROUBLE WITH TEXTUALITY

But of course the claim of the private is one of the public's chief entertainments and most cherished abstractions, and to speak of it at all—certainly to speak of it here, me to you—is to render it something quite intirely which it is not.

There would seem to be no point in writing, or the point would seem to be so circumscribed, repressively desublimated, rendered functionary and so on, that there might as well be no point. Burns enters the world and the world takes him in. The mills of scholarship turn, turn and grind exceedingly fine, sifting all into the one story of a harvest brought to market: from his *Poems, Chiefly in the Scottish Dialect* to our Kilmarnock Edition, Burns is processed into an object of textual analysis or theoretical import, or an object of biographical merit, an object of pedagogy (a scandal! a model!), and the challenge of the Preface is noted, categorized (a typical prefatory maneuver after all, the text's claim to a life beyond criticism), and dispatched. (We do live on Horse Island, in the basement of the Archive, with the talking Heids.) The story Burns's Preface tells (in hints) of negation, denial, refusal—the ither story in which Rab is King in the Court of Equity—is itself negated, denied, refused, becomes simply part of the story of accommodation, the story of the one story, world without end, the story of Litcrit, amen, amen yea and so on.

Everything fits into this story—that's the beauty of it. The Industry of Letters recognizes no horizon it does not attain and supersede. Litcrit swallows Burns as a maw might—hardly an effort, it seems, he just drops in and he's gone (but Rab remains unrecovered). Litcrit is locked in epanadiplosis itself, as all cultural activity is in sad mad Theodor's Administered World, where "the system's claim to totality," etc.—like the Scots with their blastet incubus, held in the implacable, impalpable embrace of the modern monologos, the Story of the One Story.

> Forspoken still in Embro,
>   Scoatlan's douce
> Sly Purgoatory o thi randy
>   yuppies
>   —Crawford

But if Burns is to be read under such conditions, he must yet be made strange. Litcrit has its own incubus, and Burns is a spell against it.

10

(I'm telling a big story here myself—angel, I know it—and stories are easy to tell, I know, and not to be believed. I don't see what alternative I have. Big stories in one way or another are the only

story we tell—Litcrit is one of them—and it's in the context of that
story [the Story of the One Story, the story of monologos], that by
means of various negative dialectics we imagine a world other. ['Tis
not too late, as the good Lord {Tennyson} says.] The Big Story em-
phasizes [to negate] borders, limits [anxious that Itself isn't big
enough? isn't Everything? isn't Paradise Displayed?], and doobles
within itself into a myriad imagined contradictions [like the by-
products of some sort of radioactive decay], emanations, instabilit-
ies, principles of uncertainty, poetics. Anywhere out of this world,
non? Old hat.

I realize too that this is the same story as the Morris story—
writing paradise dislocated. All this talk of contradiction, of exile,
loss, and redemption. The recuperation of the estranged, the resis-
tance of the estranged to recuperation. [Weapons against the
nightmare of history: Stephen D. has silence, exile, and cunning;
Burns has Scots, fucking, and song.] Do not move. Let the wind
speak. Or Kafka's parable:

> The expulsion from Paradise is in its main significance eternal: Conse-
> quently the expulsion from Paradise is final, and life in this world ir-
> revocable, but the eternal nature of the occurrence (or, temporally
> expressed, the eternal recapitulation of the occurrence) makes it nev-
> ertheless possible that not only could we live continuously in Paradise,
> but that we are continuously there in actual fact, no matter whether we
> know it here or not.[16]

Paradise is the state other than the state which proscribes states
other than itself—paradise contra claustrophobia, contra death.
[Every story is Paradise Lost, even the story of Paradise Regained.]
In Paradise nothing changes, neither progress nor death is there,
nothing is proscribed, all desire fulfilled: all Art speaks Paradise—
the refusal to be stupefied. My particular paradise [in which I own
stock through Morris & Burns] is informed in broad strokes by
Adorno's Administered World and Gramsci's political hegemonies
or opposing directions, by negative dialectics, by Bataille's glorifi-
cations of waste, of excess, of what will not be assimilated, of what
remains beyond—that's what makes it a paradise, it remains be-
yond; informed by the cultural politics of capitalism, of getting and
spending late and soon, of that particular world so much with us,
and—this is what makes it a paradise too—by the vision [negative,
dialectical] of a body freed from that world: this world, ours.

The Big Story I have in mind, the one that Litcrit tells, that Lit-
crit [we might say] naturalizes, includes the barbarities and envi-

ronmental despoliations and manic enterprise of the American
century so-called, the Death of God, the Death of Art, the end of
history, the end of the world, the inexorable progress of social
order [of agriculture and technology, of colonization and postcolo-
nial management], the quite staggering progress of knowledge—
the Story [in Hayden White's phrase] of "the odor of the ideal,"
the Story of [the long arm of] the Law.[17]

But the Story of the Big Story is a digression.)

11

This is the world in which I move uninvited, profane on a sa-
cred land, neither me nor mine, but me nonetheless. The story
began long ago . . . it is old. Older than my body, my mother's,
my grandmother's. As old as my me, Old Spontaneous me, the
world. For years we have been passing it on, so that our daugh-
ters and granddaughters may continue to pass it on. So that it
may become larger than its proper measure, always larger than
its own insignificance. The story never really begins nor ends,
even though there is a beginning and an end to every story, just
as there is a beginning and an end to every teller. One can date
it back to the immemorial days when a group of mighty men
attributed to itself a central, dominating position vis-a-vis other
groups; overvalued its particularities and achievements;
adopted a projective attitude toward those it classified among
the out-groups; and wrapped itself up in its own thinking, in-
terpreting the out-group through the in-group mode of rea-
soning while claiming to speak the minds of both the in-group
and the out-group.

—Trinh T. Minh-Ha

So far then: Burns is a slave, Burns is unread—his characteristic
response to the former condition perhaps accountable in part for
the latter. (Can a slave be heard by Men who imagine their society
to be one of Liberty and Equality? It's a free country, isn't it?) Rab's
letter to Willie privately defies the power of calculation and claims
an identity and an experience apart: incommensurable, subver-
sive, mocking—a raspberry blown for M'Lord. The Kilmarnock
Preface approaches that same power in the open, in public, both
more and less directly, in a posture of seduction, of appeasement
and resistance, claiming still a world apart. This claim, though, is a
dicey one, a matter of negativities, an emanation without effective
power (a kingdom in exile): how to operate in such circumstances?

This is Burns's question. How to write for publication, or present
for publication what he writes with no view to the press—how to

write for Edinburgh and London—how to embody and offer himself without surrendering himself? How to be an Author without being authorized, without cancelling himself? Without paying devotion to slavery? How not to be swallowed? How to be free?

The question, of course, is ours (or mine) as well as Burns's. But Burns's short answer is: by means of the vulgate and the vulgar, of Scots, fucking, and song—and this is in part why his work is a pleasure to us, although a pleasure made available in its unavailability. His perspective on the question is *not* ours. (Or as Crawford puts it, in his "Address" to Burns: "Yuir proablems ernae oors.") In our own time we may fairly share the assumption, with Burroughs, that "To speak is to lie, to live is to collaborate" etc., but this is precisely an assumption that Burns doesn't, quite, make: rather, he recognizes the conditions that make for these imperative infinitives, and he also recognizes another condition, available to him in a way not available to us, a condition of freedom—leave it to a slave, no? Burns *can* imagine a speech that doesn't lie, a life without complicity, a condition, an imagination, not indentured to the service of social inequality, a condition of absolute equality, a troth-speech.[18]

Let's have it, then.

> O I ha'e Silence left
>   —"And weel ye micht,"
> Sae Jean'll say, "efter sic a
>   nicht!"
>   —MacDiarmid

4

Scots

12

Eᴀᴄʜ ᴏꜰ ʙᴜʀɴꜱ'ꜱ ᴄʜᴀʀᴀᴄᴛᴇʀɪꜱᴛɪᴄ ɢᴇꜱᴛᴜʀᴇꜱ ɪɴ ᴛʜᴇ ꜰɪᴇʟᴅ ᴏꜰ textuality (the land of the living, if not the place of hope) is a gesture of disappearance, the language of troth a language of erasure. Poems chiefly in the Scottish dialect are poems calculated to find a remote ear. For the most part Burns doesn't even offer them to public hearing—only eighty-four of the 632 items collected in Kinsley's edition appear in the various editions of *Poems* Burns published—and when he does offer them for general appraisal, they appear as missives from some Beyond, in a tongue of the diminishing. He collects his pieces for friends (as in the Glenriddell MSS), encloses songs in letters, incises poems into pub windows, works anonymously for Mr. Johnson and Mr. Thomson. For the Crochallan Fencibles, it seems, he gathers/emends/produces a collection of bawdry—the text, apparently, called *The Merry Muses of Caledonia*—his hand in which it is impossible to determine. Scots, vulgarity, obscenity, privacy, anonymity: the textual Burns is designed to resist its condition.

Dᴇ Vᴜʟɢᴀʀɪ EʟᴏQᴜᴇɴᴛɪᴀ

Scots is the chief thing, *sine qua non*, both banner and embodiment of Burns's troth. To write in Scots, for Caledonia's Bard, is to fight monologos with monologos: to engage Poems of "our language" chiefly in this Dialect is to worry the space (debatable land) between "language" and "our," and to find a border where no borders are presumed to be.

A few doggerel, Scotch rhymes: the Scottish vernacular carries a discounted value (Our Prices Can't Be Beat! Everything Must Go!)—as when the ghostly Preface writer refers to Ramsay and Fergusson ("these two justly admired Scotch Poets") and the epithet "justly" inserts itself with oily ease, planting a presumption of doubt (as if doubt were inherent) in the relation between the Scottishness and the value of Poets. To write Scots is, to begin with, to stand outside the prevalent conventions of the normative, to affirm a negativity.

What such a (low) vantage might mean is a question as various as Scottish literature, but whatever it means must assume the form of a dooble tongue: Scots is always written (as much for Burns as for Tom Leonard or Gavin Douglas, renumbering his *Eneados*, or William Dunbar, who refers to "reverend Chaucere . . . / As in oure tong ane flour imperiall")[1] in the consciousness and material linguistic presence of English, is never simply another language but a language linked to another in its bones, a twinned galaxy in an awkward rotation—a language with an incubus.

Such a condition, of course, is a serious threat to the vital spirit of the language (as Morgan says, "[making] it all the more difficult for the Scottish writer to develop integrally"), and the long history of writing in Scots—from the dialect of Burns through the synthetics of MacDiarmid and the neologisms of *Sharawaggi*—testifies to the struggle to keep body and soul together. But the condition of Scots—the condition of the discounted, of the hopelessly contingent—is not only a cause for lament, a matter of the Flowres of the Forrest; rather, in good postmodern theory-of-the-marginal fashion, this very contingency of Scots, its perpetual relationality, confers upon it a powerful critical vantage on what is, after all, the condition of language itself.

Look at any page. The Center may claim to define itself in terms it claims to authorize, but what defines any Center is necessarily the margin it both creates and negates: every page in every tongue is dooble. Every language, too, no matter how dominant or precarious its position (Adamic language, Latin, lingua franca, English), stands in relation: it goes without saying. What distinguishes marginalized tongues is their necessarily more self-conscious embodiment of this common condition, and of the political weight it carries.

So Scots, the marked form, turns around and marks its marker: Ingliss, Doric, Scots, Lallans, Southron, English, all are revealed to be limited categories—an anxious proposition, if an unavoidable one, for any language, and one that only a thriving language is in a position (falsely) to deny.

To write in Scots is to resist the consumption of writing, or at least to seek it as a specialized case—a demand for the making of allowances, a slave's insurrection, an oxymoron. To be sure, the tongue is consumed: the Kilmarnock Preface announces the event, and the early reviews elaborate the process, from Henry Mackenzie's "Heaven-taught Ploughman" right on down. Consumption, as Adorno teaches, is unavoidable, even "our most secret innervations" fodder in an exchange market. But the world remains, for Burns, unconsumed, and Scots is its tongue.

In relation to English—and in the standard parlance of criticism, drawn in this case from Imperial Egypt—Scots (even the most highfalutin Scots) is a case of the demotic, which is always a category of the given. The hieratic, to which the demotic is opposed, *is* the given, and thus needs no name—giving way typically, when a name is needed, to mandarin, the litcrit metaphor shunted further east. The invisible hieratic bears the odor of the ideal upon the air we breathe in public discourse. To speak of the demotic is thus to render it neutralized, to deny it power apart from the hieratic, of which it is merely, by definition, a simplified and debased form.

The demotic, however, makes its own claim of universality, no less totalizing than the claim of the hieratic. Ask Dante:

> the vernacular speech is that which we acquire without any rule, by imitating our nurses. There further springs from this another secondary speech, which the Romans called grammar. . . . Of these two kinds of speech also, the vernacular is the nobler, as well because it was the first employed by the human race, as because the whole world

Yi write doon a wurd, nyi sayti yirsell, that's no thi way a say it. Nif yi tryti write it doon thi way yi say it, yi end up wi thi page covered in letters stuck thigithir, nwee dots above hof thi letters, in fact, yi end up wi wanna they thingz yid needti huv took a course in phonetics ti be able ti read. But that's no thi way a *think*, as if ad took a course in phonetics. A doant mean that emdy that's done phonetics canny think right—it's no a questiona right or wrong. But ifyi write down "doon" wan minute, nwrite doon "down" thi nixt, people say yir beein inconsistent. But ifyi sayti sumdy, "Whaira yi afti?" nthey say, "Whut?" nyou say, "Where are you off to?" they don't say "That's no whutyi said thi furst time." They'll probably say sumhm like, "Doon thi road!" anif you say, "What?" they usually say, "Down the road!" the second time—though no always. Course, they never really say, "Doon thi road!" or "Down the Road!" at all. Least, they never say it the way it's spelt. Coz it *izny* spelt, when they say it, is it?

—Tom Leonard

makes use of it, though it has been divided into forms differing in pronunciation and vocabulary.[2]

The local and the global (indeed, for Dante, the cosmic) become indistinguishable here, and the relation between demotic and hieratic is reversed: the vernacular not a debased form of grammar but an unregulated form—quite anither metaphor.

(Perhaps it is best to say that the vernacular and the grammatical, the demotic and the hieratic, the vulgate and the cultured, haunt one another, and that we recognize the synthesis of the two as a high achievement: in Dante, Chaucer, Rabelais, Shakespeare, Cervantes, Joyce . . .)

In any event, the demotic does not call itself demotic, and names itself never by an abstraction. The body of the demotic is its only name, as that great (primitivist) hieratic Wallace Stevens has it:

> Throw away the lights, the definitions,
> And say of what you see in the dark
>
> That it is this or that it is that,
> But do not use the rotted names.[3]

In such a dark the tongue moves. The tongue is not consumed.

13

My dear Mensch,

Burns writes in Scots because Fergusson and Ramsay showed him it could be done, and because it serves his own purposes as a slave who would speak to a false world without speaking falsely. The vulgate is unruled.

Since you asked.

Your Wordsworth, who credits Burns with his first instruction in the poetic uses of the language of real men, pursues quite different ends. He may scrap one kind of hieratic discourse (the tongue of O Phoebus and so on) because it doesn't quite work anymore, but the effect he seeks from the demotic impulse is nonetheless one of a hieratic refinement, a transcendental tongue. (Lyricized ballads, as you say.) Burns's tongue is not transcendental but a tongue of compeers. We eavesdrop, as Wordsworth eavesdrops, but Burns does not eavesdrop: he speaks as if no one is listening but those who love him.

Your foolish friend, &c.

14
In the name of the NINE. Amen!

We, ROBERT BURNS, by virtue of a Warrant from NATURE, bearing the date the Twenty-fifth day of January, Anno Domini one thousand seven hundred and fifty-nine, POET-LAUREAT, and BARD IN CHIEF, in and over the Districts and Countries of KYLE, CUNNINGHAM and CARRICK, of old estate, To our trusty and well-beloved WILLIAM CHALMERS and JOHN M'ADAM, Students and Practitioners in the ancient and mysterious Science of Confounding Right and Wrong.

RIGHT TRUSTY:

Be it known unto you, That whereas in the course of our care and watchings over Order and Police of all and sundry the MANUFACTURERS, RETAINERS, and VENDERS of POESY; Bards, Poets, Poetasters, Rhymers, Jinglers, Songsters, Ballad-singers, &c., &c., &c., &c., &c., male and female—We have discovered a certain [bawdy?], nefarious, abominable and wicked SONG or BALLAD, a copy whereof We have here inclosed; Our WILL THEREFORE IS, that YE pitch upon and appoint the most execrable Individual of that most execrable Species, known by the appellation, phrase, and nickname of THE DEIL'S YELL NOWTE: and after having caused him to kindle a fire at the Cross of AYR, ye shall, at noontide of the day, put into the said wretch's merciless hands the said copy of the said nefarious and wicked Song, to be consumed by fire in the presence of all Beholders, in abhorrence of, and terrorem to, all such COMPOSITIONS and COMPOSERS. And this in nowise ye leave undone, but have it executed in every point as this Our Mandate bears, before the twenty-fourth current, when IN PERSON We hope to applaud your faithfulness and zeal.

Given at Mauchline this twentieth day of November, Anno Domini one thousand seven hundred and eighty-six.
GOD SAVE THE BARD![4]

Letter no. 58 is a document from the unapproved minutes of an unauthorized court of equity, the inscription of a local Bardship, an obeisance to the Muses, apparently an enclosure for a piece of bawdry, a note to say "see you in a few days," and a takeoff on the hieratic, like the letter to wise & witty Willie, only this time upside-down rather than inside out.

Written on the verge of Burns's visit to Edinburgh following the publication of his Poems, cast in the language of an imperious order—We, Robert Burns! Be it known that!—this piece trumpets the vulgate not only in its mocking appropriation of the Highest

---

Grammar (the vulgate's Lord and presumed Master) but also in its celebration of bawdy, nefarious, abominable, wicked tendencies (linguistic and otherwise) among the body politic. The ancient and mysterious Science of Confounding Right and Wrong precisely *is* the vulgate, the local, the discourse of exceptions, particularities, impulses, Polish grandmothers, unruled periods, eccentric moralities, and not necessarily rational animal veracities. Burns speaks here, with a warrant from Nature, in a tongue of the most exalted totalitarian proclamation—perversely—for an ear most particularly private. The vulgate is what makes Letter no. 58 a joke.

15

If the thrust of the vernacular for Burns is a stab at the Order of Right and Wrong—anither story than Hail Britannia!—then the reception history of his work is its elaborate parry: a counter-gesture sometimes inflamed, sometimes worried, sometimes casual, and almost always as self-contradicted as my own Improvisations here. The self-contradiction is the important part. The vernacular as an object of study, of critical attention, of analytic discourse, *is* a contradiction, invites—makes unavoidable—self-contradiction. Burns's book is offered for consumption, and illuminates the illusions of its consumers.

Immortal Memory

Can it be possible, that when I resign this frail, feverish being, I shall still find myself in conscious existence! When the last gasp of agony has announced that I am no more to those that knew me, & the few who loved me; when the cold, stiffened, unconscious, ghastly corse is resigned into the earth, to be the prey of unsightly reptiles, & to become in time a trodden clod, shall I yet be warm in life, seeing & seen, enjoying & enjoyed? Ye venerable Sages & holy Flamens, is there probability in your conjectures, any truth in your many stories, of another world beyond death; or are they all alike baseless visions & fabricated fables? If there is another life, it must be only for the just, the benevolent, the amiable, & the humane; what a flattering idea, then, is a World to come! Would to God I as firmly believed it, as I ardently wish it!
—Burns, to Mrs. Dunlop, 13 December 1789

The cranial bones were perfect in every respect, if we except a little erosion of their external table, and firmly held together by

their sutures; even the delicate bones of the orbits, with the tri-
fling exception of the *os unguis* in the left, were sound and unin-
jured by death and the grave. The superior maxillary bones
still retained the four most posterior teeth on each side, includ-
ing the *dentes sapientiae*, and all without spot or blemish; the *inci-
sores, cuspidati*, &c., had, in all probability, recently dropt from
the jaw, for the *alveoli* were but little decayed. The bones of the
face and palate were also sound. Some small portion of black
hair, with a very few grey hairs intermixed, were observed
while detaching some extraneous matter from the occiput. In-
deed, nothing could exceed the high state of preservation in
which we found the bones of the cranium, or offer a fairer op-
portunity of supplying what has so long been desiderated by
phrenologists—a correct model of our immortal poet's head;
and in order to accomplish this in the most accurate and satis-
factory manner, every particle of sand, or other foreign body,
was carefully washed off, and the plaster of Paris applied with
all the tact and accuracy of an experienced artist. The cast is
admirably taken, and cannot fail to prove highly interesting to
phrenologists and others.

Having completed our intention, the skull, securely inclosed
in a leaden case, was again committed to the earth precisely
where we found it.

—*Dumfries Courier*, April 1834

Shortly to say, is nane can tell
The halle condicioun off a threll.

— John Barbour

For Burns's first reviewers and for much of the nineteenth cen-
tury, the vulgate nature of his work is the most important thing
about it; in the twentieth century Burns's vulgate is simply histori-
cized, appearing no longer either to pose a threat or suggest a pos-
sible desire's excitement. For those first reviewers, his Life and his
Work form twin monoliths for the scrutiny of the moral imagina-
tion; by the twentieth century the authority of biographical criti-
cism wobbles significantly, itself edging into a state of vulgarity,
and the Work is found to be a kind of footnote, insufficiently cen-
tral to be of more than passing regard—there's no Burns left.

The earliest review of the Kilmarnock *Poems* comes as an un-
signed notice in the *Edinburgh Magazine, or Literary Miscellany* of Oc-
tober 1786 and introduces the themes that will dominate the
discussion for years to come: the apparent gulf that separates
Burns from the world to which he (now) makes address is the criti-
cal point of interest, the point that must be resolved before any
further business might be conducted.

> Who are you, Mr. Burns? will some surly critic say. At what university have you been educated? what languages do you understand? what authors have you particularly studied? whether has Aristotle or Horace directed your taste? who has praised your poems, and under whose patronage are they published? In short, what qualifications entitle you to instruct or entertain us?[5]

This list of questions is admirable for the precision with which it delineates the terms of a contract, which Burns, having put his poems into general circulation, might be presumed to have signed. Like the "form" to which various specimens of Osmond Dips's body are appended in "Horse Island," the form of Burns called forth here is of paper—a matter of identifying documents, of entitlement. Institutional affiliation, linguistic command, curricular history, classical allegiance, current sponsor: these are the sites of validation and judgment, beyond which "Mr. Burns" might be said to be of no account—this surly critic, at least, hardly looks up from his desk.

Our Miscellaneous critic, however, who imagines this interrogation, is himself more kindly disposed. Although Burns's poems "may probably have to struggle with the pride of learning," he notes, "yet they are entitled to particular indulgence." For this condescending fellow, Burns is "indeed a striking example of native genius bursting through the obscurity of poverty and the obstructions of laborious life" (Low, *CH*, 64). But if this critic's judgment deviates from the surly standard, his indulgence is nevertheless the mark of a border crossed—"bursting through" indeed, a cultural divide named here by violence.

"He is said to be a common ploughman; and when we consider him in this light, we cannot help regretting that wayward fate had not placed him in a more favoured situation." ('Tis a pity indeed.) Here it is lowliness of station in general, and not Scots per se, that impedes an audience from receiving the thrust of Burns's poems in gentle fashion—that, and "a dash of libertinism, which will keep

> Thus the hearsomeness of the burger felicitates the whole of the polis.
>
> —Joyce

some readers at a distance"—but the class issue and the language issue shadow one another inescapably, in spite of exceptions one might make ("the doric simplicity of Ramsay, . . . the brilliant imagination of Ferguson"), and the point is the same: Burns, like "the Character Horace gives to Ofellus," is a case of "*Rusticus abnormis sapiens, crassaque Minerva*" (Low, *CH*, 64). The sign of the vulgate overdetermines the whole: the incubus is its obsessional spawn.

"Surprising effects of Original Genius, exemplified in the Poetical Productions of *Robert Burns*, an Ayrshire Ploughman" (Low, *CH*, 67), Henry Mackenzie's instantly famous review, appeared two months later in the *Lounger*—the name of this as of several other contemporary periodicals (*General Magazine and Impartial Review*, *Universal Magazine*, *New Town and Country Magazine*) fully redolent of the new cosmopolitan milieu. Privilege and Presumption open their door (someone has knocked) and, taking a moment to adjust their faces, are quite pleased by what they see: an exemplum no less. Mackenzie takes the conceit of the Edinburgh Miscellany and gives it a shine that illuminates its deepest self-regard; the seeds of this review are scattered throughout Burns's reception history.

What Character would Horace give to Mackenzie? A central figure among the literati, publisher not only of the *Lounger* but of the *Mirror* as well (another organ of self-regard), author of *The Man of Feeling* ("a book," Burns claims, "I prize next to the Bible"),[6] and Comptroller of Taxes for Scotland too, he is poised to speak for a vantage that makes every claim to be representative.

The tony opening lets us know where we are (Burns is several paragraphs off yet):

> To the feeling and the susceptible there is something wonderfully pleasing in the contemplation of genius, of that supereminent reach of mind by which some men are distinguished. In the view of highly superior talents, as in that of great and stupendous natural objects, there is a sublimity which fills the soul with wonder and delight, which expands, as it were, beyond its usual bounds, and which, investing our nature with extraordinary powers, and extraordinary honours, interests our curiosity, and flatters our pride. (Low, *CH*, 67)

This is the rhetoric of a select club in which nature is invested, curiosity interested, and pride flattered: a connoisseurship of the most exalted discrimination which takes in *every*thing and turns it to account—an account (a mirror) of the club itself, the whole world (beyond, even, the soul's usual bounds) reduced to a tickling of refined taste. "Wonderfully pleasing" catches the tone just so.

Before we even get to the question then of Ayrshire ploughmen and native genius bursting out of poverty and obscurity, the *Lounger* review makes clear that poverty and obscurity are mere epiphenomena, that the real question has little to do with Ayrshire and everything to do with establishing and sustaining the self-image of Mackenzie's readership. (The Kilmarnock *Poems*, of course, are concerned with that self-image themselves, but in a different self-interest.) The approval of the literati—"that superior place, which the enthusiasm of its patrons

> Mass culture is a system of signals that signals itself.
> —Adorno

would have assigned it" (Low, *CH*, 68)—is the prize and the main point of interest: poetical productions are commodities by means of which our taste can appreciate itself (thereby appreciating in value—a profitable business).

In such a context the matter of the vulgate can only be a curiosity—if that much—a hieratic name for the demotic, a category of special dispensation. "The language in which most of [Burns's] poems are written" is indeed the "one bar . . . opposed to his fame" (Low, *CH*, 69): "Even in Scotland, the provincial dialect which Ramsay and he have used, is now read with a difficulty which greatly damps the pleasure of the reader; in England it cannot be read at all, without such a constant reference to a glossary, as nearly to destroy that pleasure" (Low, *CH*, 69). It is further necessary to write off the "spirit of libertinism and irreligion" which these poems "breathe"—which is easy enough

> Reduced as it is to the pursuit of cultural goods, the spirit demands that these goods themselves are not genuinely experienced. The consumer must only know how to deal with them in order to justify his claim to be a cultivated person.
> —Adorno

to do when "we consider the ignorance and fanaticism of the lower class of people in the country where these poems were written" (Low, *CH*, 70). *Noblesse oblige* tolerates even "some exceptionable parts of the volume he has given to the public, which caution would have suppressed, or correction struck out" in a Subjunctive Scotland of the literati class. No worries, then, in the end: "Some of his productions . . . are almost English" (Low, *CH*, 69), and many display recognizable categories of worth—solemnity, sublimity, "the tender and the moral," the "truly pastoral." Burns is just like us, it seems, even if we're not just like him. His disappearance is well under way.

Mackenzie does mean to praise Burns: "if I am not greatly deceived, I think I may safely pronounce him a genius of no ordinary rank," a "Heaven-taught ploughman" of "uncommon penetration and sagacity," "rapt and inspired melancholy," "fully intitled to command our feelings, and to obtain our applause" (Low, *CH*, 68–70). Burns's Muse is even to be considered "the champion of morality, and the friend of virtue" (Low, *CH*, 70)—or rather, intitled to be pronounced such (feel free, please, to applaud). It's just that Mackenzie's voice is the voice of a king's liege subject; when he says "I hope I shall not be thought to assume too much, if I endeavour to place [Burns] in a higher point of view, to call for a verdict of his country on the merit of his works, and to claim for him those honours which their excellence appears to deserve" (Low, *CH*, 68), he evokes only the humility of a favored class, a posture courtly power is pleased to assume. (He also mirrors the fear of a tyrant's wrath, a fear which trembles under the polished surface of courtly discourse.) But as he puts it in *The Man of Feeling*, "One is ashamed to be pleased with the works of one knows not whom."[7]

The review ends with a call for patronage, and (again) it is the patronage—not the patronized—that draws our eye. Burns must not be made "to seek under a West Indian clime that shelter and support which Scotland has denied him":

> I trust means may be found to prevent this resolution from taking place; and that I do my country no more than justice, when I suppose her ready to stretch out her hand to cherish and retain this native poet, whose "wood-notes wild" possess so much excellence. To repair the wrongs of suffering or neglected merit; to call forth genius from the obscurity in which it had pined indignant, and place it where it may profit or delight the world; these are exertions which give to wealth an enviable superiority, to greatness and patronage a laudable pride. (Low, *CH*, 70–71)

Burns, of course, cannot trust that means may be found (for much of anything at all), which is precisely why his poems come to this venue as if from another country. If Adorno is right that the "transfer of the use value of consumption goods to their exchange value contributes to a general order in which eventually every pleasure which emancipates itself from exchange values takes on subversive features" (Adorno, *The Culture Industry*, 34), then Mackenzie's role here is to keep this *emigré manqué* within familiar bounds, to spread his means over Burns's prepos-

> to find some kind of counterpoise to the struggles of a world, always an alien scene, a task uncouth to the poetical mind
>
> —Burns

terous or lamentable ends. Enviably superior wealth, laudably proud greatness and patronage, the capacity to rescue the pining indignant maiden from obscurity, to repair wrongs of suffering and make a profit in the bargain: these belong not to Burns but to us. Burns speaks to Power—that's what Mackenzie makes clear: whatever Burns may say (of the penetrating, the sagacious, and the like), Mackenzie only hears applause for himself. One would be ashamed otherwise.

> What parades as progress in the culture industry, as the incessantly new which it offers up, remains the disguise for an eternal sameness; everywhere the changes mask a skeleton which has changed just as little as the profit motive itself since the time it first gained its predominance over culture.
>
> —Adorno

The matter of patronage is a characteristic, recurring note in the early reception (and remains a critical issue even now, even if Burns, his widow, and his orphans are no longer materially concerned in its outcome, and even if we no longer speak of patronage with the bald clarity of eighteenth-century culture industry figures).

One month before Mackenzie's review appears, one Allan Ramsay of Ochertyre (not, of course, *the* Allan Ramsay) writes to the editor of the *Edinburgh Evening Courant* complaining of "the number of . . . Peers, Nabobs, and wealthy Commoners" in Ayrshire, "not one of [whom] has upon this occasion stepped forth as a patron to this man"—"a reflection on the county and a disgrace to humanity" (Low, *CH*, 65). This prompts a reply from G. H. (probably Gavin Hamilton) of Glasgow, noting that "the gentlemen of Airshire . . . have taken particular notice of the Author," having "subscribed for, or bought up" the bulk of his production, and that "Ramsay's reflection upon the county does therefore little credit either to his information upon the subject or to the politeness of his stile" (Low, *CH*, 66). *The New Annual Register, or General Repository of History, Politics, and Literature, for the Year 1786* (another redolent mouthful) has "our rural bard . . . justly entitled to the patronage and encouragement which have been liberally extended toward him" (Low, *CH*, 75). The literatus writing for the *Critical Review* in May 1787, who finds it "to be regretted, that the Scottish dialect, in which these poems are written, must obscure the native beauties with which they appear to abound, and renders the sense often unintelligible to an English reader," opines nevertheless:

Should it, however, prove true, that the author has been taken under the patronage of a great lady in Scotland, and that a celebrated professor has interested himself in the cultivation of his talents, there is reason to hope, that his distinguished genius may yet be exerted in such a manner as to afford more general delight. (Low, *CH*, 80)

The matter seems to be settled by December, following the publication of a second edition in Edinburgh (in May) and a third in London (in November), when the *Monthly Review* is pleased to mention "the numerous and respectable list of subscribers prefixed to the volume before us": "It appears that [Burns] has been very liberally patronized by an indulgent Public; and we rejoice to see that he may now have it in his power to tune his oaten reed at his ease." ("John Barleycorn, a Ballad" is singled out among the poems new to the Edinburgh edition: "As this piece is written *in English*, it will be relished alike by the southern and the northern reader" [Low, *CH*, 90].)

The effect of all this jousting, name-calling, speculation, self-justification, and pastoral fantasy is of a kind of anxious but unflappable respectability. With the Edinburgh edition, it seems, Burns has been, if not quite admitted to the club, at least admitted on the premises: poems in hand, he appears on the scene as an object (in the words of the Monthly Reviewer, "an article of some curiosity"), but the subject of the initial reception is the appetite, taste, and digestive apparatus of the consuming (feeling, susceptible, enviably wealthy, superior) class—the curiosity of an indulgent Public, the capaciousness, authority, and delicacy of the maw. Our own maw, too—this respectability as much ours (to maintain, defend, and capitalize upon) as any eighteenth-century Nabob's.

Every tongue has the same tale. The *Catalogue of Five Hundred Celebrated Authors of Great Britain; the Whole Arranged in Alphabetical Order* for 1787 offers this item:

BURNS, Robert. A ploughman in the county of Ayr in the kingdom of Scotland. He was introduced to notice by a paper in a periodical publication, called the *Lounger*, and his poems were published in the year 1787. Mr. Burns was upon the point of embarking for America, when he was prevented from executing his intention by a letter, exciting him to the further pursuit of his literary career, by doctor Blacklock. (Low, *CH*, 20)

Burns here, in the glare of the eminence of Mackenzie and Blacklock, is abstracted out of his own catalog entry. His poems appear, as if without his initiative, from an erroneous kingdom (and in the wrong year)—only after his introduction to notice and in the course of being prevented from executing his intention. His status as a (tenant) farmer is further reduced to that of a plough-man—Mackenzie's term reproducing itself—a figure defined by its functionary relation to the whole. As in the Kilmarnock Pref-ace—or as in the Drunk Man's vision of a different kip—Burns dis-appears, but here it is into constitutive consumables: a matter, again, of Rabbie we'd hardly know ye. . . .

16

Perhaps the only place Burns *can* conceivably appear is on Horse Island, and then only through the medium of Mrs. Semphill's ghost. With the Kilmarnock poems, Rab of Mossgiel's construction of himself in the third person (as his Bardship Robert Burns) ef-fects a kind of disappearance of himself—a Houdini act, these *Poems*, a dooble tongue embodying what vanishes—and this disap-pearance of himself (my wording here awkward enough to be apt, perhaps) stands in a complex relation to his subsequent disappear-ance and reconstitution in the Court of Public Opinion, a dooble relation at once mirror and refusal before-the-fact of that Court's judgment. The power of the court reaches ever outward, the lite-rati casting its ever-widening (feeling and susceptible) net—and those who would come before the bench (or creepie-chair) for jus-tice are assured of finding a set of laws: the supplicant is to be pro-cessed and dismissed.

Among other things, the taste of the literati for judicious delimit-ation speaks (in doobleness itself) a tongue of fear and repres-sion—the tongue of industrial culture (which Adorno will lash helplessly and sharply with his own). "On the Ayr-shire Plough-man Poet, or Poetaster, R. B.," in *Animadversions on Some Poets and Poetasters of the Present Age, Especially R——T B——S, and J——N L——K. With a Contrast of Some of the Former Age. By James Maxwell, Poet in Paisley* (1788), casts Burns in the role of unsurpassed "cham-pion of Satan, none like him before," an "infidel scoffer" by whom "are the laws both of God and man broke" (Low, *CH*, 93–94). Max-well is particularly agitated by Burns's lines "Written by Somebody in the window of an inn at Stirling on seeing the Royal Palace in ruins" (Burns disappearing again, transparent as glass, into Some-body), the lines beginning "Here Stewarts once in triumph reigned, / And laws for Scotland's weal ordain'd," and ending un-humbly enough:

A Race outlandish fill their throne;
An idiot race, to honor lost;
Who know them best despise them most.—[8]

(When he seeks help in pursuit of "the excise idea," Burns is "question'd like a child about my matters, and blamed and schooled for my Inscription on Stirling window," by "a great Person, Miss N[immo]'s friend, M{rs} Stewart," as well. "Why will Great people not only deafen us with the din of their equipage, and dazzle us with their fastidious pomp, but they must also be so very dictatorially wise?" [Letter no. 189, 27 January 1788].)[9] Burns is not wise, is not "sober" (Low, *CH*, 93), is not good: "Tho' some take his part . . . / . . . and value his lies, / By consequence then they the scriptures despise" (Low, *CH*, 94). Maxwell's got it right, in fact: and although in most literary circles nowadays it may be difficult to be deemed an infidel (the question of fidelity to scripture having grown a more technical matter), unless we see that Burns *is* an infidel (or can be taken for one) we must miss the point of his reception.

An infidel, a barbarian, a bastard: William Cowper, who finds Burns's book "a very extraordinary production," nevertheless professes "despair of meeting with any Englishman who will take the pains that I have taken to understand him" ("I lent him to a very sensible neighbour of mine; but his uncouth dialect spoiled all; and before he had half read him through he was quite *ram-feezled*"), and submits that "It will be a pity if he should not hereafter divest himself of barbarism, and content himself with writing pure English, in which he appears perfectly qualified to excell" (Low, *CH*, 91). A parish minister in Scotland before turning London literatus, John Logan observes in the *English Review* that Burns is "a *natural*, though not a *legitimate*, son of the muses," that "vulgarity and commonplace . . . occupy one half of the volume"; and in a letter to Henry Mackenzie adds (with pith o' sense and pride o' worth?) the drollery that "no man should avow

> I never respect him with humble veneration; but when he kindly interests himself in my welfare, or still more, when he descends from his pinnacle, and meets me on equal ground in conversation, my heart overflows with what is called *liking*. When he neglects me for the mere carcase of greatness, or when his eye measures the difference of our points of elevation, I say to myself, with scarcely any emotion, what do I care for him, or his pomp either?
> —Burns, on Dr. Blair

rakery who does not possess an estate of 500 [pounds] a year" (Low, *CH*, 76, 78–79). The *Monthly Review* reprints excerpts in which "We have used the freedom to modernise the orthography a little, wherever the measure would permit, to render it less disgusting to our Readers south of the Tweed"—and laments the weary labor of the reviewing class, forced to wade through the pressing mass of cultural product: "We never reckon our task fatiguing, when we can find, even among a great heap, a single pearl of price; but how pitiable is our lot, when we must toil and toil, and can find nothing but tiresome uniformity, with neither fault to rouse, nor beauty to animate the jaded spirits!" (Low, *CH*, 73–74). (The barbarians no doubt would turn from the gate and run, if they knew how rough it was inside.) And Hugh Blair, doctor, minister of the High Church, and Professor of Rhetoric and Belles Lettres at Edinburgh, famously advises various deletions of indecencies, licentiousness, and exceptionable turns of phrase, including whole poems "which in my opinion ought not to be published" for fear of "burlesquing the Scriptures," and in order to "preserve the fame of Virtuous Sensibility, & of humorous fun, without offence" (Low, *CH*, 82).

In every case the burden of the tune is the prerogative of the consuming public to expect something very like tireless uniformity, to demand what it can use and to transform what it can't use—or what refuses it—into something, at least, after labelling, discardable. (Horse Island, which operates along similar lines, nevertheless discards nothing.) Here the chief means of producing such goods (or bads) is through the mediation of a figure identified as "Genius." This figure both certifies what is valuable in the product, and excuses what is not: the object is in either case dispensed with. The manufacture of Genius, as of its analogy (or by-product) "the Poet," at once provides a container for the exceptionable, the licentious, the infidel burlesque, the wayward (and so on), and allows for its ready consumption by the virtuously sensible.

George Thomson, writing in the *London Chronicle* on the occasion of Burns's death in July 1796, calls it "the powers and failings of genius." (This is the same Thomson to whose *Select Collection of Original Scotish Airs* Burns contributed so many songs, and to whom Burns begins Letter no. 511: "Let me tell you, that you are too fastidious in your ideas of Songs & ballads.")[10] "He had genius," Thomson discerns, "starting beyond the obstacles of poverty," although wont to be "wasted in those haunts of village festivity, and in the indulgences of the social bowl, to which the Poet was but too immoderately attached in every period of his life"

(Low, *CH*, 99). These indulgences and wasting haunts of life in the vulgate are to be regretted, surely, but they are (again) not too much to be worried over. When "a coarse edition of his poems was first published at Dumfries" (or wherever), "they were soon noticed by the gentlemen in the neighbourhood," and "Proofs of such uncommon genius in a situation so humble, made the acquaintance of the author eagerly sought after"—a genius which, if coarse, is yet not beyond the refinement of gentlemen. (Thomson, in any event, never did make the acquaintance of the author—he and Burns never met—which is one reason his account here reads like such a cartoon, and gets so much wrong.) "A subscription was set on foot for a new edition of his works, and was forwarded by the exertion of some of the first characters in Scotland. The subscription contains a greater number of respectable names than almost have ever appeared to any similar production," Thomson declares:

> Burns was brought to Edinburgh for a few months, everywhere invited and caressed, and at last one of his patrons procured him the situation of an Exciseman, and an income somewhat less than 50 l. per ann. We know not whether any steps were taken to better this humble income. Probably he was not qualified to fill a superior station to that which was assigned him. (Low, *CH*, 100)

Genius, it seems, isn't worth much, even if it is (as Mackenzie says) wonderfully pleasing to contemplate, to caress a little while. Although Burns's "manners refused to partake the polish of genteel society" and although "his talents were often obscured and finally impaired by excess," as a Genius, at least, these lamentable developments are readily enough explained (Low, *CH*, 100). Burns is brought to Edinburgh, taken in for a season, his secret Identity— i.e., Native Genius—like an inoculation *contra vermibus*.

The point is, again, "an opportunity to his admirers and the public, at once to pay a tribute of respect to the genius of a Poet, and to erect a substantial monument of their own beneficence" (Low, *CH*, 101). A letter to *Universal Magazine* in June 1787— covering an enclosure of one "judicious Critique on the Poems, which I met with in the 97th Number of the *Lounger*, a very ingenious periodical Paper lately published at Edinburgh by the Authors of the *Mirror*, and now collected, like that entertaining Work, into three Pocket Volumes," and noting with fastidious pleasure "a very noble Subscription in Favour of this untutored Bard"—is most particularly unsigned: "I am, &c. A Friend to Genius" (Low,

CH, 87)—a pledge, again, of liege service. The making of Genius
is an industry like any other in those (in our) industrious days. The
border between Exceptionality and Exceptionability is tightly
maintained—"thi Hadrian's Waa o ther Culchur / Jammin yi
oot"[11]—by means thereof. Insufficient caution, suppression, and
correction, are taken up, tolerated, and indulged by the steely ma-
ternal bosom of thi biggars o waas—for "Poets are seldom cautious,
and our Poet had, alas! no friends or companions from whom cor-
rection could be obtained" (Low, *CH*, 70)—and the self-gratifica-
tion of "more exalted situations" (Low, *CH*, 86) continues
profitably to announce itself.

17

> I am, and have been, ever since I came to Edin{r}, as unfit to
> write a letter of humour, as to write a commentary on, The
> Revelation of Saint John the Divine, who was banished to the
> Isle of Patmos, by the cruel and bloody Domitian, son to Ves-
> pasian and brother to Titus both Emporers of Rome, and who
> was himself an Emporer, and raised the second or third Perse-
> cution, I forget which, against the Christians, and after throw-
> ing the said Apostle John, brother to the Apostle James
> commonly called James the greater to distinguish him from an-
> other James who was, on some account or other, known by the
> name of James the less, after throwing him into a caldron of
> boiling oil from which he was miraculously preserved, he ban-
> ished the poor son of Zebedee to a desart island in the Archipel-
> ago, where he was gifted with the Second Sight, and saw as
> many wild beasts as I have seen since I came to Edin{r}; which,
> a circumstance not very uncommon in story-telling, brings me
> back to where I set out.—
> —Burns, to [William Chalmers], 27 December 1786

It's one thing to say (as the books generally say) that Burns had
to contend with the taste and judgment of Gentle Society, and an-
other thing to encounter that fact, to feel that Society's tongue in
your ear: this is one difference between us and Burns, the differ-
ence between assuming the power of that Society and standing
outside it.[12]
The persona of his humble Bardship is Burns's takeoff on the
rhetoric of the Poet Genius industry. (It's also his bid for a commis-
sion in that industry—"I have likewise warm friends among the
Literati"[13]—and at the same time a claim to power from an alterna-
tive [Caledonian] tradition—where Stewarts once in triumph
reigned.) Burns invites his poetical coronation—anticipates,

mocks, and plays it for what it's worth, sublimates and transforms it into a (dooble) figure at once of acceptable worth and of unconvertibly alien authority. He is to be, that is, like St. John the Divine (poor bastard son of Zebedee, St. Rab the Rhymer), both consumed and miraculously preserved, a very emblem of independence subordinated, transcendental vision swallowed up, the Second Sight (and refusal) of an inhuman order.

The Sign of the Powers and Failings of Genius, as it develops over the course of the next century, assumes the form of a dooble fascination with the Life & the Work of Burns—a development that Burns anticipates as well in his ghostwritten Kilmarnock Preface. The interest in Burns's life is indeed extraordinary—no comparable literary figure comes to mind for the sustained intensity of his biographical presence (the Scottish Tourist Board even designating a cluster of Ayrshire sites "Burns Country"—that old kingdom in exile—a shrine to the departed flesh)—but whereas for Burns the point is precisely the fundamental (even radical) entanglements of Work & Life, their refusal to come apart into separable pieces (the better to eat you up), for the Literati this proves an impossible point to follow.

> When I have pressed him to tell me, why he never applied himself to acquire the Latin, in particular, a language which his happy memory would have so soon enabled him to be master of, he used only to reply, with a smile, that he had already learnt all the Latin he desired to know, and that was "*Omnia vincit amor*," a sentence that from his writings and most favourite pursuits, it should undoubtedly seem that he was most thoroughly versed; but I really believe his classic erudition extended little, if any, farther.
>
> —Maria Riddell

The biographical Burns makes its claim, of course, as early as the earliest reviews, and with his death appears to find its way considerably smoothed. When Thomson remarks on "the powers and failings of genius," he parses the matter neatly in two: "Of the former, his works will remain a lasting monument; of the latter, we are afraid that his conduct and his fate afford but too melancholy proofs" (Low, *CH*, 100). A month later (August 1796), a "Character Sketch" by "Candidior" appears in the *Dumfries Journal*, "offering to the public a few at least of those observations which an intimate acquaintance with Burns, and the frequent opportunities I have had of observing equally his happy qualities and his failings for several years, have enabled me to communicate," and as a way of countering "misrepresentation and calumny" (Low, *CH*, 102). This piece is in fact by Burns's friend Maria Riddell, and is later reprinted in Currie's edition: like Currie's text itself, and like Mackenzie's, it is a founding document of our Bard's biographical mythography. Riddell follows Mackenzie's broad-minded line on her poor friend's questionable morals—

> The eccentric intuitions of genius too often yield the soul to the wild effervescence of desires, always unbounded, and sometimes equally dangerous to the repose of others as fatal to its own. No wonder then if virtue herself be sometimes lost in the blaze of kindling animation, or that the calm monitions of reason are not invariably found sufficient to fetter an imagination, which scorns the limits and restrictions that would chain it to the level of ordinary minds. (Low, *CH*, 106)

—and she accepts, no less than Mackenzie or Thomson, that such matters are to be considered quite apart from the question of the Work: "a literary critique I do not aim at" (Low, *CH*, 107). Defending his Character or attacking his Character, the question of the Life begins (via passionate concern) its slow exile from any notice whatsoever—enters, that is, the field of consumption.

Burns, as might be expected, approaches the matter of his Life from quite another perspective. The Kilmarnock Preface would appear to make it as difficult as possible for the world at large to regard *Poems . . .* as either simply literary—an affair of an increasingly familiar (i.e., textual) kind—or simply *not* literary, a biographeme of more broadly cultural (i.e., moralitarian) import. Consider what looks to be a book of poems, but note that it proceeds "unacquainted with the necessary requisites for commencing Poet by rule," in an alien "native language," and involves the witnessing of "rustic compeers," grounded in what Carlyle calls "local habitation" (Low, *CH*, 362)—hardly a book of poems, anyway, to which standard critical principles might be applied. Or consider the book otherwise, making "every allowance for Education and Circumstances of Life"—a kind of anthropological criticism—but note Theocrites and Virgil, representatives of the textual standard for one who here, after all, "appears in the public character of an Author." Biographical and textual considerations impinge upon one another here, and impinge as well upon the presumed reader of such a document. The Life & the Work are not to be pried apart.

Burns's (defensive) strategy for appearing before the world is a matter of maintaining himself against both textual appropriation and biographical reduction (another version of St. John the Divine's story, you might say). He makes both a claim of the textual and a claim against the textual, which together represent (in Donald Low's quaint phrase) "his independence as a poet" (Low, *CH*, 9)—a claim of power and a claim of freedom, we might say, the power both of intervention and of resistance, freedom both *to* and *from*. His mode is biotextual.

But this composite mode is insupportable in the context of the culture industry, and its disintegration begins, as we see, immediately upon reception. The biotextual is a utopian claim of the dooble tongue, deployed precisely at the incapacities of the current order: which order nevertheless receives it dis- and re-assembled—a Life & a Work—for consumption, an object not of independent (contradictory) identity but of fashionable use, the literati's pet after all.

> An open grave is a furrow syne.
> —Hamish Henderson

With Dr. Currie's effort to salvage for the widow and orphans what the debt to nature leaves remaining, the Life & the Work of Burns achieve their partitioned apotheosis. Currie's edition leaves traces, spoor (or spores, sprouts), all across the nineteenth century: *The Works of Robert Burns, with an Account of his Life* (4 vols.) out of Liverpool in 1800 inaugurates the series, which includes reprints and new editions generally "with a criticism on his writings, etc." from Aberdeen in 1824; Edinburgh in 1815 ("to which is prefixed a review of the life of Burns and of various criticisms on his character and writings; by Alexander Peterkin"), 1818 (once from Thomas Nelson, once from James Robertson and Stirling and Slade), 1819, 1820 (once from Ogle, Allardyce, and Thomson, once from John Orphoot), 1831, 1837, [?1851]; Glasgow in 1816, 1821, 1843–44 ("with an essay on his genius and character; by Professor Wilson, also numerous notes, annotations and appendices"), 1867; London in 1800 (from Creech, of Edinburgh, through T. Cadell and W. Davies, new editions issued in 1801, 1802, 1803, 1806, 1809, 1813 and 1814), 1819 (once from William Allason, once from John Bumpus, once from James Thomson), 1823 (twice again), 1824 ("with an enlarged glossary"), 1825, 1828, 1830, 1833, 1834, 1841, 1844, 1846, 1866 (a "national edition" edited by one William Wallace!), 1875; Belfast in 1805, 1807; Baltimore in

1816; Boston in 1848 ("exhibited under a new plan of arrange-
ment" with no less than "a complete glossary"); New York in 1830,
[?1840], 1855, 1856, 1869; Philadelphia in 1804, 1831, 1835, 1836,
1842—a list restricted in this case only by the *Catalogue of Robert
Burns Collection in the Mitchell Library* (1959) and by the appearance
of the words Currie, Work & Life. The edition I work from is *The
Works of Robert Burns: with An Account Of His Life, and Criticism On
His Writings. To which are prefixed, Some Observations on the Character
and Condition of the Scottish Peasantry. By James Currie, M.D.——A
New Edition, with many additional poems and songs, From the latest Lon-
don Editions, Embellished With Thirty-Three Engravings on Wood* (2
vols., New York: Printed by J. Booth and Sons, 1832)—one, by
chance, not to be found at the Mitchell.

18
FORSPOKEN

Some books are lies frae end to end,
And some great lies were never penn'd:

—Burns

I maun consult some learned clark
Aboot this wanton modiewark.

—Burns

The Work & Life of Burns is an object of anxiety, of contention,
the biotextual composite form Burns claims for it a kind of taboo
to be handled carefully (against the wrath of gods), broken down,
and reconstituted under a spell of magical ritual recitation—
literatied—made knowable and safe. But to put the Work & the
Life together is to acknowledge that they have already come apart.
    Currie's edition is in a sense an attempt to defuse the potentially
combustible nature of the material—the vulgate body, after all,
quite a proper object for a doctor's ministrations. As he puts it in
his dedication of the second volume "To Captain Graham Moore,
of the Royal Navy": "The task was beset with considerable difficul-
ties, and men of established reputation naturally declined an un-
dertaking to the performance of which, it was scarcely to be hoped
that general approbation could be obtained by any exertion of
judgment or temper":[14]

To secure the suffrages of such minds, all topics are omitted in the writ-
ings, and avoided in the life of Burns, that have a tendency to awaken

the animosity of party. In perusing the following volumes no offence
will be received, except by those to whom even the natural erect aspect
of genius is offensive; characters that will scarcely be found among
those who are educated to the profession of arms. (iv)

The professionally armed are the readers ideally protected from
the taint of this material, and all others are hereby warned. But
measures have been taken—no cause for alarm, ladies and gentle-
men, the authorities are in total control—and both Life & Work
can now be presented to Virtuous Sensibility.

The Life comes elaborately wrapped—a heavily inscribed trope
of editorial practice—as if with only a wee absence in the middle.
Burns's letters make up the bulk of the volume (159 pieces of
"General Correspondence"—much lopped, emended, misdated,
with recipients misattributed—ninety more of "Correspondence
Between Mr. Thomson and Mr. Burns," one to Captain Grose,
and one, by brother Gilbert, "containing some particulars of the
History of the foregoing Poems")—and these letters, which "not-
withstanding some specimens of bad taste, occurring here and
there, . . . are certainly entitled to no mean place in the department
of literature to which they belong" (in the words of a later editor,
Robert Chambers), are intended, apparently, to show "the charac-
ter and history of the Poet himself, who is here seen in the undis-
guise of his veritable nature." Certainly they maintain a powerful
hold on the reprint imagination for a century to come. As Currie
notes, however, these letters themselves (like the Poems and Songs
which fill the first volume) "afford but an inadequate proof of the
powers of their unfortunate author" (iii): living or dead, Burns is
a mocking imp of the textual.

But the doctor is undaunted: the makeshift of the letters is bol-
stered by every sort of supplemental validation, from the dedica-
tion to the Royal Navy ("which, in our own days, emulates on
another element the superior fame of the Macedonian phalanx, or
of the Roman legion, and which has lately made the shores of Eu-
rope and of Africa resound with the shouts of victory, from the
Texel to the Tagus, and from the Tagus to the Nile" [iv]) through
eight pages in double columns of "Prefatory Remarks, on the
Character and Condition of the Scottish Peasantry," through the
"Life of Burns" itself (another seventy pages), including a brief
"Memoir respecting Burns, by a Lady," and a substantial "Criti-
cism on the Writings of Burns, including observations on poetry in
the Scottish dialect, and some remarks on Scottish literature" (v),
through an "Advertisement to Dr. Currie's Edition of the Corre-

spondence" ("It is impossible to dismiss this volume, of the Corre-
spondence of our Bard, without some anxiety as to the reception
it may meet with" [79]), to three appendices—the last a "Letter
from Mr. Gilbert Burns to the Editor, approving of his Life of his
Brother; with observations on the effects of refinement of taste on
the labouring classes of men" (x)—an edifying apparatus indeed.

Currie's approach to the Life is essentially anthropological, an
affair of distance, and of distance overcome. ("To such an office,"
he observes of this editorial undertaking, "my place of residence,
my accustomed studies, and my occupations, were certainly little
suited" [iii]—but this is almost a qualification.) He sensibly divides
the subject "of the Scots" into five: "church establishment," "ab-
sence of poor laws," "music and national songs," "laws respecting
marriage and incontinence," and "domestic and national attach-
ments" (v). And if the tale thus told "will not, perhaps, be found
unworthy of attention," this is largely because the anthropological
here is happily found to speak a Nationalist, British tongue. "The
subject," Currie says, "is, in a great measure, new." "Scotland has
produced persons of high distinction in every branch of philoso-
phy and literature," he goes on, "and her history, while a separate
and independent nation, has been successfully explored" (success-
fully from whose point of view, one might ask):

> But the present character of the people was not then formed; the na-
> tion then presented features similar to those which the feudal system
> and the catholic religion had diffused over Europe, modified, indeed,
> by the peculiar nature of her territory and climate.

—And her tongue.—

> The Reformation, by which such important changes were produced on
> the national character, was speedily followed by the accession of the
> Scottish monarchs to the English throne; and the period which elapsed
> from that accession to the Union, has been rendered memorable,
> chiefly, by those bloody convulsions in which both divisions of the is-
> land were involved, and which, in a considerable degree, concealed
> from the eye of the historian, the domestic history of the people, and
> the gradual variations in their condition and manners. Since the
> Union, Scotland, though the seat of two unsuccessful attempts to re-
> store the House of Stuart to the throne, has enjoyed comparative tran-
> quillity; and it is since this period that the present character of her
> peasantry has been in great measure formed, though the political
> causes affecting it are to be traced to the previous acts of her separate
> legislature. (1)

"Presented features"—this (not to mention "bloody convulsions") is doctor talk, and indeed the Character and Condition of the Scottish Peasantry appears here to be that of a patient. Its "separate and independent" body is a thing of the past (even if its autopsy—utopsy?—has yet to be performed): Burns's poetry "displays, as it were embalms, the peculiar manners of his country" (8), and what concerns us immediately here is rather the formation of a present character—a dependent, unseparated body, Frankenstein's monster again, perhaps, or the monster's bride—under the meliorating beneficence of a dooble accession (although concealed from the eye of the historian). "Political causes" of "the national character" may indeed be "traced to the previous acts of her separate legislature"—but the "effects" of such law belong, as everything not lost belongs, to the present, and

> may be considered to have commenced about the period of the Union; and doubtless it co-operated with the peace and security arising from that happy event, in producing the extraordinary change in favour of industry and good morals, which the character of the common people of Scotland has since undergone. (1–2)

(At this point we are referred to Appendix I, Note A [an appendix to a prefatory note, mind you: the suasions of swaddling], for "a short account"—four pages in double columns—"of the legislative provisions respecting" the business of schools for the poor [216].) "Since the Union," in short, "the manners and language of the people of Scotland have no longer a standard among themselves, but are tried by the standard of the nation to which they are united" (7), and if the prognosis is excellent, it is not necessarily for the patient. The procedures of critical care, at least, can be trusted to render all containable, even death itself intelligible, the corpse antiseptic.

Currie gets a deserved bashing in the critical literature, but he also provides what is quaintly called yeoman service in handing down to us, at this great remove, such a sharp picture of the controlling interest of his times. Scotland (unlike Horse Island, and in another way unlike Growing Britain) is a vanishing of people before the enticements of history's "natural course":

> By the articles of the Union, the barrier was broken down which divided the two British nations, and knowledge and poverty poured the adventurous natives of the North over the fertile plains of England; and more especially, over the colonies which she had settled in the East and West. The stream of population continues to flow from the North to the

South; for the causes that originally impelled it, continue to operate; and the richer country is constantly invigorated by the accession of an informed and hardy race of men, educated in poverty, and prepared for hardship and danger; patient of labour, and prodigal of life. (2)

Appendix I, Note B invokes Adam Smith on the "free export of corn" as a model for the explanation of "the free export of people"—along with Sir James Stewart's "late truly philosophical *Essay on Population*" and "the Statistics of Sir John Sinclair"—by way of justifying this natural and invigorating development. (At least invigorating in part: "The unhealthy climates into which they emigrate, the hazardous services in which so many of them engage, render the mean life of those who leave Scotland [to speak in the language of calculators] not perhaps of half the value of the mean life of those who remain" [218].) Scotland is the raw material of labor, the colonialization of the colonized, a romance of manliness in the service of fertility, an allegory of poverty and the prodigal. Britannia sails on with her calculators working overtime, and Burns—he of "the Character and Condition of the Scottish Peasantry"—climbs aboard, "the expiring genius of an ancient and once independent nation" (8). It is the Burns we still have today.

Its manifest by this Map, which is founded upon undoubted Authority, how easy it would be to settle the most advantageous Fishery in the World here, and also with small Charge to make Rivers navigable, for Carrying timber to the Sea side, for there grows excellent good Fir &c in these parts, so that if things were rightly managed, there would be no occasion to go to Norway for Wood or to Newfound-land for fish; seeing North Britain can Plentifully furnish us with both.

—The North Part of Great Britain Called Scotland, with Considerable Improvements and many Remarks not Extant in any Map. According to the Newest and Exact Observations. By Herman Moll Geographer. (1714)

"Unfortunately the correctness of his taste did not always correspond with the strength of his genius; and hence some of the most exquisite of his comic productions are rendered unfit for the light"—a footnote lists "Holy Willie's Prayer; Rob the Rhymer's Welcome to his Bastard Child; Epistle to J. Gowdie; the Holy Tulzie, &c." (3)—but this, obviously, is the least of the problems Burns represents. Currie's task is to name the disease, and where it cannot be excised, to treat it, to render it at least intelligible ("Knowledge has, by Lord Verulam, been denominated power" [2]) if not innocuous.

"The direct influence of physical causes on the attachment between the sexes is comparatively small, but it is modified by moral causes beyond any other affection of the mind," the doctor observes in his practice:

> Of these, music and poetry are the chief. Among the snows of Lapland, and under the burning sun of Angola, the savage is seen hastening to his mistress, and everywhere he beguiles the weariness of his journey with poetry and song.

(Another footnote: "The North American Indians, among whom the attachment between the sexes is said to be weak, and love, in the purer sense of the word, unknown, seem nearly unacquainted with the charms of poetry and music.—*See Weld's Tour*" [5]. In the summer of 1993, the lobby outside the reading room of the Burns Collection at the Mitchell carried an exhibit of North American Indian artifacts—garb and tools—and more locally potted Indian history: kindred in vanishing.) Music and poetry and the attachment of the sexes, along with other dubious attachments, are indeed the subject here, and Currie's task is to make of it an object, the better to be swallowed.

19

For a' that, Currie does manage to step aside quite effectively, and let his subjects speak for themselves. He begins his Life proper (after one paragraph summarizing Burns's course from birth to death, and one by way of introducing Dr. Moore—"well known for his *Views of Society and Manners on the Continent of Europe, Zeluco*, and various other works"—one "of many persons distinguished in the republic of letters" from whom "the strength and originality of [Burns's] genius procured him the notice") with Burns's own autobiographical narrative letter to Moore, dated Mauchline, 2d. August, 1787.

Burns's letter (no. 125) is, like the Kilmarnock Preface, another preemptive strike against cant and calumny, an effort to engineer (in part) his own reception in the republic of letters—a cultivating tool, like a plough.[15] "I will give you an honest narrative, though I know it will be often at my own expense," Burns writes:

for I assure you, Sir, I have, like Solomon, whose character, excepting in the trifling affair of *wisdom*, I sometimes think I resemble—I have, I say, like him, *turned my eyes to behold madness and folly*, and, like him, too frequently shaken hands with their intoxicating friendship. (9)

To be like Solomon except in the affair of wisdom is a bit like being Christlike only in the matter of one's association with women of ill repute. Burns here announces, if quietly and politely, a tapsalteeri- zation of standard categories:

After you have perused these pages, should you think them trifling and impertinent, I only beg leave to tell you, that the poor author wrote them under some twitching qualms of conscience, arising from suspicion that he was doing what he ought not to do: a predicament he has more than once been in before. (9)

Burns's "history of myself" may be "a whim," which "may perhaps amuse you in an idle moment"—a bit of the marginal prodigal— but what he has to say (after "rambling over the country" and being "now confined with some lingering complaints, originating, as I take it, in the stomach") represents a kind of breach: a version of Currie's own trepidatious venture into the same territory.

"I have not the most distant pretensions to assume that charac- ter which the pye-coated guardians of escutcheons call a gentle- man."[16] Burns identifies himself here not against the bearers of escutcheons—gentlemen—per se, but against those who wear their livery: at the Herald's Office in Edinburgh ("that granary of hon- ours") he reports finding "almost every name in the kingdom" but his own—quoting Pope, "My ancient but ignoble blood / Has crept through scoundrels ever since the flood"—his own pretensions and assumptions having nothing to do with any noble calling to wealth, honor, or service: "Gules, Purpure, Argent, &c. quite dis- owned me" (9). His position, perhaps even more definitively than either Dr. Moore or Dr. Currie is in a position to appreciate, is wholly anither story.

(Burns draws the point out in a note he appends to a transcrip- tion of this letter, by another hand, in the Glenriddell MSS [1791]:

Know all whom it may concern, that I, the Author, am not answer- able for the false spelling & injudicious punctuation in the foregoing transcript of my letter to D{r} Moore.—I have something generous in my temper that cannot bear to see or hear the Absent wronged, & I am very much hurt to observe that in several instances the transcriber has injured & mangled the proper name & principal title of a Personage of the very first distinction in all that is valuable among men, Antiquity, abilities & power; (Virtue, every body knows is an obsolete business) I mean, the Devil.—Considering that the Transcriber was one of the Clergy, an order that owe the very bread they eat to the said Personage's exertions, the affair was absolutely unpardonable.—R. B.—[17]

The devoted slave of an absentee master, R. B. is a defender of principally titled distinction, of true spelling and judicious punctuation, of Personages, to whom Virtue is a mere parenthetical nod—and a joke. He comes from so far beyond the pale that it's hard to tell who's outside looking in: the Devil's pardon is a questionable grace.)

Burns is "born a very poor man's son," which means for him principally "stubborn ungainly integrity" and "headlong, ungovernable irascibility"—"disqualifying circumstances" for any place but the most locally defined. It is a position that, characteristically, he both claims and refuses. Like Currie, he insists on the determining force of Class (even while transgressing its borders):

My social disposition, when not checked by some modifications of spirited pride, was like our catechism definition of infinitude, *without bounds or limits*. I formed several connexions with other youngsters who possessed superior advantages, the *youngling* actors, who were busy in the rehearsal of parts in which they were shortly to appear on the stage of life, where, alas! I was destined to drudge behind the scenes. It is not commonly at this green age that our young gentry have a just sense of the immense distance between them and their ragged play-fellows. It takes a few dashes into the world to give the young great man that proper, decent, unnoticing disregard for the poor, insignificant, stupid devils, the mechanics and peasantry around him, who were perhaps born in the same village.

Unlike Currie, however, he resists his own commodification. Of an early period when "my father's generous master died; the farm proved a ruinous bargain; and to clench the misfortune, we fell into the hands of a factor," he notes:

A novel writer might have viewed these scenes with some satisfaction; but so did not I; my indignation yet boils at the recollection of the s——l factor's insolent threatening letters, which used to set us all in tears. (10–11)[18]

A novel writer, an anthropologist, a doctor of belles lettres encounter a terrain which only presumption can open to them.

The course Burns charts runs from the inescapable through the unaccountable, and ends in wayward social pleasures:

> I saw my father's situation entailed on me perpetual labour. The only two openings by which I could enter the temple of Fortune, was the gate of niggardly economy, or the path of little chicaning bargain-making. The first is so contracted an aperture, I never could squeeze myself into it;—the last I always hated—there was contamination in the very entrance! Thus abandoned of aim or view in life, with a strong appetite for sociability, as well as from native hilarity as from pride of observation and remark; a constitutional melancholy or hypocondriasm that made me fly from solitude; add to these incentives to social life, my reputation for bookish knowledge, a certain wild logical talent, and a strength of thought, something like the rudiments of good sense; and it will not seem surprising that I was generally a welcome guest where I visited, or any great wonder that, always where two or three met together, there was I among them. (11–12)

First disowned and now abandoned, Burns refuses economy itself: for "perpetual labour" there is no alternative, but such monologic, as always, discovers its own contradictions.

Among these is "the sin of rhyme" (a splendidly Scottish Presbyterian formulation) which Burns specifically identifies with "This kind of life—the cheerless gloom of a hermit, with the unceasing moil of a galley slave"—and with "a bewitching creature" of fourteen years old, "a year younger than myself," to whom Burns forms his first romantic attachment:

> Among her other love-inspiring qualities, she sung sweetly; and it was her favourite reel to which I attempted giving an embodied vehicle in rhyme. I was not so presumptuous as to imagine that I could make verses like printed ones, composed by men who had Greek and Latin; but my girl sung a song, which was said to be composed by a small country laird's son, on one of his father's maids, with whom he was in love! and I saw no reason why I might not rhyme as well as he; for, excepting that he could smear sheep, and cast peats, his father living in the moorlands, he had no more scholar-craft than myself. (11)

The laird's son smearing sheep and casting peats (by mere accident of his *locus patris*) is a rich touch, and makes Burns's point more vividly than argument: contradiction abounds. Stealing the tune of the laird's son (himself—is it preposterous?—in love with a servant!), Burns makes his characteristic claim of *nevertheless*. Poetry, Love, Folly of every description, Rusticity, definitive Locality, alien Economy, Song: these, for the Bard, are not forspoken, not con-

sumed but consuming, resistant modes of possibility—a Work &
Life as one.

20

Of course Poetry, Love, Folly and the rest *are* forspoken by Cur-
rie as by Mackenzie and the rest and yet others still to come. Burns
is lionized, sanctified, romanticized, purged, and ultimately
shelved (in one way or another) for his achievement of these sites,
and Britannia (for the moment) sails on. These (conceptual) colo-
nies are *not* lost: Burns is weeded, pruned, lopped, sprayed, virtu-
ally decontaminated, held in a place of honor (for a season
masquerading as the ages), and rendered nugatory. Poetry, Love,
Folly, the Deil, the vulgate offer (as the case may be) a *frisson* of
profundity or certainty or self-congratulation, nothing like a resis-
tant mode of possibility—very like a whale, rather.
This is the problem of reading Burns.

> "A strong imagination brings
> on the event," say the scholars.
> —Montaigne

Burns is out of the loop and at the center of the universe. Cut
off or barred from any social network worthy of the name, any that
by any reckoning would count, he persists nonetheless, in the lu-
carne of his pestiferous dungeon, at the center of an elaborate so-
cial network—just one with no Business to mediate it. He describes
for instance having "engaged several of my school-mates to keep
up a literary correspondence with me," and notes:

> I carried this whim so far, that though I had not three farthings worth
> of business in the world, yet almost every post brought me as many
> letters as if I had been a broad plodding son of day-book and ledger.
> (12)

"I felt as much pleasure," he adds, "in being in the secret of half
the loves of the parish of Tarbolton, as ever did statesman in know-
ing the intrigues of half the courts of Europe."
What is Burns doing here? (A predicament he has more than

once been in before.) Is he elevating Tarbolton to the storied eminence of the Gentle & Polite, Inc.? Is he lowering the latter to the former, amatory and political intrigue the lowest common denominator of manic ephemera? Is he turning a phrase away from elevation and debasement alike? He makes two points: that the World of the Local and the World of the Center are isolate, and that the claim of each is equal. Whether the estimation of Burns by Society in any way approaches the estimation Burns makes of himself is a matter of none but circumstantial interest.

On the verge of "leaving my native country for ever," making "what little preparation was in my power for Jamaica," he tells Dr. Moore,

> I resolved to publish my poems. I weighed my productions as impartially as was in my power; I thought they had merit; and it was a delicious idea that I should be called a clever fellow, even though it should never reach my ears—a poor negro driver;—or perhaps a victim to that inhospitable clime, and gone to the world of the spirits! I can truly say, that *pauvre inconnu* as I then was, I had pretty nearly as high an idea of myself and of my works as I have at this moment, when the public has decided in their favour. . . . To know myself had been all along my constant study. I weighed myself alone; I balanced myself with others; I watched every means of information, to see how much ground I occupied as a man and as a poet; I studied assiduously Nature's design in my formation—where the lights and shades in my character were intended. I was pretty confident my poems would meet with some applause; but, at the worst, the roar of the Atlantic would deafen the voice of censure, and the novelty of West Indian scenes make me forget neglect. I threw off six hundred copies, of which I had got subscriptions for about three hundred and fifty—My vanity was highly gratified by the reception I met with from the public; and besides I pocketed, all expenses deducted, nearly twenty pounds. (14)

"This sum came very seasonably," Burns adds, "as I was thinking of indenting myself, for want of money to procure my passage." Our Bard here makes virtually no distinction between slavery and escape from slavery, and virtually an absolute distinction between private and public (or "Publick," in Burns's own unCurried usage) estimations of worth. (Is Burns in imagination negro himself? Is he driving imaginary negros as a hired hand drives an owner's men? Is this "poor negro-driver" vision of disappearing beyond the reach of hearing—short of death, still the land of the living if not the place of hope—an act of service or of domination?) In one way or another the man is indentured, "master of nine guineas" cash and otherwise without prospects: but the value appraised to his work (as to his existence) is a measure of nothing.

When Dr. Blacklock turns the key, then, his letter "opening new prospects to my poetic ambition," the event signifies no kind of validation. Simply, "the baneful star which had so long shed its blasting influence in my zenith, for once made a revolution to the nadir," which unaccountable heavenly intervention signifies only "nearly twenty pounds," and a "delicious" (if untenderable) flash of "vanity." Burns goes to Edinburgh to see about a second edition (and an imaginary income), and "At Edinburgh I was in a new world" (14)—a match for any West Indian scene. As for the critics, surly and/or condescending, who sift the Bard in their fine meshes, for Burns himself the Local overdetermines all, the matter to be resolved before any further business might be conducted.

The difference, perhaps, between Burns and his patrons, is that for the patrons (those early consumers) there is nothing *but* this business to conduct—the relation of the Scots local to capitalized Society (as it Represents Itself) being the only question worth looking into—whereas for Burns other questions loom: the fate of his farm, for instance, or the course of that baneful star. He comes to Auld Reekie "without a single acquaintance" (14), emphasizing his distance, always, just as his admirers would have him do: but the new world he comes to assumes one thing about that passage, and he assumes another.

For Currie, this is a difference without a distinction. The good doctor lops off the end of Burns's letter to Moore, and interpolates an editorial invention: the sentence "Whether I have profited, time will show." But Burns makes no such speculation, writing instead:

> You can now, Sir, form a pretty near guess what sort of a Wight he is whom for some time you have honored with your correspondence.—That Fancy & Whim, keen Sensibility and riotous Passions may still make him zig-zag in his future path of life, is far from being improbable; but come what will, I shall answer for him the most determinate integrity and honor; and though his evil star should again blaze in his meridian with tenfold more direful influence, he may reluctantly tax Friendship with Pity but no more.—[19]

Burns again disappears into the third person, answering for the "Wight he is," and the "zig-zag in his future" recalls the letter to Willie Nicol (or looks ahead, as this is six years earlier), those zigzag wanderings that defy all the powers of Calculation. If he is to profit from entering into the new world of a literati season, it will not be as himself.

21

HIS SOVEREIGN GOOD PLEASURE

So much for unalloyed essence. At this point Currie reassumes overt control of the narrative (beginning again, or we might say, properly, "Robert Burns was born on the 25th day of January, 1759, in a small house . . ." [14]), adding some "annotations" made by Gilbert Burns upon Robert's letter to Dr. Moore, and a letter from John Murdoch ("a principal means of my brother's improvement," in Gilbert's phrase [16], "the preceptor of our poet," in Currie's [21]), by way of extending and corroborating his story.

Murdoch may be an easy figure to ridicule. Burns's teacher when Robert was a boy at Alloway and Mt. Oliphant, and again briefly at his school in Ayr (the building still stands) when Robert was a teenager, he is the first figure in our Bard's correspondence associated with the institution of letters, and his pretentiousness is hard to miss—referring, for instance, to the Alloway cottage (in his retrospective letter of 1799, which Currie prints) as a "mud edifice," "tabernacle of clay," and "the argillaceous fabric above-mentioned" (21–22). The "continuous search for pretentious synonyms," Daiches says, "was characteristic of Murdoch's method of instruction."[20] The man is nevertheless—or for this very reason—one to reckon with: he represents a site of the substitution of language.

In Burns's own account to Dr. Moore, Murdoch appears only in passing, and is unnamed: "Though it cost the schoolmaster some thrashings, I made an excellent English scholar; and by the time I was ten or eleven years of age, I was a critic in substantives, verbs, and particles" (10). (I will let that stand in for Murdoch's more rational representation of his pupil's character and curriculum.) It appears that he taught Robert well—a degree of command in French, too—and that Burns was grateful to him. But Gratitude, for Burns, is always—at least always in situations of social inequality—a site fraught with prickles. He writes to his former teacher twice (in 1783 and 1790) and otherwise names him only twice in passing—this out of 710 letters extant. The 1783 letter (no. 13) is the earliest extant to someone beyond his immediate sphere: addressed "Schoolmaster in Stapleinn buildings London," it is an address to a master in more than a casual sense.[21]

Its occasion, apparently, is unknown. Burns begins:

> As I have an opportunity of sending you a letter without putting you
> to that expence which any production of mine would but ill repay; I
> embrace it with pleasure to tell you that I have not forgotten, nor never
> will forget, the many obligations I lie under to your kindness and
> friendship.

This is Burns, as it were, making a first trip to London (four years
before his first to Edinburgh), making a figure of himself before
eyes that represent not so much the judgment of love (framed in
the dozen earlier extant letters by friendship, family, or sex) as the
judgment of some less warm interest.

(If this distinction is obvious enough—degrees of intimacy deter-
mining modes of discourse—for Burns it is nevertheless definitive:
not obvious enough, that is, to obviate repeated notice, a point not
to concede but to elaborate, to seize in its fatefulness. If it is a given
that power is by degrees immediate, personal, local, or mediated
by distance, the implementation of an abstraction—a model, again,
of Scottish experience in Burns's British world—the letters make
this given problematic. They [typically, as here] reflexively con-
struct, rather than assume, the relation of intimacy to judgment,
and claim for judgment always a local address.)

A political discourse: the tone of Burns's opening sentence is one
of self-deprecation and a kind of terse humility, informed (if not
quite by gratitude) by "the many obligations" of "your kindness
and friendship"—what might, in other words, be expected, warm
words with a chilled edge. At any rate, if Burns never will forget
what he owes to Murdoch, it is a debt—he goes on to make plain—
that he does not intend to repay: this letter is a kind of (elegant)
sneer at a creditor.

Self-deprecation, then, but also a presumption that Murdoch
possesses no measure fit for "any production" he might receive
from him—that Murdoch could not, or would not, recognize the
currency. Burns, in any case, is no longer his young charge. The
student only approaches his teacher here on the condition that
their correspondence *not* be regarded as an exchange, but as a one-
way transmission. A mirror (and reversal) of masterly discourse:
the slave speaks, the master listens, and for this letter at least—
whatever obligations loom otherwise—nobody owes anybody any-
thing.

Burns appears to go out of his way to disappoint Murdoch, to
deny the master his desire:

I do not doubt, Sir, but you will wish to know what has been the result of all the pains of an indulgent father, and a masterly teacher; and I wish I could gratify your curiosity with such a recital as you would be pleased with; but that is what I am afraid will not be the case.

This is a masterful performance in its own way, deploying the language of power (of obedience, of total indebtedness) in a syntax of refusal—a gesture of deference with, again, a thumb at the nose (as in the discourse of thy devoted slave, or the curse that closes the Kilmarnock Preface).

I have, indeed, kept pretty clear of vicious habits; & in this respect, I hope, my conduct will not disgrace the education I have gotten; but, as a man of the world, I am most miserably deficient.—One would have thought that, bred as I have been, under a father who has figured pretty well as an homme des affaires, I might have been what the world calls, a pushing, active fellow; but, to tell you the truth, Sir, there is hardly anything more my reverse.

Murdoch's role in the boy's breeding here cannot be said to have effected a human object that would gratify the investment: the master is not to be pleased. Far from the *homme des affaires* his father paid Murdoch to equip the boy to become, the figure Burns draws of himself here instead appears (if not quite a beast or a reptile) quite intirely without resources:

I am quite indolent about those great concerns that set the bustling, busy Sons of Care agog; and if I have to answer the present hour, I am very easy with regard to any thing further.—Even the last worst shift of the unfortunate and the wretched, does not much terrify me: I know that even then, my talent for what country folks call "a sensible crack," when once it is sanctified by a hoary head, would procure me so much esteem, that even then—I would learn to be happy.

Thus identifying himself with country folks, and happiness with irony, Burns warns Murdoch against presuming (from the perspective of the Capital beyond the Capital) to take his pupil's measure; if he appears here to flaunt his delinquency and the lowness of his aspirations, this is paradoxically both to acknowledge and to render of no account his good Sir's frame of reference.

The implication difficult to avoid is that Burns *is* in fact (if not in one respect, then in general) a disgrace to the education he has gotten, and that this hardly concerns him: a stance beyond repudiation, an appropriation (and dismissal) rather *of* Murdoch *by*

Burns, a claim of independence that is unremarkable, a given—powerlessness without subjection: a Scottish fantasy.

(Perhaps, contrarywise, Murdoch is meant to be flattered by this unco tongue—perhaps no repudiation at all, but gratitude, rather, or at least the recognition of obligations to kindness and friendship—perhaps he is a loving master [of the kind Caesar and Luath, twa dogs, might honor], no mean thing. Burns's 1790 letter [no. 405] refers to "a life the early years of which owed so much to your kind tutorage" [but is otherwise taken up with arranging for Murdoch to contact brother William Burns, currently in London, which "poor fellow will joyfully wait on you as one of the few surviving friends" of Burns *père*].[22] The figure Burns draws of himself, unterrified of penury, is perhaps meant to represent a posture of noble humility—scorn, not for the obligations of his education but for the foolish Sons of worldly Care: perhaps Murdoch is proud of his "sincere friend, and obldged humble Serv{t}," who values moral clarity above the trappings and comforts of achievement. [Burns is talking to a pedagogue, after all.] But the unpublished Bard insists:

> one of the principal parts in my composition is a kind of pride of stomach; and I scorn to fear the face of any man living: above every thing, I abhor as hell, the idea of sneaking in a corner to avoid a dun—possibly some pitiful, sordid wretch, who in my heart I despise and detest. 'Tis this, and this alone, that endears eoconomy to me.

If humble frugality is a virtue, it functions here as rage.)

The one concession Burns makes to his former master—apart from his apparently accidental avoidance of vicious habits—is to note that "In the matter of books, indeed, I am very profuse." He lists the Bible, Shenstone's "Elegies," Thomson, Mackenzie's *Man of Feeling*, Sterne's *Sentimental Journey*, and Macpherson's *Ossian*, as the "glorious models after which I endeavour to form my conduct," and as total compensation for the otherwise derelict state of his fortunes.

But if this profusion of books *is* compensation for the rest, the joke is on *some*body: a matter more, perhaps, of "abundant recompense" (soon to become a soothing, hopeful, dark and edgy watchword) than of any compensation recognized to be full (or even adequate). " 'Tis incongruous, 'tis absurd," Burns writes, "to suppose that the man whose mind glows with sentiments lighted up at their sacred flame . . . can . . . descend to mind the paultry conccerns [*sic*] about which the terrae-filial race fret, and fume, and vex themselves"—but the matter is conspicuously without weight in this world:

> O how the glorious triumph swells my heart! I forget that I am a poor, insignificant devil, unoticed [*sic*] and unknown, stalking up and down fairs and markets when I happen to be in them, reading a page or two of mankind, and "catching the manners living as they rise," while the men of business jostle me on every side, as an idle encumbrance in their way.—But I dare say I have by this time tired your patience . . .

The escape-trails of the heart (and of art), a fundamental trope of the Romantic imagination—at once omnipotent and null—is rendered here in the fullness of its self-contradiction. Burns's glorious triumph is a bitter pill, even before Mr. Creech reels him in, and takes him under that inky wing.

22

From Gilbert's tongue we hear:

> I doubt not but the hard labour and sorrow of this period of his life, was in a great measure the cause of that depression of spirits with which Robert was so often afflicted through his whole life afterwards. At this time he was almost constantly afflicted in the evenings with a dull headache, which at a future period of his life, was exchanged for a palpitation of the heart, and a threatening of fainting and suffocation in his bed in the night-time. (17–18)

"At this time" refers to Burns's middle adolescence, with his and Gilbert's "father growing old (for he was now above fifty,) broken down with the long continued fatigues of his life, with a wife and five other children, and in a declining state of circumstances," and young Robin "the principal labourer on the farm" (17). (Murdoch's gloss on this spot in the hagiographic iconography runs, more trippingly, thus: "But now the plains of Mount Oliphant began to whiten, and Robert was summoned to relinquish the pleasing scenes that surrounded the grotto of Calypso; and armed with a sickle, to seek glory by signalizing himself in the fields of Ceres—and so he did; for although but about fifteen, I was told that he performed the work of a man" [22].) Unlike Robert, and certainly unlike Murdoch, or Mackenzie, or Currie, Gilbert has no particular use for the Mythology of Poverty.

On the subject of equality, inequality, and love, Gilbert observes of Robert:

> He had always a particular jealousy of people who were richer than himself, or who had more consequence in life. His love, therefore, rarely settled on persons of this description. When he selected any one out of the sovereignty of his good pleasure, to whom he should pay his particular attention, she was instantly invested with a sufficient stock of charms, out of a plentiful store of his own imagination; and there was often a great dissimilitude between his fair captivator, as she appeared to others, and as she seemed when invested with the attributes he gave her. (18)

The sovereignty of Love is an old trope as good as new even still (examples too numerous to mention). Gilbert's brother embodies this ancient romanticism in its identification with other sites of sovereignty vexed—Scotland/England, vulgate/text, Life/Commerce: he supplies the capital for each of these battles in the poor negro-driver's rebellion.

> Though a love were given as perfect
>   as heroism against circumstances,
>   unhesitant, undoubting, hopeless,
>   sore, blood-red, whole;
>   though the unspeakable love were given,
>   it would be only as if one were to say
>   that the thing could not happen
>   because it was unspeakable.
>   . . . .
> There is no knowledge, no knowledge,
>   of the final end of each pursuit,
>   nor of the subtlety of the bends
>   with which it loses its course.
>
> —Sorley MacLean

Currie resumes the tale with the formation, in 1780, of the Tarbolton Bachelor's Club, "our poet, his brother, and five other young peasants of the neighbourhood" comprising "a society . . . the declared objects of which were to relax themselves after toil, to promote sociality and friendship, and to improve the mind." The details of the gathering are plain:

> The laws and regulations were furnished by Burns. The members were to meet after the labours of the day were over, once a week, in a small public-house in the village; where each should offer his opinion on a given question or subject, supporting it by such arguments as he

thought proper. The debate was to be conducted with order and decorum; and after it was finished, the members were to choose a subject for discussion at the ensuing meeting. The sum expended by each was not to exceed three pence; and, with the humble potation that this could procure, they were to toast their mistresses, and to cultivate friendship with each other. (25)

A kind of Socratic Church,[23] the TBC clearly claims a (sovereign) site apart from the judgment of our medical editor, who nevertheless must make sense of it somehow.

A "curious document, which is evidently the work of our poet," the *History of the Rise, Proceedings, and Regulations of the Bachelor's Club* dates from 1782 (a sort of belated charter, a declaration of independence after-the-fact) and begins, as on an oaten reed, to a strain of Ceres:

> Of birth or blood we do not boast,
> Nor gentry does our club afford;
> But ploughmen and mechanics we
> In Nature's simple dress record.
>
> (25)

The theme is commonplace by now—the ploughmen's tune from beyond the pale—and a site, nae doot, where Burns and Currie meet (which is not to say common ground). For Burns and his Bachelors the situation is this: given that "the principal view of every man in every station of life" "ought" to be "to become wiser and better," and given that "by far the greater part of mankind are under the necessity of *earning the sustenance of human life by the labours of their bodies*":

> In short, the proper person for this society is, a cheerful, honest hearted lad, who, if he has a friend that is true, and a mistress that is kind, and as much wealth as genteelly to make both ends meet—is just as happy as this world can make him. (220)

Among Tarbolton bachelors, in short, a proper person is one who pretends to nothing.

The Tarbolton Bachelor's Club first convenes "upon the evening of the 11th of November, 1780, commonly called Hallowe'en" (24–25), and indeed is a matter of restless spirits liberated to walk the earth. Its articles of governance call for the election of a new "president" at the end of each meeting, and a discourse in which every mind is spoken. The relation of this radically local utopia to the world of the fairs and the markets ("when I happen to be in them") is one of absolute separation: "No member, on any pretence whatever, shall mention any of the club's affairs to any other person but a brother member, under the pain of being excluded" (220).

> Every man proper for a member of this society, must have a frank, honest, open heart; above any thing dirty or mean; and must be a professed lover of one or more of the female sex. No haughty, self-conceited person, who looks upon himself as superior to the rest of the club, and especially no mean-spirited, worldly mortal, whose only will is to heap up money, shall upon any pretence whatever be admitted. (220)

Currie, however, has other fish to fry. He accommodates the Bachelor's Club by conceiving of it as a kind of training cell for entry into polite society, a veritable engine for the generation of superiority—and from superiority, election, and from election, privilege, and from privilege, (almost) all powers of calculation and command. He hazards his tuppenny thus:

> Though some attention has been paid to the eloquence of the senate and the bar, which in this, as in all other free governments, is productive of so much influence to the few who excel in it, yet little regard has been paid to the humbler exercise of speech in private conversation; an art that is of consequence to every description of persons under every form of government, and on which eloquence of every kind ought perhaps to be founded. (27–28)

Perhaps that last bit about what "ought perhaps to be" is a function of the rhythmic requirements of Currie's rhetoric here, or perhaps not: in any event, what the sentence proposes—the superior usefulness, the approbability of the thing—is virtually the antithesis of the TBC's favored modes of intercourse. The site Currie defines is an imperialist one, where the Club itself is separatist.
He thus praises the endeavor:

> The philosophical mind will dwell with interest and pleasure, on an institution that combined so skilfully the means of instruction and of happiness, and if grandeur look down with a smile on these simple annals, let us trust that it will be a smile of benevolence and approbation. (26)

But "persons of every description" functioning "under every form of government" are not exactly *people*, at least not as the TBC conceives of people, functioning as honest, open hearts; the self-instruction and happiness of these (few) people are indeed the aim of the Club, but not with a view toward any horizon (or judgment) beyond its own.

"And happy had it been," Currie adds,

> after he emerged from the condition of a peasant, if fortune had permitted him . . . to have fortified his principles of virtue by the purification of his taste; and given to the energies of his mind habits of exertion that might have excluded other associations, in which it must be acknowledged they were too often wasted, as well as debased. (28–29)

Fortune, alas, as we know, did not, but each Tarbolton Bachelor remains—"just as happy as this world can make him."

23

Quoth Dr. Currie:

> We have dwelt the longer on the early part of his life, because it is the least known, and because, as has already been mentioned, this part of his history is connected with some views of the condition and manners of the humblest ranks of society, hitherto little observed, and which will perhaps be found neither useless or uninteresting. (30)

Perhaps indeed neither useless nor uninteresting, at least to those ranks themselves (less humble than Currie might think). "His history is connected with some views" (views, no less, that have "already been mentioned") and thus is the thing known (though "hitherto little observed"). But "There is no knowledge, no knowledge," quoth Sorley. The Tarbolton Bachelor's Club is an exemplum of nothing, for any but its own members.

A SEASON IN HELL

To find a Polite name for Burns's skinny-ass vulgate self, to re-name the Local (the vulgate in buckskin breeches) in the tongue of its erasure: this is the impulse (the only recourse, it would seem) that runs through the reception history. At Edinburgh, as Currie notes, "To use an expression of his own, [Burns] found himself, 'suddenly translated from the veriest shades of life,' into the presence, and, indeed, into the society of a number of persons, previously known to him by report as of the highest distinction in his country" (34), and whose response to Ayrshire Man reflects the observation (a wee understated perhaps) that "in Edinburgh, literary and fashionable society are a good deal mixed" (35).

Burns thus is "suddenly translated" upon his arrival in Embro into several etymologies: he is a consumable bard, he is a ladies' man and a man's man both, he is an exemplum of proudly elemental independence and (a little further down the road) a cautionary tale of the wasted and debased. One pictures several exhibits, some perhaps with anthropomorphized capercaillies, in the Hall of Unnatural History at the Archive on Horse Island.

24

Caledonia's Bard is both a recognized trademark and a claim to a free radical identity (or a claim, at least, to a larger latitude): Burns's trick is to maintain the distinction, and Currie's is to collapse it. His humble bardship does well enough in Edinburgh, Currie tells us:

> On the motion of this nobleman [James, Earl of Glencairn], the *Caledonian Hunt*, an association of the principal of the nobility and gentry of Scotland, extended their patronage to our bard, and admitted him to their gay orgies. He repaid their notice by a dedication of the enlarged and improved edition of his poems, in which he has celebrated their patriotism and independence in very animated terms. (35)

RB seems indeed to have been brought within the fold, and placed in proper relation to the powers that be; but Currie quotes only a bit of Burns's Dedication to the 1787 Edinburgh edition, which, out of context, may appear to settle questions which the full text renders more problematic.

Burns does praise "the *Noblemen and Gentlemen* of the Caledonian Hunt" as "those who bear the honours and inherit the virtues of their Ancestors," in whom "the blood of [Scotland's] ancient heroes still runs uncontaminated," and from whose "courage, knowledge, and public spirit, she may expect protection, wealth, and liberty." Nevertheless:

> Though much indebted to your goodness, I do not approach you, my Lords and Gentlemen, in the usual stile of dedication, to thank you for

past favours; that path is so hackneyed by prostituted Learning, that honest Rusticity is ashamed of it.—Nor do I present this Address with the venal soul of a servile Author, looking for a continuation of those favours: I was bred to the Plough, and am independent. I come to claim the common Scottish name with you, my illustrious Countrymen; and to tell the world that I glory in the title.[24]

Plain and simple, and uncontaminated blood notwithstanding, what Burns comes to claim is equality, and he claims it not as a right that might be granted (or not) but out of his own independence. (The Dedication is signed "Your most devoted humble servant"—but if humble service does not mean inequality, then what does it mean? Love? And what would Love mean in such a connection?) The Bard moves to a different measure, a different dictate, a different subservience:

The Poetic Genius of my Country found me as the prophetic bard Elijah did Elisha—at the *plough*; and threw her inspiring *mantle* over me. She bade me sing the loves, the joys, the rural scenes and rural pleasures of my natal Soil, in my native tongue: I tuned my wild, artless notes, as she inspired.—She whispered me to come to this ancient metropolis of Caledonia, and lay my Songs under your honoured protection: I now obey her dictates.[25]

So it wasn't Dr. Blacklock, after all, who whispered in his ear.

> Tell them wha hae the chief direction,
> *Scotland* an' *me's* in great affliction . . .
>
> —Burns

In the summer of 1791, two English gentlemen, who had before met with him in Edinburgh, paid a visit to him at Ellisland. On calling at the house they were informed that he had walked out on the banks of the river; and dismounting from their horses, they proceeded in search of him. On a rock that projected into the stream, they saw a man employed in angling, of a singular appearance. He had a cap made of a fox's skin on his head, a loose great coat fixed round him by a belt, from which depended an enormous Highland broad-sword. It was Burns. He received them with great cordiality, and asked them to share his humble dinner—an invitation which they accepted. On the table they found boiled beef, with vegetables, and barley-broth, after the manner of Scotland, of which they partook heartily. After dinner, the bard told them ingenuously that he had no wine to offer them, nothing better than Highland whiskey, a bottle of which Mrs. Burns set on the board. He produced at the same time his punch-bowl made of Inverary marble; and, mixing the spirit with water and sugar, filled their glasses, and invited them to drink. The travellers were in haste, and besides, the flavour of the whiskey to their *southron* palates was scarcely tolerable; but the generous poet offered them his best, and his ardent hospitality they found impossible to resist.

—Currie

For Currie there is little more to tell. Once Burns disappears back into himself (if he ever really appeared in the first place: maybe Rab isn't Tam but the demon who gets a piece of his mare's tail)—once Burns is consumed—there's only a little tidying up to do.

The Life closes with a long disquisition on Reason (with the observation that "the occupations of a poet are not calculated to strengthen the governing powers of the mind, or to weaken that sensibility which requires perpetual control, since it gives birth to the vehemence of passion as well as to the higher powers of imagination" [55], as well as quotations

> He carried his disregard of money to a blameable excess.
> —Currie

from "Quinctilian" in the original Latin untranslated, and from a "Philosophy of Natural History" by Mr. Smellie), culminating in a vision of Imagination and Understanding in exemplary combination (although not, alas, in Burns)—a kind of unified field theory of eighteenth-century Moral Philosophy—and a further carefully informed discussion of the comparative dangers and appeals of wine and opium, "the pleasures and pains of intoxication, as they occur in the temperament of sensibility" (58).

Burns, in the meantime, has died, and Currie notes that he dies neither in debt nor with anything much to leave the flesh of his posterity, as if (to employ the language of calculators) he never (economically speaking) existed at all. Hence Currie's own work: to provide for the widow and weans, whose "hope in regard to futurity depends on the favourable reception of these volumes from the public at large" (54), to provide what Burns himself would or could not—to capitalize what Burns spent. In the end, and with perhaps the trifling exception of the *os unguis*, this is a Life & a Work marvellously preserved in death, an exemplary specimen for the Archive. Robert Burns (the cold, stiffened, unconscious, ghastly corse) disappears into posterity. Electrodes, anyone?

25

What's *done* we partly may compute,
But know not what's *resisted*.

—Burns

Angel dear & devilish—

I've gone on, I know, and on, my reading is repetitious and obsessive, I know. I want to have drawn a closed, broken circle over and over again, the argument steeping in the image: Burns unread, unreadable, unrecuperable, Burns thy devoted slave, Burns the subversion of pretense to Social Order—and unredeemable even in these terms. (An old trope of Burns, after all: the trope of Freedom.) If I go on too long it is because (as we learn at the Marriage of Heaven and Hell) you never know what is Enough unless you know what is more than enough—and because, if I must produce a consumable Burns, I want to make that fact awkward (as it is): I want Burns to consume you, me, the others, not the other way round. Impossible.

I could sum up this whole treatment of Currie's work on Burns in a sentence—have written that sentence in different forms several times already throughout. We can pop Burns into our canon and blow him to the top of Olympus—but I don't see how this is going to get us any closer to the subject. The subject is impossible in any case. The vulgate will only speak itself, will not be spoken for. I can only try to speak with it, as in a translation to a tongue anathema to it: can only try to turn my own tongue inside out. I don't have to tell *you*.

Dr. Currie, *c'est moi:* my tongue too parries, neutralizes the vulgate, and like Dr. Currie I imagine that I too, at least, recognize the splendor of the creature, the specimen, as I watch it expire.

Reception history can take us only so far, angel: the doctor's breath is upon us all, the incubus of Social Order, of Valuation, Appropriation, Textuality—Litcrit's VAT. Burns remains . . . around the corner, his Scots tongue remains beyond the ken of the literary, a mode of troth our own methods and measures have always already written off. Eventually we learn to read the Life and Work in a modern way—Daiches, among others, shows us how in the '50s—and invaluable work is done: I think especially of McGuirk on the "polemical reversal of Calvinism" running throughout Burns's work, and on the *sentimental* generally, the functioning of sensibility, feeling, and passion in a social-historical context of insensibility, reason, and restraint.[26] I admire these works more than I know how to show, have learned from them with real pleasure (there's that sentimental tradition again!)—but what I can't shake (my own incubus) is the sense that the essential question is always the same ("if Burns is to be reconstituted as a major poet" is how McG puts it),[27] always a question of assimilation, accommodation, accreditation, and thus always—at least in the realm of Burns's Sovereign Pleasure—beside the point: our voices, our interests, our own self-contradictions betray him. Do not speak, let the wind speak . . .

I agree that Arnold got it about right, even if for mostly the wrong reasons: he appreciates Burns, as you note, but (with a sniff or two from his fine nose) places him essentially beyond the ken of "appreciation." In the Scotch zone. Different standards apply, there's not much that *we* can say or see here: the claim Burns makes is not part of Our Big Story. (Matthew knows: Investments "appreciate"—and RB is not an investment.)

MacDiarmid sees the problem too: " 'Immortal memory.' Immortal fudge!"[28] Everywhere the Bard is betrayed, and where he is not betrayed he is lost, unremembered—these are the only alternatives. It's Horse Island again.

So Scots stands against the imperial administration of production and consumption, and is thus perfectly designed to occupy a cubicle in the office of that administration: Scots itself self-contradicted. Which is not to say that it is unfree: is to say that it is unknown, an alien spore (better: a native spore) somehow untouched tho covered in fudge.

Scots, fucking, and song.

God help us all, &c.

26
KILMARNOCK ON MY MIND

The early reception shows that Burns's work is defined by its (self)identification with the vulgate, and that the vulgate is always (for the literati industry) a problematic category: but the Order of Valuation and Appropriation, the institution of letters in the modern state, is unfazed. If Scots is a thrust at the Order of Right & Wrong, and if the reception history is that thrust's elaborate parry, then this parry must be said to have been nimble and effective.

The latter reception history follows the same pattern as the initial reception, only the issues don't matter anymore—they've been absorbed. The vulgate tongue no longer threatens (at least not *that*

vulgate tongue), Jacobitism means nothing, licentiousness is too ir-
relevant to be mentioned (or we too whatever to be ruffled by it),
the "failings of genius" has become a quaint phrase, the ardor of
poets, the excesses of inspiration grow ironic or . . . the problem
remains but fades, and Burns fades with it. The triumphal march
of Good Taste and Textuality puts him in his place (edging his way
out the door).

(But Burns's Scots vulgate does not even register such judg-
ments. A fig for those!)

By subordinating the Work to the Life of Burns, in fact, the eigh-
teenth and early nineteenth centuries would appear to have recog-
nized something—to have sensed the limits of the textual condition,
to have appreciated the possibility of some power that resists textu-
alization—that we here at the end of the twentieth cannot: for we
have been schooled longer, and more aggressively, in the curricu-
lum of textual power. In any event, the reception history considered
most broadly marks a largely successful effort to appropriate the
Life & Work both, to neutralize and accommodate Burns's vulgate
sensibility, to turn it to textual account, and in the end to find it
largely wanting. The rest, for us, is all rear-guard action.

Which brings us to Kilmarnock: here Burns makes his own ef-
fort to address the question directly—the question of the relation
of the vulgate to the discourse of empire, the discourse of English,
of the commercial maw, of the literati—to step forth from the com-
pany of the likes of Willie Nicol, and to make the best of a bad situ-
ation.

I will put the situation thus: in addressing us, the literati, Burns
addresses an industry—call it Litcrit—of production and con-
sumption, specializing in services pertaining to cultural represen-
tation and reproduction. (Or so it is readily construed.) Within this
industry, various interests compete for attention, for sway, for
market share—for power: and if the terrain competed over may
seem ethereal at times, the struggle is no less real for a' that, the
consequences no less material. The business in which we are en-
gaged, the business of cultural representation and reproduction, is
the serious business of establishing (and revising) what questions it
is possible to ask. Litcrit is a custodian of critical consciousness as
well as an instrument of social control.

But Burns comes along, himself very much concerned with
questions of cultural representation and reproduction, and insists
that these questions are not to be regarded in terms of production
and consumption. He insists that cultural representation and re-
production occur somehow beyond the reach of social control—his

vision is a utopian one, ultimately—where neither the poetic work nor the poet's life is a commodity. He makes this argument explicitly and repeatedly throughout the Kilmarnock texts, and again in the very form and framing of those texts. Production and consumption here, as a metaphor for writing and reading, is imagined in every poem to provide an inappropriate, or otherwise inadequate, frame of reference.

What then *is* a poem when it is not a commodity? Burns's answer, chiefly, is that a poem is a performance—and this is a metaphor that raises a wholly different set of questions (the answer to which, for Burns, is chiefly Scots). Unlike a commodity, a performance cannot be reproduced: although it can be recorded, this is less to reproduce than to translate it. (The performance itself, for instance, always includes the audience [if only an audience of one], as well as other specific circumstances affecting the performer, and these can never be duplicated.) A recording can be commodified, but not a performance—it vanishes more resolutely than pork belly futures.

Thus, although Burns does submit both poems and songs to the market's appraising eye, what he provides in effect are recordings—translations from the performative to the textual—and not the thing itself, not the performance, of which (it is important to reiterate) no adequate account can be made. Burns's work exists to say: Something there is, in the world of cultural representation and reproduction, of which your instruments can make no account. The sun may never set on the British Empire, but its light does not shine over all.

Song, of course, is one of Burns's names for this spectral or penumbral zone of the performative, and perhaps its chief name, where he starts out and where he's headed in the end, where he inhabits the performative condition most fully—but Scots is another name for it, and in his role as professional Author, his first name for it. Scots for Burns makes an independent claim for itself (even in the context of its relation to more dominant English and a world of dependencies) largely through its embodiment of performative principles.

The performative and the textual, the vulgate and the mandarin, meet in Kilmarnock: Burns's book dramatizes just this, beginning with its title—with its tongues in relation—an engine for registering the intimacies and exclusions of Georgian language north of the border.

> Just now I've taen the fit o' rhyme,
> My barmie noddle's working prime,

My fancy yerket up sublime
       Wi' hasty summon:
Hae ye a leisure-moment's time
       To hear what's comin?

                   —Burns

In one way or another, each of the Kilmarnock texts contrives its audience—that is, its book-reading audience—that is, us—as an irrelevance, or at least an accidental party to the discourse of *Poems, Chiefly* . . . . What we look for in a poem, like what Mackenzie, Currie, & Co. look for, whatever it may be, we may find: but this is inessential to the poems' own conceptions of themselves, which have to do not with production and consumption but with performance. The performative is a different kip, and a further doobling of Burns's tongue.

Of the thirty-six items listed as "Contents" in the Kilmarnock edition, twenty are in the form of epistles or otherwise direct addresses: "The Author's Earnest Cry and Prayer, to the Right Honorable and Honorable, the Scotch Representatives in the House of Commons," "Address to the Deil," "The Death and Dying Words of Poor Mailie" (to Hughoc, "a neibor herd-callan"), "Poor Mailie's Elegy" (to "a' ye Bards on bonie DOON!"), "To J. S****," "A Dream" (to the King), "The Auld Farmer's New-Year-Morning Salutation to his Auld Mare, Maggy," "The Cotter's Saturday Night, inscribed to R. A. Esq.," "To a Mouse," "Epistle to Davie, a Brother Poet," "To a Mountain-Daisy," "Epistle to a Young Friend," "On a Scotch Bard Gone to the West Indies" (to "A' ye wha live by crambo-clink, / A' ye wha live and never think," and "a' ye rantan core, / Wha dearly like a random-splore," among others), "A Dedication to G. H. Esq.," "To a Louse," "Epistle to J. L*****k, an old Scotch Bard," "———to the same," "———to W. S*****n, Ochiltree," and "———to J. R******, enclosing some Poems." Better than half of the volume, in other words, is presented as for ears other than our own, and occasionally from a mouth other than Burns's. All are chiefly in Scots (with "To a Mountain-Daisy" and "Epistle to a Young Friend" being problematic cases). "The Twa Dogs" is in the form of a conversation (in Scots) between the titular characters. Twenty-one pieces in all, then, embody their performativity in immediate terms—and leave the Reader outside an imagined door, listening in.

This leaves five poems in English, four songs (one chiefly Scots, three in English), a clutch of Epitaphs and Epigrams in Scots and English, four poems in Scots—"Scotch Drink," "The Holy Fair," "The Vision," "Halloween"—and "A Bard's Epitaph," which begins with a mild touch of dialect and moves quickly to its "FINIS" in English.

The Epitaphs are the only poems in the book that explicitly imagine their readers to be specifically the readers of this book— the only ones that wholly let us in. The Epitaphs represent a kind of wholly public tongue, a tongue that does not discriminate between audiences; all the same, one is required to be somewhere (when reading an epitaph) that one in fact is not (when one is reading the book)—namely, at the spot where "Here lies ***"—in order to fit the bill, and so even here, as an audience, we are miscast. The Songs give their tunes, but their audience too (as the audience for any song printed in a book) is elsewhere, their textual condition an unstable one. The English poems are plainly texts, or presented as such, apparently lacking a performative dimension, with no specificity regarding who speaks to whom: but of course this English is an exclusive dialect as well, and leaves out many. (Burns himself may be said to be missing from these poems.)

The four remaining Scots poems, which may be taken to be addressed to a general audience (to a readin' republic, to us), would seem to represent a different order of Burns's art, an effort to bridge (or at least acknowledge directly) a more public gap. "Scotch Drink," "The Holy Fair," "The Vision," and "Halloween" do function in this way, as if the textual condition were here at least an appropriate one. But the placement of these poems within the sequence of the book as a whole tells a slightly more complicated story. The story told by the structural arrangement of the Kilmarnock volume is a story about audience, the effect of which is to make all tongues (and all ears) problematic.

Beyond the performative dimension of individual texts in themselves, the arrangement of these pieces constitutes a further performance—a kind of structural narrative (even a biographical narrative, ending with the Bard's own epitaph), each poem a moment in a sequence proceeding, as all performances proceed, in one direction, each moment following another and being followed in turn. (This is one way in which the performative resists objectification, and casts a wry eye on the ministrations of absolute value: performance knows only relative values.) If we consider the Kilmarnock in this light as a performance (as opposed to, say, a book of poems—the sequence of which, less fully determined by forward motion, allows for readerly rearrangement), if we examine the volume as a discrete sequence, what do we hear?

27

The arrangement of the Kilmarnock poems is a little puzzling.
—Kinsley

Performing the Kilmarnock:[29]
The book begins with a conversation between twa dogs: we are thus immediately conceived in the condition of outsiders, eavesdropping in more than the usual sense. (Crossing linguistic borders here entails both new intimacies—inside a dog's head! a lord's head! poor folks' heads!—and old exclusions.) The poem launches the book in the mode of a destabilized textuality, a conversational model of discourse (the abrupt ending of the poem, without summation, helps too): Scots here is a tongue of more tongues than one, and a record of a performance, a tongue without a textual center. The third voice in the poem, the narrator of this "ance upon a time" tale, is indeed addressed to us—but only in the most generic way: it is the dogs themselves, "unco pack an' thick thegither," who represent audience here most immediately—they, unlike us, know with whom they are engaged. Thus, uncouth, do we enter the discourse of *Poems, Chiefly* . . . .

(If we seek to situate ourselves in our own language in relation to this Scots, we must recognize from the start that ours is only one of several, and here not a privileged one—that the discourse of Burns's book has other origins and other intentionalities: we are, after all, as the Preface notes, the Press for whom [or which] none of these poems was composed.)

"Scotch Drink"—the very heart perhaps of Matthew Arnold's Scottish fantasy if not of Burns's—comes next, ushered in by a bit of Solomon's Proverbs (xxxi: 6,7) done in Scots: and while this most local of poems does indeed include us among its audience, it does so more by allowing than by inviting us. "Ye Scots wha wish auld Scotland well, / Ye chief, to you my tale I tell:" like the twa dogs, the bitterly aroused Bardie of "Scotch Drink" depends upon a presumption of intimacy, of the "unco pack and thick thegither," to which we ourselves—those of us who are not auld Scots—are not party. Words playing in public do not play equally for all. This poem is the first of the four in which Burns addresses the question of a generalized Reader, an audience other than one specifically (or originally) indicated (or intended), and this Reader is decidedly marginal.

Being marginal is better than being generic, perhaps, and better than not existing at all—our imagined condition(s) in "The Twa Dogs." But if "Scotch Drink" allows for an advance of a kind on the Reader's part, the third poem pushes us further off than we were to begin with—almost off the edge of the page. "The Author's Earnest Cry and Prayer" is the first of the Poems in the book to assume the form of direct address wholly to someone not ourselves: "Ye Irish lords, ye knights an' squires, / Wha represent our Brughs an' Shires, / . . . / To you a simple Bardie's pray'rs," is how it begins. We (the Reader) are not wholly absent—the presence of an epigraph conjures us, as does the word "Author"—but only just. Further evidence of our exclusion from the performative community of this poem is given in a footnote referring to "A worthy old Hostess of the Author's in Mauchline, where he sometimes studies Politics over a glass of guid, auld Scotch Drink," and in the closing line of the poem, in which Burns signs off, "While Rab his name is." The footnote is a concession to our readerly presence, but Rab bent over his study hardly takes notice—*we* don't call him by his name. The Reader here is a given of no account—like the Poor themselves, seen from the other side.

(Thus again, whatever Mackenzie, Currie, & Co.—whatever we ourselves—may find to say about the Kilmarnock poems, however much and many the fruit of our readings and researching, all is explicitly to be recognized as a kind of untruth [or at least trothlessness], as interpolation, interposition, intervention, appropriation, and none of it is to be considered as touching upon the essential social contract that these poems recognize: a metaphor for Burns's own sovereign subjunctive Scotland, bounteous natural/cultural resource imagined untouched by British predation.)

So we come, in timely fashion, to "The Holy Fair"—a place whaur a' kinds meet, after a fashion, and (after "Scotch Drink") the second of the four Kilmarnock poems to embody the possibility of our own (the Reader's) presence most directly. If each of the first three poems in the book (even "Scotch Drink") allows us into its discourse somewhat tenuously—and only to emphasize our lack of primary access—this fourth poem would appear more openly exposed to our view (for which it was not composed): a risky move for a nervous Bard, but one for which he's been preparing us since the Preface. "The Holy Fair" opens with an English epigraph (and not a parodic one, as in "The Author's Earnest Cry"—this is the first moment at Kilmarnock in which English speaks for itself) and then moves gently into its narrative: the tale of a private moment, to begin with, cast in a tongue of public design. (This poem also marks the first appearance here of Burns's nine-line stanza, which he uses again only in "A Dream," "Halloween," and "The Cotter's Saturday Night," poems [however privately conceived] that in one way or another engage a more public, urban, or English audience.)[30] In a public space, however private the moment, we are in the company here of FUN, SUPERSTITION, and HYPOCRISY: the riddles of allegory paradoxically legible to all. But when the poem moves into its more public setting—the Fair itself, "the holy spot"—it becomes, again paradoxically, more local, and we turn out to be eavesdroppers and Peeping Toms again after all. A "we" appears (in stanza 8) to which we do not belong—not those of us in Edinburgh, London, or the ex-colonial outposts—and the text begins to accrue cyphers the significance of which (however well modern editorial science can decipher them) we are presumed not to recognize. (One of the cyphers is "K*******ck," a kind of joke *avant la lettre*.) Again we are made party to a poem in which whatever we may comprehend is quite explicitly a function of our being inappropriately placed to tender a full response. (Laughing at Universal Folly is not the same as laughing at ministers Moodie, Smith, and the rest.) Burns comes to the Fair at the invitation of FUN: we are put in the position of one who doesn't quite get the joke. But who invited us, anyway?

The next five poems, each a direct address of one kind or another, put us squarely again in the position of eavesdroppers, privy to a discourse in which we have no part: whatever interpretive rights we might claim here are clearly extraneous to the economy of discourse that these poems imagine. "Address to the Deil" (in spite or because of its epigraph from Milton) makes our identification with the addressee most fundamentally problematic—can we interpret as the Devil would? and what would that mean?—at the same time that Burns identifies himself with that Personage most familiarly. The discourse of an unorthodox religion succeeds the discourse of orthodoxy (delivered by cyphers in "The Holy Fair"), and leaves us naebody to be our own cypher. (Now the risk is ours: to be let in on the joke requires a kind of blasphemy—to imagine ourselves Satan, or someone with whom Satan might speak, to have Satan's Ear in two senses, a dooble risk.) The fuss calculated to ensue—in the form, for instance, of Maxwell's evangelical *Animadversions* on Burns's depravity—is testimony to the success of our Bard's maneuver here: the poem makes a wee world of words in which the unco guid have no easy footing. (Sandinista Burns: no pasarán!) And this world, the world of "a' [the deil's] doings,"

from its beginning "Down to this time," is identified wholly with
"a' Lallan tongue, or Erse, / In Prose or Rhyme"—the tongue of
Burns's compeers, not ours.

"The Death and Dying Words of Poor Mailie," "Poor Mailie's
Elegy," "To J. S****," and "A Dream" pursue the same displaced
relation to audience, with the Addresses to the Deil and to the King
serving as bookends to this movement of the Kilmarnock composi-
tion. The extreme sentimental thrust of the Poor Mailie poems is a
measure of any Reader's naturally more sober (and/or conde-
scending) perspective on these matters, which is acknowledged in
the insistent subtitles: "The Author's Only Pet Yowe,/An Unco
Mournfu' Tale." Burns introduces us to Mailie and Hughoc (who
is at once the one figure who may be said to be speaking here, and
the only one who, as it were, does not speak) and then the remain-
der of the poem is given over to the sheep's speech—all but the
closing couplet, which returns us to Burns's narrative voice. (The
quotation marks which open Mailie's discourse, however, are
never closed—a transcription error—and thus in these last two
lines Sheep and Bard may be said to be speaking with one—a doo-
ble—tongue.) We find ourselves in the same relation to the occa-
sion of this poem as we do in "The Twa Dogs," listening in: if
Mailie seems all too human ("But ay keep mind to moop an' mell, /
Wi' sheep o' credit like thysel!"), this is only an illusion of perspec-
tive—the creature inhabits a country ("amang the dead" now)
whose border the Reader cannot cross (without ceasing to be the
Reader).

"Poor Mailie's Elegy" demands of us too an intimacy—an imme-
diacy of response—that the Reader is ill-equipped to provide: the
poem gives us an "I" and a "Bardie" named "Robin"—the speaker
here is not Burns, exactly, although Burns does supply the record-
ing of his speech—and a local band of "a' ye Bards on bonie
DOON! / An' wha on AIRE your chanters tune!" to whose com-
pany we are, again, most (un)likely strangers.

In moving to this point through a succession of direct addresses
from which we ourselves are pointedly removed (however much
we may project ourselves among their concerns), we have moved
from discussions of broad public issues—between the twa dogs,
with the lords in Parliament, at the Holy Fair—into discussions of
an apparently more restricted (unco mournfu') compass. The first
Epistle follows, "To J. S****," and we are thus here at what would
appear to be a first climax of the book's composition: the unmedi-
ated tongue unbound in intimacy. The only concession made to
the Reader here—wholly otherwise a voyeur—is the epigraph in

English from Robert Blair's *The Grave* (1743), a bland apostrophe to "Friendship" ("solder of Society!") which serves as a kind of calling card, ushering the poem in to our attention. But the poem that follows this introduction is the most intimate of all the Epistles in the book (with the last one, "Epistle to J. R******, Enclosing some Poems," an analogous case): as if the person let into our parlor amiably were to turn and address an imaginary companion—which in the Kilmarnock context is precisely what is happening.

The occasion of this poem ("Just now I've taen the fit o' rhyme") is quite wholly without transcendental value, the moment of inspiration random, the Reader equally accidental. And the whole book of *Poems* is cast backward and forward from this point in such improvisational terms: "This while my notion's taen a sklent, / To try my fate in guid, black prent," means one thing to James Smith, another to the Reader of a bound volume—the emptiness of fun has a different value in either case—but the impulse of Rhyme without Reason holds sway over both. "Sworn foe to sorrow, care, and prose, / I rhyme away," "nae rules nor roads observin." (Burns's resistance here is specific. Gavin Sprott: "Made-up roads did not exist, but rather routes or tracks," but "the means of effecting improvement were . . . coming together—a combination of wealth, organization and the growth of markets. . . . In 1766 the first turnpike trust to start made-up road construction in Ayrshire was formed.")[31] Burns is a kind of Jolly Beggar here, a creature no kin to "ye, douse folk, that live by rule, / Grave, tideless-blooded, calm and cool." The "zig-zag" of his letter to Willie Nicol appears here too—moving beyond the Powers of Calculation—and in the end Burns disappears entirely from our sight, alone with Jamie, "Whare'er I gang." This first Epistle, and the close of the first major movement of the book, presents a bardic persona that emphatically has no use for us.

Such is the figure who turns next to address the King. After the interlude with Mailie and Jamie, "A Dream" marks a return to public discourse (and the nine-line stanza of "The Holy Fair") as engaged from a most private vantage. (Writing in response to "the Laureate's Ode," Burns here at once engages the most public audience imaginable and an audience so private as to appear inconceivable: "sure an uncouth sight to see.") Asleep in a dream, the "humble Bardie" speaks as familiarly and preposterously to the King as to Auld Hornie himself; the

> His politics always smelt of the smith's shop.
> —Dr. Blair, on Burns

Reader here again appears (spectrally) only in the epigraph and explanatory note, which again seek to smooth the way, to request allowances for such impertinence. The epigraph, in fact, rhymes Reason with Treason, quite literally asserting a (treasonous) Rhyme beyond Reason—a world beyond any the Reader might wish, perhaps, to claim. (McGuirk: "If the Auld Licht considered 'Address to the Deil' Burns's most shocking poem, this satire was his most offensive [of the poems in the Kilmarnock volume] to the wealthy and landed. . . . In Burns's day criticism of the Hanoverians was assumed to signify loyalty to the Stuarts. Jacobitism was worse than treasonous in Edinburgh—it was unfashionable, lower-class, an obstacle to patronage.")[32] And this poem too (like "Twa Dogs," "Holy Fair," "To the Deil," and "To J. S****") ends without particular closure, as if again its impulse, and not its wholeness, were all that mattered. (Unfinished, improvised, and in its own way regal, a poem like this holds no brief with our meddling concerns.) "A Dream" makes for a post-climactic climax in the composition of the book, as if a parting volley in the Bard's argument on behalf of an unrestrained Scots tongue.

But "A Dream" is followed by "The Vision," and the title alone signifies a shift toward something comparatively more encompassing still, more fully authorized, more officially revealed. In the context of the Kilmarnock texts, in fact, "The Vision" is the one poem most directly addressed to an audience of Readers (more so even than "Scotch Drink" and "The Holy Fair," which are only partly so, or than "Halloween," which follows immediately). Swinging to the opposite pole in the Poems' economy of discourse, then, "The Vision" makes for yet a further, antithetical climax: a voice, an assumption about audience, that has been repeatedly and explicitly hemmed in throughout, here finds a kind of full embodiment—only here, rather than the voice of intimacy, it is the voice of full-dress public discourse that has its moment. Nothing in this poem suggests that the Reader is any other than an appropriate audience. (Daiches complains about the poem's move, in the second Duan, "into standard neoclassic English, both in vocabulary and in properties," and notes that "long before we hear of Shenstone's 'bosom-melting throe' we have become aware that the poem has become a piece of posturing for a genteel audience"—and notes as well that this poem "was much worked over by Burns before it saw publication"—all of which is to make the same point: "The Vision" is a piece prepared for a certain kind of consumption, hitherto merely indirectly glimpsed in this book.)[33] But to what exactly—here at our widest portal of ingress—is the Reader a full party? A "digressive Poem," Burns's note informs us to begin with, with a

nod to the alien heroics of Ossian, and a vision, first, of squalor
rather ripe—rats in the rafters and all. (As Crawford has it: "pit
that in yir pipe, Noam!") Here too, again, rhyme stands beyond
the reach of reason, and if the poem lets us in (as it aims to) it does
so without concession—Burns is still "stringing blethers up in
rhyme / For fools to sing." And when "COILA," his "SCOTTISH
MUSE" appears ("a tight outlandish Hizzie, braw," "bounded to
a district-space"—a kind of administrative functionary among the
Genius class), she speaks with an authority undiminished by her
relative powerlessness: a rhyme with Burns's own projection of
himself in the voice of the poem as a whole—a dooble Duan of un-
defeat. "The Vision" lets us in to let us know that *our* place is else-
where.

"Halloween," which marks the halfway point of *Poems*, follows,
and makes most unmistakably explicit the question of audience
that the book has been pursuing and parrying from the start; I
read the construction of the Kilmarnock book backward from this
point, with the second half constituting a further series of varia-
tions on the same pattern. "Halloween" comes wrapped not only
in the (by now familiar) English epigraph—from Goldsmith, this
time—but also in footnotes on virtually every page (including a
note to the title itself) and a prefatory note to explain the occasion
of all this apparatus. (Kinsley observes that these notes "were made
more comprehensive, circumstantial, and 'literary' for the Kilmar-
nock edition.")[34] It is a public poem—or a poem made public—in
a way that no other Kilmarnock poem, not even "The Vision," will
quite allow. Yet the public dimension of this poem is a matter
wholly imposed upon it, "for the sake of those who are unac-
quainted with the manners and traditions of the country where the
scene is cast." The arcanely specific nature of the proceedings de-
scribed, "the unusually heavy mixture of dialect" (Kinsley), the
spectral autobiography of Rab and Nelly in stanza 6, and (again)
the abrupt termination of the poem (a catalog with barely a nod
toward closure)—all embody a community no mere Reader could
ever hope to plumb. The footnotes only make our estrangement
from this culture of discourse more apparent, turning each of us,
like Currie, into an anthropologist.

28

These last four poems bring the book to a kind of doobly dou-
bled consummation—"To J. S****" and "A Dream" representing
the fullest reach of a private discourse, "The Vision" and "Hallow-

een" the fullest reach of a public. The relations and exclusions between the private and the public are thus established: the Reader, that public creature, is a party to these Poems only as a voyeur or an imperialist, is party to the object of voyeuristic or imperialist desire—as an unwarranted imposition, an uninvited guest, a poor relation. The Reader, in fact, is an object of indulgence on Burns's part here, and not the other way round (as the Preface might be construed to suggest): "unpublic" discourse made public is not public discourse. Placed into public circulation, the Kilmarnock poems nevertheless withhold themselves for other purposes.

The arrangement of the poems dramatizes this independence of purpose. Following the quartet of variations on privacy and publicity, which closes the first half of the book, the second half opens with a further quartet—the last in Scots before English comes to dominate the arrangement, and so yet another climax, a further consummation of the dooble tongue's desire—and each of these four Scots poems ("The Auld Farmer to his Auld Mare," "The Cotter's Saturday Night," "To a Mouse," and "Epistle to Davie") makes a claim to consideration as the most intimate discourse yet presented. The Reader is again, in each poem, an absent figure of no account; we are neither the horse nor the mouse nor Davie nor Robert Aiken, the addressee of the Cotter piece. If this latter seems more readily to include the general Reader in its address—as it was indeed seized upon, by the literati, as an exemplum—the effect is nonetheless to include one for whom the address cannot mean what it is intended to mean. Our own judgments on the pious sentiment of this poem have nothing to do with Aiken's, just as our judgments on the others have nothing to do with Davie's or the beasts'.[35] "To a Mouse," to be sure, has spoken (and speaks still) to a great many people,[36] but whatever it says to us we can only turn to hindsight or to foresight—the *present* only toucheth mousie, and touches not us.

"Epistle to Davie" brings to a close the chiefly Scottish portion of *Poems*, with an explicit and characteristic statement of the position of Scots in relation to whatever World might otherwise interpose itself. "I set me down, to pass the time, / And spin a verse or twa o' rhyme, / In hamely, *westlin* jingle"—the Scots moment, for Burns, is typically improvisational, a performative moment which stands only, we might say, in accidental relation to its textual condition here. Burns's (and David Sillar's) own relation to the great world at large is much the same: accidental and without consequence. From this unpromising vantage Burns considers "how things are shar'd; / How *best o' chiels* are whyles in want, / While *Coofs* on countless thousands rant"—and concludes that beggary ("the last o't, the warst o't") is no terrible prospect, to be avoided at all cost, but a "comfort" in fact "nae small." He stands with his friend, like "Commoners of air" (a choice pun), at once at the center of the world and at its very margin of impoverishment and hopelessness—and Scots is the tongue of this territory. This Scots is specifically a kind of antithesis to English: upon pronouncing the lowest social condition "a comfort this nae sma'; / . . . / Nae *farther* can we *fa'*," the Epistle shifts with stanza 4 into English, chiefly, with the westlin' jingle returning to finish the stanza—"We'll sit and *sowth* a tune; / Syne *rhyme* till't, well time till't, / And sing't when we hae done"—and to dominate the next several stanzas. (English returns with stanzas 9 ["O, all ye *Pow'rs* who rule above!"] and 10, which bear no trace of Scots vocabulary or orthography—before Scots comes "skelpan" back with stanza 11, to conclude the poem.) Improvised Scots performance, presented specifically as for someone not ourselves ("wha scarcely tent us in their way, / As hardly worth their while"), the Epistle represents as the tongue of all that matters, the tongue of all that is truly shared—not titles or rank or wealth or power or education, but the heart alone. Scots is troth-speech, a transcendental claim.

One would think, here, that the book might rightly be at an end. But "Epistle to Davie" is followed by a series of poems on a different plan entirely—poems in English, and quite entirely at the disposal of (that relatively newfangled bugaboo) the Readerly gaze. The first of these—"The Lament, Occasioned by the Unfortunate Issue of a Friend's Amour," our introduction to the world of a chiefly English tongue, the beginning of a second book—is concerned with the loss of love (and follows the Epistle's closing apostrophe to all "ye tender feelings dear!"); because the poem also concerns Burns's relations with Jean Armour (although Burns appears here in disguise, as "a Friend"), we know that the love he laments is lost under the compulsion of Law (in the form of Jean's father)—Love circumscribed by Law, another model of the Scots/English scenario.

"The Lament" is an English poem, but its form is "the common medieval one—the *balade* . . .—which became popular with Scottish medieval poets, particularly Henryson, Dunbar, and Lindsay, and was known to Burns from Ramsay's *Ever-Green*": a Scots poem after all, of the finest pedigree (if not the finest quality).[37] When Burns's "Friend," rising to his tune, invokes old "Phoebus," we are sent back (again) to the end of "Epistle to Davie," when "The ready measure rins as fine, / As *Phoebus* and the famous *Nine* / Were glow-ran owre my pen" (and the Nine send us back to "We, Robert Burns," the Bard's proclamation re: wicked Song)—Scots again penetrating (impersonating, mocking, appropriating, inhabiting, and subverting) the politest tongue.

"Despondency, an Ode," provides more of the same. Cast in an English of quite opaque abstraction (Kinsley notes that the ode's occasion was "probably" the same as that of "The Lament,"[38] i.e., James Armour interposing himself between his daughter and her plighted lover, Rab of Mossgiel—but you'd hardly know this from the textual evidence), the poem is quite wholly made available, it would seem, to any Reader whatsoever: English a tongue for no ear in particular, and a tongue in which Burns disappears more fully even than behind a disguise. "Despondency" is a world of cyphers. And even here the Scots tongue, as in "The Lament" however silently, makes its claim to anither order unextinguished—like a kingdom in exile. The Ode assumes the stanza form of "Epistle to Davie" (a poem that will not end, it seems), which is also "the measure of the Cherry and the Slae," as Burns observes—"a poem by Alexander Montgomerie," Kinsley notes, known to Burns "from Watson's *Collection* (1706) and Ramsay's *Ever-Green* (1724); . . . the stanza is quoted by James VI as one example of 'cuttit and brokin verse, quhairof new formes are daylie inuentit.' "[39] "Ye sons of Busy-life, / Who, equal to the bustling strife, / No other view regard!," aspire, among other things, to English, and "Despondency" gives it to them: but all aspiration is futile here, where Scots is rendered skeletal, a cultural foundation erased.

Thus "Man Was Made to Mourn, a Dirge." We are still in the world of English (although Burns places himself here "Along the banks of AIRE"), again with a Scots undertow—and this time the linguistic politics of the situation are made explicit (even if not readily evident). Brother Gilbert tells us of Burns that "he used to remark to me, that he could not well conceive a more mortifying picture of human life, than a man seeking work. In casting about in his mind how this sentiment might be brought forward, the elegy *Man was made to mourn* was composed," to which comment Kinsley appends Burns himself, in a letter of a later date (no. 264, 16 August 1788) to Mrs. Dunlop: "Man is by no means a happy creature.—I do not speak of the Selected Few, favored by partial Heaven . . . I speak of the neglected Many, whose nerves, whose sinews, whose days, whose thoughts, whose independance, whose peace, nay, whose very gratifications & enjoyments, the instinctive gift of Nature, are sacrificed and sold to those few bloated Minions of Heaven!" Burns goes on to mention "an old Scots Ballad, 'The life and age of Man,' " which Kinsley notes "refers to the year 1653 and has Burns's title as refrain,"[40] and James Dick gives the fuller story:

> The year 1653—when the ballad was written—was a sorry time for Scotland, and at no period since Edward I had the independence of the country been more menaced. The General Assembly had met, and were discussing much controversial matter, when a general of Cromwell's army entered, and ordered the Assembly to dissolve and the members to follow him. "Broad-based" Baillie the Covenanter describes this unheard of atrocity, and how the ministers and elders were conducted a mile out of the town, and forbidden to meet more than three in number, under pain of imprisonment. English Commissioners were appointed to administer public business, and the country for a short time was entirely under English control.[41]

Burns's Dirge, for which (as Dick notes) he "made use of the old ballad," memorializes these events: in this context, *Made to Mourn* means (doobly) both Created so that we may Mourn, and Compelled to Mourn—the old Calvinist suffering and the new (dare we say Jacobite?) social/political grievance are both brought to bear upon this text. Rather than English, we might say that "Man Was Made to Mourn" is a poem of Scots in interdiction.

The Dirge, further, is cast (after the first stanza) entirely in the form of direct address—that auld Scots propensity: another case of listening in on a discourse not designed for us, another performance transcribed. Burns's is the ear here, not ours. And the Song (in fact, the first in the book) Burns set to an Irish melody[42]—a further colonial decoration to the British history this piece embodies so obscurely.

All of the English Poems are generic pieces: the lament, the ode, and the dirge above are followed by another dirge ("Winter"), a prayer ("In the Prospect of Death"), and an apostrophe ("To Ruin")—and each bears the same thematic burden as well, of which the titles alone are sufficient indication. Each bears within it, too, a Scots possibility: "To Ruin" in the Cherry and the Slae stanza (of "Epistle to Davie"), "A Prayer" in "the familiar measure of the Scottish metrical psalms," "Winter" in the joke with which it ends—turning the grand formulaic tone of its English on its head. (The Bard himself makes a spectral appearance in "Winter," in "tumbling brown, the Burn comes down" and "roars frae bank to brae:" another wee free Scots impulse, hiding in plain sight.)

In the midst of this series of English poems comes "To a Moun-
tain-Daisy, on turning one down, with the Plough, in April—
1786"—the linguistic politics of which is a bit more plainly
problematic. This poem, with its opening echo of "To a Mouse,"
brings us back both to Scots and to direct address, and the stanza
is Standard Habbie, the most recognizable of the Scots forms: but
with the third stanza, and quite thoroughly from the fifth stanza to
the end, the poem shifts (or reverts) to English as the discourse
itself becomes more abstract, generalizing from the particulars of
the daisy. ("Epistle to a Young Friend," which comes after "To
Ruin" and introduces a second series of chiefly Scots poems, fol-
lows the same pattern.) Scots is, as it were, struggling to resurface
through this middle passage of the Kilmarnock book—or English
has come (for the moment at least) to wield its Imperial sonorities
over all: neither Scots nor English is to be silenced.

At this—yet another!—critical juncture in the sequence of the
poems, the claims of Scots and English are similarly poised—or
further, brought to a kind of mutual interpenetration: and it is
here that the final stanza of "To a Mountain-Daisy" makes a direct
address to the putative Kilmarnock Reader ("Ev'n thou who
mourn'st the *Daisy's* fate")—the one such event in the whole vol-
ume—the climax, perhaps, of its chiefly English movement (only
"Ruin" to follow before Scots chiefly returns). When this Reader
(we gentle folk ourselves) at last makes an appearance—or rather,
when our appearance is at last recognized, like Burns in the draw-
ing rooms of Edinburgh—we are given to know (in English, so that
anyone might understand) that

> Stern Ruin's *plough-share* drives, elate,
> Full on thy bloom,
> Till crush'd beneath the *furrow's* weight,
> Shall be thy doom!

Ingratiating words from our Ploughman Poet. The whole world
gets ploughed—the mountain-daisy, the "artless Maid" bedded
and abandoned, the "simple Bard" (this appellation the single
Scots impulse in an otherwise English stanza), Love and Poetry, all
human worth, and "Ev'n thou," even the Reader—Burns gets his
coulter under everything.

With "Epistle to a Young Friend," *Poems* is brought back home
to Scots—if fitfully—and back to direct address (not, that is, to Us)
essentially for the rest of the book. The stanza of this Epistle, Kin-

sley tells us, "was not uncommon in English poetry and had been used in Scots by Ramsay"[43]—an inversion of the pattern in "To Ruin," "A Prayer in the Prospect of Death," "Man Was Made to Mourn," "Despondency," and "The Lament," English poems composed in Scots forms—and English, as in the "Mountain-Daisy," comes again to dominate the latter passages of the poem as it grows less "Sang" and more "Sermon." But the piece is addressed to Andrew Aiken (son of the Robt. to whom Burns inscribes "The Cotter's Saturday Night"), the presentation is improvisational ("Let time and chance determine"), and Scots holds sway over the first half of the poem ("Och" appearing twice, in stanzas 3 and 6, as one measure of this dominance): this is a performance, again, to which the Reader has not exactly been invited, or a text that resists its textualization. (McGuirk notes that Burns's Epistles were not necessarily "extemporaneous in composition," their "general moral reflections" composed first "and, many months later, introductory and concluding stanzas tailored to the recipient;"[44] again, what is significant to my reading is simply that the Epistles are presented as if for specific recipients, and thus as if not for Readers.) As befits its position as (yet another) structurally transitional piece, this Epistle is divided virtually down the middle between Scots and English—Scots in the first six stanzas, English (cued by "Dame Fortune") in the latter six—and drawn back to Scots in the end (or at least to the perspective of *ploughman phrase*") with a punch line (as in "Winter") that turns the sermon on its head: English can only be sustained so far.

This, in a sense, is the chief thrust of *Poems*' linguistic politics: English can only be sustained so far, and only for certain purposes—and cannot speak to or for a whole range of Scots experience, which zigzags beyond the ken of the Powers of Calculation. (The point is nothing new: I'm merely arguing that the book's structural composition makes it as well.) The remaining seven poems (before a series of songs and one of epitaphs, epilogues, in effect, to the book) are all deep in the intimacies of a chiefly Scots tongue—a return to power for Scots, in the parable of the book's construction, like a wee Jacobite dream.

"To J.S****," "Epistle to Davie," and "Epistle to a Young Friend" establish the epistolary form as a critical issue in Kilmarnock: the former marks most plainly at an early juncture the Reader's fundamentally voyeuristic relation to the text, and the latter two frame the English portion of the book—as if to define, at the borders, a Scots mode. Five of the seven remaining poems (excluding songs and epitaphs) are epistolary, as if we have crossed that

border in fact; the other two are "To a Louse" and "On a Scotch
Bard Gone to the West Indies," and each of these as well embodies
the vulgate in the most extreme terms imaginable as an alien (or
alienated) category of experience.

"On a Scotch Bard" comes first: after the encroachments of En-
glish, it seems, there is no other course but flight. The community
Burns claims for himself here, far from a community of Readers,
is of a congeries of Jolly Beggars—"A' Ye wha live by sowps o'
drink, / A' ye wha live by crambo-clink, / A' ye wha live and never
think," "a' ye rantan core" of "auld, cantie KYLE"—of which he is
the *"Laureat"* (a most unofficial post): he speaks of himself in the
third person, as already gone, an economic, political, and emo-
tional refugee from the straight and narrow new world order. The
return of Scots to chiefliness at this point in *Poems* is heavy with
refusal and subordination—a self-contradicted vision of the uto-
pian and the colonial.

"A Dedication, to G**** H******* Esq" follows—a further occa-
sion for delineations of dominance and subordination. The piece
is a kind of misplaced preface—an intimate version of (and reply
to) the public Preface—which is careful to discriminate between
subordination and subservience, and to claim for Burns and his
Protectors alike a troth altogether untouched by official pieties and
political explanations. Placed at the start of the volume, such a text
might appear as if Burns were to have farted upon entering the
room (instead, we get the mellifluities of the Preface); placed here,
near the end, it takes on the appearance of an essential statement.

Burns owes nothing to Hamilton, or to anyone, beyond what
plain human worth demands—the familiar message. Burns again,
in making this claim to a world governed by the requirements of
Patronage, disappears into namelessness ("It's just *sic Poet*"), and
into the voice of "each poor man's *pray'r*": another way of honoring
independance, protecting against falsity, against the breaking of
troth, against all "art o' *legal* thieving" and *"sound believing."*
C——lv——n and all the rest gae hang: Rab places the whole book
in Gavin's hands, in Gavin's image, and against all expectation—
that wee Jacobite flourish again (like phosphor of Culloden), im-
pulse of Scots unbound.

The "Louse" too, which follows, in this context embodies an un-
likely heroism (among other things), a champion of the vulgate
sensibility answering to nobody, emblem of desecration as revela-
tion. The Louse, "Detested, shunn'd, by saunt an' sinner," occu-
pies a category beyond even the Devil, beyond all categories, and

observesna distinctions itself—Common Ground as no one's ground, a state free of pretense. But the Louse in "To a Louse" is not simply a Scots banner; it is also a measure of Scots alienation. *"To see coursels as others see us!"* is to see ourselves radically reduced. The Louse at any rate is not listening: Scots a direct address to an audience utterly unequipped to notice, a tongue divided against itself.

And so the book winds down into intimacy. The four epistles that round out the text (before Songs and Epitaphs wrap it up, the fourth epistle "Enclosing Some Poems" as if the Kilmarnock itself) are arranged in a progression of intimacies (the first two to a virtual stranger, the next to a friend in the Muse from Mossgiel, the last to an old farming friend from Tarbolton) and in a progression from most polite to rudest: the epistles to Lapraik concern the exchange of verse and good fellowship between Bards, the epistle to Simson concerns matters of Poetry and Kirk doctrine, and the epistle to Rankine concerns Poetry and fornication. A progression, too, of responses: Lapraik, famously, responds to the first epistle, perhaps somewhat dutifully, not in verse (as requested) but with a prose letter, which occasions the second epistle he receives, in which Burns is left working against the will of his own Muse, a man without an ear without a tongue—while the final epistle, "To J. R******, Enclosing Some Poems," as Kinsley notes, "doubtless had an enthusiastic response from the company of his 'ramstam' friends."[45] Burns exits the Kilmarnock clear about the company he keeps.

Response is what all of these Poems, and these closing Epistles most explicitly, ask for—and what the textual condition, again, is not most suitably equipped to provide. The textual condition is the public and polite condition, the Value Added condition, the imperial political and colonial economic condition—where what Rob wants belongs to an economy quite wholly ungoverned, the economy we might say of a conversation, exalted in verse. It is a world in which the literati would lose all of their regulatory powers.

"This freedom, in an *unknown* frien', / I pray excuse," he says in his first epistle to Lapraik, hoping to "forgather, / An' hae a swap o' *rhymin-ware*, / Wi' ane anither." Three weeks later, in his second epistle to Lapraik, Burns is still waiting for a free response—operating, so to speak, in the absence of an economy that would make sense of his discourse—and while he waits, goes on to damn "Fortune" ("She's but a b——tch"), to proclaim himself sovereign ("*I, Rob, am here*"), to propose a new "*charter* of our state, / 'On pain o' *hell* be rich an' great,' " and to pit the "followers o' the ragged Nine" against the "sordid sons o' Mammon's line." This freedom too he prays his Reader excuses.

To winsome Willie Simson, next, he becomes more explicit yet: "My curse upon your whunstane hearts, / Ye Enbrugh Gentry!" COILA reappears, not the grudging balksome "ramfeezl'd hizzie" of the previous epistle (nor, contrarily, the "tight, outlandish *Hizzie*" of "The Vision," where hers is the will and his the resistance), but a figure, rather, while comfortably established ("Till echoes a' resound again / Her weel-sung praise") yet "like some unkend-of isle" quite utterly off the map ("Besouth *Magellan*")—a place of "*Bardies*" but "Nae *Poet*." These same "*Bardies*" are the ones, in the Postscript to the epistle, who might be hoped to "ken some better" what to do with the moon other than subject it to the logic and cant of religious doctrine ("what they mean / By this *new-light*"): "plain, braid lallans" is a tongue that renders the Kirk, and all the "bluidy" business of the order it upholds, a thing of no account, a "clatter." The title of Bard—even the aspiration to Bardship—confers a certain immunity, establishes a community and economy with no stake in the dangerous foolishness of the rich and the great. With winsome Willie, as with wise & witty Willie (whose devoted slave RB is), Burns has a conversation in which the language of Power is turned on its ear.

"O Rough, rude, ready-witted R******"—the final epistle, to John Rankine, has a rip at the Hypocrite Kirk too, but in the end goes further in its attack on Gentle Society. Again the occasional mode is an exchange of verse ("I've sent you here, some rhymin ware")—but this time the desired response is apparently forthcoming ("Yon *Sang* ye'll sen't"), or at least promised: after the epistles to Lapraik, a kind of consummation. Burns's tongue here embodies a community of "unregenerate Heathen[s], / Like you or I," based on "*dreams* an' tricks" and ("when ye hae an hour to spare") improvised versification and songcraft—a radical community that spares no quarter to what "monie godly folks are thinkin." Indeed this is a piece of which Dr. Blair says "the whole poem ought undoubtedly to be left out of the new edition." (It was not.) The bulk of the poem is taken up with an elaborate metaphor of shooting down "a *Paitrick* to the *grun*', / A bonie *hen*," representing, as Kinsley tells us, the quick courtship and subsequent "pregnancy of Elizabeth Paton, a servant girl at Lochlie, who bore [Burns] a daughter on 22 May 1785." (" 'The description of shooting the hen,' said Hugh Blair obtusely, 'is understood, I find, to convey an indecent meaning, tho in reading the poem . . . I took it literally,

and the indecency did not strike me.' ")[46] Burns is casually rapa-
cious—is assessed a fine—and vows a campaign of aggressive
houghmagandie to come, either here at home "owre moor an'
dail" or herding kye "in Virginia!" In either place he is a Bard
under siege: at once unfree and undaunted. "It pits me ay as mad's
a hare; / So I can rhyme nor write nae mair"—the Bard con-
strained nevertheless refuses silence—"But *pennyworths* again is
fair, / When time's expedient." He signs off "Your most obedi-
ent"—which, addressed to a peer (like "Thy devoted slave" to Wil-
lie Nicol, only in a different key), makes Obedience (and Service,
Subservience, and Power) an altogether different proposition than
what "the *Poacher-Court*" or (as he puts it elsewhere) "the hough-
magandie pack" has in mind: fornication as radical politics (an-
other old story), a body's resistance to (or zigzag from) the Powers
of Calculation. And here the *Poems*, properly, end.

> "*Economics*: Old Greek word for the art of keeping a home
> weatherproof and supplied with what the householders need.
> For at least three centuries this word was used by British rulers
> and their advisers to mean *political* housekeeping—the art of
> keeping their bankers, brokers and rich supporters well sup-
> plied with money, often by impoverishing other householders.
> They used the Greek instead of the English word because it
> mystified folk who had not been taught at wealthy schools. The
> rhetoric of plutocratic bosses needed *economics* as the sermons
> of religious ones needed The Will of God."—from *The Intelli-
> gence Archive of Historical Jargon*
>
> —A. Gray

Burns by now has disappeared many times, though, has effaced
(and exalted) himself in these Poems in countless ways, as if on the
run even as we answer his knock at the door: disappearance seems
to be an essential feature of Bardic power, a measure of Bardic
troth. Now he disappears a few more times—into songs, epitaphs,
and finally his own epitaph. This material, like a coda to the vol-
ume, exhibits a variation of the Kilmarnock pattern as a whole—in
Scots, chiefly, at first, moving into English, with Scots returning, a
bit, in the end; in the coda, the proportion of English is greater,
and Scots returns less convincingly.

The first "Song," "It was upon a Lammas night" (tune: "Corn
rigs are bonie"), is a Scots number, and, as it reads on the page, is
conceived most specifically for the "Annie" it addresses. The sex-
ual liaison the song celebrates is a consummated one (in a past, re-
cent or distant it is impossible to determine, which lends the weight
of troth to the refrain "I'll ne'er forget") and a matter of quite

wholly mutual consent—of "sma' persuasion" and blessings all
around. The second "Song, Composed in August" ("Now westlin
winds, and slaught'ring guns"), is rendered in English, chiefly (al-
though "it is notable," as Kinsley observes, "that when Burns re-
vised the song for [*Scots Musical Museum*] about four years later, he
strengthened the thread of Scots in the diction"),[47] and its
"PEGGY dear" is virtually a cypher: she is named but once, in the
fourth stanza, and is otherwise the occasion for a generalized medi-
tation on pleasure and "the charms of Nature." (Burns apparently
made copies of this song both for Peggy Thomson of Kirkoswald—
his "Charmer"—and, slightly modified, for famous Jeannie
"Armour.") The sexual liaison this song celebrates is unconsum-
mated—a song of expectation rather than memory. The formulaic
mode, and the English, carries through the third "Song" (tune:
"Gilderoy") as well, and here again "ELIZA" appears, cypher-like,
with hardly a personal memory attached: Burns in fact is staging
his impending emigration yet again (as in, most recently, "To
J. R******"), and the world he leaves behind is English, and emp-
tying fast.

One last song, "The Farewell" to "MASONRY and SCOTIA
dear!"—his Brethren of St. James's Lodge, like his rustic compeers
in the Preface, embodying a secret society lurking within the En-
glish (like a virus), in this case even discoursing in English—and
then, an end to trump all means and ends, the epitaphs: a kind of
Public Discourse to be sure (Readers Welcome), but a Public with-
out distinction, a Public universally *low*—and a Public that must
come to the text (and not the other way round) in order to read
aright. The epitaphs are (in fancy) specific to a place—"Below thir
stanes," "An' here his *body*": gravesites that Kilmarnock Readers
are less likely to stand before than they are to take ship to Jamaica.
We are left outside, offscreen, lurking at the end of *Poems* as at the
beginning.

Robert Aiken and Gavin Hamilton, both still alive by normal
reckoning, get the two penultimate epitaphs—Burns leaving us ex-
plicitly with another round of inscription and dedication to his in-
tended audience—and Burns himself gets the last. Anonymous for
his last Houdini act, he turns the book itself into a gravesite. But
the Reader, as likely mourner, is again miscast: unless we are "a
whim-inspir'd fool," "a Bard of rustic song," or one whose "judg-
ment clear" is inadequate to "life's mad career," we are not invited
to attend or expected to understand. The gravebook we hold in
our hands—like any headstone—presents us with a choice, or
(continuous series of) choices, regarding who we take ourselves to

be. Not "Who are you, Mr. Burns," but who are we? That is the question.

(It is a question that Mackenzie & Co. address only to decide [before the fact, as it seems] that we, whatever we may be, are unquestionable. The questions are all for the Heaven-taught Ploughman; for us, the reflected glory of discriminating taste and refined understanding.)

When Burns, opening his closing stanza, says "Reader attend," he may be talking only to the whimsical fool and rustic Bard et al., or he may be talking to us indeed, and what he says will signify differently, depending. "Know, prudent, cautious, *self-controul* / Is Wisdom's root" we can well imagine Drs. Blair, Blacklock, Moore, and Currie applauding in the sagacity of their eminent positions: but to Burns it would seem, in the context of the volume closing now upon itself, that self-controul plays to a different tune—in the key not of self-restraint but of independance, of self-controul as sovereignty, a condition to be sought and honored, as the stanza tells us,

> —whether thy soul
> Soars fancy's flights beyond the pole,
> Or darkling grubs this earthly hole,
>   In low pursuit. . . .

29
PERFORMANCE BOUND

The Kilmarnock is a book that keeps coming (climax after climax) and then keeps ending: the poems trickle out into a series of fragmentary epistles (the epistolary form being by nature fragmentary), then a clutch of songs is appended, then a farewell, then an epitaph and epigrams, more epitaphs, and finally the Bard's own epitaph. This arrangement is one way in which Burns marks his book as a performative model of discourse. The book's registry of voices, or of the relations between voices, is another way.

The vulgate itself is of course yet another way, the vulgate by definition radically situational, localized, sensitive to specificities of audience, designed for immediate response. The vulgate's power, in a textual empire, is in its resistance to textuality, and it manages this resistance in part through its assumption of the performative dimension of language.

(The textuality of the Kilmarnock is impure: Scots, rude, improvised, fragmentary, performative, secretly biographical—a kind of contra-textuality harbored in the state of textuality [a Scottish tongue in an English mouth: a kiss, perhaps].)

Most poems, surely, are performative—it's partly what makes them poems—but the textual condition that most poems come to inhabit (certainly from Burns's time down to ours) is in important ways at odds with performance. The bias of the textual is toward what doesna change, not toward irregularities and variations: although the textual itself is a veritable engine of irregularity and variation, it seeks nevertheless to expunge this quality in itself, or where it cannot be expunged at least to account for it. Performance has its own modes of permanence, its own regularities and ultimate orders, but these are givens rather than aspirations: performance aspires in the opposite direction, not toward ultimacy but toward audience, toward the relational and the relative.

> Know me by the voice
> That speaks outside my choice
> And speaks our double breath
> Into this formal death
>
> —W. S. Graham

The performative is a kind of postmodern transcendental value, and as such a Romantic category too. The untouched thing— uncapitalized, unadministered, unfalse (unfalsified): troth. But postmodernism ironizes troth along with everything else—or at least situates it in an evermore impermeable web of lying signs. Burns's troth, if no more hopeful in the end, is more present to him as (at least) a defeated possibility. Scots is his first public name for this troth: on the verge of an imagined escape across the ocean, Burns performs his *Poems* against the encroaching world of the textual and all the forms of social control elaborated in that world. But the Kilmarnock proves an unsustainable enterprise—the market, finally, will not bear it—and (cutting his losses) Burns falls back, for the bulk of his short life, upon more durable modes of contradiction.

5

Sang & Mowe

THE WELL-KNOWN STORY IS TOLD IN MANY FORMS ACROSS MUCH OF Burns country. The Bard once rode into Edinburgh on an ass— well, on a horse, and to save mostly his own skin and kin: ostensibly seeking his literary fortune (looking to line up subscribers and to promote the notion of a second edition), he actually pursued a variety of interests—alive not only to the main chance but to whatever Chance might bring his way. He carried on with Mrs. MacLehose and with the servant girls and, it seems, with brothel prostitutes, and he made the acquaintance, one evening, of James Johnson, an engraver, to whose *Scots Musical Museum* he agreed to contribute a number of songs.

New schemes appear: in the end Burns doesn't sail for the Indies, and marries Jean Armour. And while he does arrange for a second expanded edition (and later a third) of his *Poems*, it is now without the expectation of salvation. Instead he returns to the farm, at Ellisland this time, to move stones with his hands, and ends up in Dumfries working for the Excise, frequently riding the horse two hundred miles in a week as the King's own blackguard slave.

All the while he contrives to generate the preponderance of material for Johnson's multivolume *Museum* (and eventually, too, for George Thomson's *Select Collection*, also voluminous), working in virtual anonymity for virtually no pay. Even more explicit: "I assure you, my dear Sir," he writes when Thomson sends him five quid in remuneration,

> that you truly hurt me with your pecuniary parcel.—It degrades me in my own eyes.—However to return it would savour of bombast affectation; But, as to any more traffic of that D{r} & C{r} kind, I swear, by that HONOUR which crowns the upright Statue of ROB{T} BURNS'S INTEGRITY!—On the least motion of it, I will indignantly spurn the by-past transaction, & from that moment commence entire Stranger to you![1]

195

D{r} & C{r}, presumably, spell Debtor and Creditor: Burns's deg-
radation is not to come so cheap, but to come for any price at all.
He politely but firmly refuses to have his Soul sodomiz'd. He helps
to organize a rural circulating library in the neighborhood of
Dumfries, he gets hassled for making certain unkosher statements
with regard to the Revolutionary Events in France, and in 1795,
as if in counter-balance, he signs on with the patriotic Dumfries
Volunteers, for whom he writes "Be BRITAIN still to BRITAIN
true, / Amang oursels united; / For never but by British hands /
Must British wrongs be righted"—a cheer which cuts both ways.[2]
    "Don't let the awkward squad fire over me," he is said to have
said of them at the end—but they did anyway; he is also said to
have levelled a parting "curse on the law agent who had written
for payment of volunteer uniform."[3] On the day he dies, self-con-
tradicted to the end, Jean bears them a son. The funeral is an event
of pomp and obscurity somehow simultaneously.

    Where has he disappeared to now? Among all these zigzags of
fortune and contingency in Burns's life *après* Auld Reekie, what
stands out most emblematically is, of course, the songwork—from
the bird's-eye view of history (at least literary history), this is the
point of these later years (unless, of course, the point is dissipation
and the failings of genius). Burns's production of songs runs to 373
numbers in Donald Low's recent compendium; his correspon-
dence with Thomson alone on the subject of song surpasses even
the sustained energy of Sylvander's with Clarinda (on quite other
subjects); and the terms in which he speaks of songs and of Song
("by that HONOUR which crowns the upright Statue of ROB{T}
BURNS'S INTEGRITY!") leave no doubt that it is here at least he
feels he can (or must) be true. Song is the rear-guard action behind
the rear-guard action of the Kilmarnock—and proves a more tena-
ble position to hold on the slippery slope of troth.
    The Excise, too, is a measure of Burns's situation in his last dec-
ade—or perhaps merely another calibration of the same measure.
Like the songwork, his work as an Exciseman situates Burns in a
world of definitive valuation—that is, of a valuation either defini-
tively established and entered in His Majesty's Books, or defini-
tively refused. Burns himself struggled with the question as early
as October 1786, before he'd even first gone off to Edinburgh, in
a letter to Robert Aiken:

    I have been feeling all the various rotations and movements within,
    respecting the Excise. There are many things plead strongly against it;

the uncertainty of getting soon into business; the consequences of my follies, which may perhaps make it impracticable for me to stay at home; and besides I have for some time been pining under secret wretchedness, from causes which you pretty well know—the pang of disappointment, the sting of pride, with some wandering stabs of remorse, which never fail to settle on my vitals like vultures, when attention is not called away by the calls of society, or the vagaries of the Muse. Even in the hour of social mirth, my gaiety is the madness of an intoxicated criminal under the hands of the executioner. All these reasons urge me to go abroad, and to all these reasons I have only one answer—the feelings of a father. This, in the present mood I am in, overbalances everything that can be laid in the scale against it.

Further, he acknowledges in a later letter, "There is a certain stigma affixed to t[he character of an] Excise-Officer"—and in still another: "I know how the word, Exciseman, or still more opprobrious, Gauger, will sound in your Ears.—I too have seen the day when my auditory nerves would have felt very delicately on this subject, but"—again—"a wife & children are things which have a wonderful power in blunting these kind of sensations."[4]

The stigma sticks still, in some quarters, two centuries later. It is common enough for the Excise to be regarded as a kind of taint on Burns's record, an ineradicable corruption in the text of his life, a kind (however excusable) of self-betrayal. Burns's own position was clearly that he had no choice—and he means by this something more than the argument of a man with his back against the wall. His

> The question is not at what door of fortune's palace shall we enter in; but what doors does she open to us?
>
> —Burns

"*Lines* Written on a window, at the King's Arms Tavern, Dumfries" argues that there is nothing else to be *but* an Exciseman, of one description or another:

> Ye men of wit and wealth, why all this sneering
>   'Gainst poor Excisemen? give the cause a hearing:
> What are your landlords' rent-rolls? taxing ledgers:
>   What premiers, what? even Monarchs' mighty gaigers:
> Nay, what are priests? those seeming godly wisemen:
>   What are they, pray? but spiritual Excisemen.[5]

Moral purity is not an option: there's no innocence available in this market. In any event, "I do not intend to borrow honour from any profession; and though the salary be comparatively small, it is a luxury to any thing that the first twenty five years of my life taught me to expect."[6]

"The poor, naked, helpless wretch, with such voracious appetites and such a famine of provision for them, is under a kind of cursed necessity of turning selfish in his own defence," he writes, and he "will stoop to anything that honesty warrants" to keep the roof from falling in—"To save me from that horrid situation of at any time going down, in a losing bargain of a farm, to misery."[7] Honest enough. Welcome to North Britain.

The world defined by the Excise—by the extension of gauging across the country into every ingle, a world of record-keeping, of equivalences, of production and reproduction and consumption—is the same world in which Burns performs his great song-work. (It is a kind of gauging itself, finally, the plumbing and notation of a folk musical idiom, but a work which nevertheless repudiates the very Powers of Calculation.) It is in this work that Burns finds his most durable mode of contradiction: turning away from "the public character of an Author," from the Press and the vision of fame, and re-submerging himself in the voice of a nameless Scottish people, Burns in his songwork pushes further into the Performative, and leaves his deepest mark on our inability to sort out what he's worth.

> I wish I was a mole in the
>   ground,
> I wish I was a mole in the
>   ground—
> If I was a mole in the ground
> I would root that mountain
>   down,
> And I wish I was a mole in the
>   ground.
> —old song

30

Song has long been a resistant category for the textual crowd—even the earliest editors recognize its otherness. Typically (as in Currie and in my mid-nineteenth century American *Illustrated Family Burns*, among many other editions) songs are listed separately from poems in the table of contents, and listed differently: not sequentially (as the poems and correspondence are listed) but alphabetically—as if, to begin with, the sequence of pages were an unfit vessel for songs, an undue confinement. The songs come from some other order, some different kip, and would seem indeed to raise questions that challenge the Order of Textual Consumption (that new world order, then as now). Song is the embodiment of the Performative Unbound (of time on the fly, of the body's expenditure)—an enterprise run to the measure of troth alone, subject to the considerations of troth, and worth almost nothing. (He did it for a song.)

> I would not write you till I could have it in my power to give you some account of myself & my matters, which by the bye is often no easy task.
> —Burns, to John Ballantine, 13 December 1786

I must speak to you, angel, of Doc Watson and Habermas and more, must speak more privately still.

Perhaps it's better to say that songs are a purer form of a tendency within poetry—the tendency toward the incommensurable, the unstable, the unfixed—which poetry in its textual form tends to negate or undermine. This tendency toward the unspeakable lies near the revolutionary impulse of Romanticism: what Romanticism calls the Natural, or, sometimes, the Imagination, or the Innocent, or Beauty, is in every case an emanation from this unnameable zone. Defying the Powers of Calculation, the unfixed forms of the poetic act—in poetry and, in exemplary fashion, in song—define the Romantic dream: a vision of the world turned inside out, or upside-down, and of the body's claims on the abstractions of the spiritual. It's a totalizing dream, too—another one of Those—and thus a self-contradicted dream as well. Big surprise.

Romanticism wants transcendence, wants the totalizing tale (to do battle with that other totalizing tale, of savage torpor, of industrial progress and its minions, its glorious hegemony); Romanticism, like its postmodern descendents, is a mirror of the sickness it seeks to cure. The text—any text—bears witness to this dooble bind: the text is the statist (static) dream of poetry—the impulse to fix it, domesticate it. Poetry moves always to shatter this dream, too, to dream another, different dream, to dream itself into somebody's mouth/ear: and Song, the despised genre, is the emblem of this further dream.

Burns no doubt wants his own transcendence (who doesn't?), but he wants something else, too, or in a different way: a transcendence down—not a rising above but a sinking below. (He wants this sinking below in many ways: in the demotic, in the sexual, in the anonymous tradition of Scottish Song—arts of disappearance.) The Performative is less a transcendental ideal than a case of transcendental materialism—an oxymoron, surely, but one that troubles all of Romanticism, and that Burns embraces with unparalleled clarity. Among transcendentals, the Performative is least idealized—among Poems, Songs are so—and most weighed down with the Real the Ideal seeks to rescue / deliver us from. Performance delivers us only to ourselves.

31

> Performance is the art form which most fully understands the generative possibilities of disappearance. Poised forever at the threshold of the present, performance enacts the productive appeal of the nonreproductive.
>
> —Peggy Phelan

Of course when we talk about the songs of Burns we talk about something other than performance, too: we talk about a reproduced corpus. Burnsong as we encounter it is largely a textual affair, and has always been so—notwithstanding Nelly Kilpatrick and innumerable other occasions, notwithstanding Burns's own (lost) singing, the organ through which the songs come to us for the most part is publication (through James Johnson and George Thomson, and later James Dick and James Kinsley and Donald Low). Burns himself conceived of many songs (unlike his poems) expressly with publication in mind: working on the *Museum* and the *Select Collection* is what propels him into this last, most fevered enterprise of his life's work. But the songs, we might say, are emblems of performativity—unless you sing one, or listen to one sung, when they become themselves.

Mrs. Hogg famously understood the problem, when she "berated Sir Walter Scott for his effort to record the passing tradition":

> There war never ane o my songs prentit till ye prentit them yoursel and ye hae spoilt them awthegither. They were made for singing an no for readin: but ye hae broken the charm noo, and they'll never be sung mair.[8]

Reading Burnsong, the charm is broken too—but it remains possible (why must it seem so odd?) to sing the words to their tunes, and

even to read in the prentit form something of the performative im-
pulses to which the songs move. Habermas says it like this: "To the
degree . . . to which philosophical and literary works and works of
art in general were produced for the market and distributed
through it, these culture products became similar to [a] type of in-
formation: as commodities they became in principle generally ac-
cessible"—but this is not to say that a commodity is all songs (or
poems or philosophical works) become.[9]

Can we begin with theory, angel? as a way of demonstrating that
we come at Song from the farthest possible reach. Peggy Phelan
puts the problem nicely:

> Performance in a strict ontological sense is nonreproductive. It is this
> quality which makes performance the runt of the litter of contempo-
> rary art. Performance clogs the smooth machinery of reproductive
> representation necessary to the circulation of capital.[10]

What Phelan means by "nonreproductive" is that performance
lives only in the despised now, here, this, and takes no part in the
great System of economic Exchange by which Capitalism defines
everything it can get into its maw:

> Performance's only life is in the present. Performance cannot be saved,
> recorded, documented, or otherwise participate in the circulation of
> representations *of* representations: once it does so it becomes some-
> thing other than performance. To the degree that performance at-
> tempts to enter the economy of reproduction it betrays and lessens the
> promise of its own ontology. Performance's being, like the ontology of
> subjectivity . . . , becomes itself through disappearance.
>   The pressures brought to bear on performance to succumb to the
> laws of the reproductive economy are enormous. For only rarely in this
> culture is the "now" to which performance addresses its deepest ques-
> tions valued. (146)

The way in which Performance attains its being, and escapes the
clutches of capitalist exchange, Phelan calls "representation with-
out reproduction" (3)—a fancy way of saying "disappearance."
The disappearance of performance—in spite of (or even accentu-
ated by) efforts to record and reproduce it—is Phelan's key. Per-
formance is the act unmarked by value—the thing that is worth
nothing—because it doesn't stick around long enough to have a
value assigned it. (And it can't be reproduced without ceasing to be

itself.) Value can only be assigned in relation to other values—can only function in a world, like that of capitalist exchange, marked by the manipulation of equivalences. But how can you equate something that exists with something that doesn't? ("Horse Island" gives one answer, the Auld and New Lichts others.) Performative exchange is marked by responses which are *not* equivalents. "Performance resists the balanced circulations of finance. It saves nothing; it only spends" (Phelan 148).

"Writing," for Phelan, "can broach the frame of performance but cannot mimic an art that is nonreproductive." Writing "relies on a substitutional economy in which equivalences are assumed and re-established. Performance refuses this system of exchange and resists the circulatory economy fundamental to it" (149). If capitalism (that text-mad system) is the negation of the now, performance is our old friend the negation of the negation.

The performative—the valueless—is in this way related, of course, to the identity politics of Scottish cultural self-consciousness. (The dichotomy of the marked and the unmarked terms plays itself out in endless circles, rippling, concentric: English/ Scots, England/Scotland, urban/rural, language/vulgate, Nation/ People, text/performance.) Both Performance and Scotchness are matters of questioning the determination of value in relation to other values, and to write about either one is to betray it. "Identity is perceptible only through a relation to an other" (Phelan 13), but performance (like Scotland under William Wallace) rejects such a relation: "Performance approaches the Real through resisting the metaphorical reduction of the two into the one. . . . Performance is the attempt to value that which is nonreproductive, nonmetaphorical" (Phelan 152).

Enough, you say? Or Too Much! Whereas "Representation reproduces the Other as the Same," "Performance, insofar as it can be defined as representation without reproduction, can be seen as a model for another representational economy, one in which the reproduction of the Other *as* the Same is not assured" (Phelan 3)— for Performance is like "the quantum" of modern physics, which "cannot be preserved, recalled, measured, and evaluated by recourse to representation's insurance policies" (Pelan 166). Capitalism, as ever, may be in hot pursuit, but songs and quarks and gluons would seem to defy its grasp.

> Sound and rhythm pose
> the elsewhere of meaning.
>
> —Steve McCaffery

The pit of theory has no bottom (one reason why it's so ill-suited to bawdry); still, where Phelan goes, I follow (a fool, perhaps, for the rhetoric, but a happy fool). The argument appears inescapable, inexorably so, a powerful organ of understandings (and the same argument the Romantic transcendental model makes): the world closes in and the imagination seeks a progressively proscribed possibility—who can blame it? From a certain (political)

> We provisionally give the name *différance* to this *sameness* which is not *identical*: . . . . *Différance* is neither a *word* nor a *concept*.
> —Derrida

vantage, every story tells the same tale: what Roland Barthes calls the pleasure of the text, or Jacques Derrida différance, or Jean Baudrillard Seduction (which "knows neither equivalence nor value" and "is, therefore, not soluble in power"),[11] or Herbert Marcuse the polymorphous perverse, or Georges Bataille waste (excess), or Peggy Phelan performance, is in every case a matter of defining a kind of thing that is not exactly a thing, and that in any case will not be talked about (without extraordinary delicacy, and even then, inadequately).[12] 'Tis something evermore about to be, or something that was and still remains (and so again, evermore will be—like Anna Livia)—but in any case what theory desires is to gain a purchase on the unspeakable (as if language were to turn against itself), to zigzag in defiance of the Powers of Calculation.

I mean not the slightest disrespect—quite the contrary— in saying that theory is like a battery of versions of Elfland (persisting under increasingly— hegemonically— tight State control): God bless the theorists, who explain to us systematically how we understand our worlds, and God save them, too, I say.

Steve McCaffery's terms get us to the heart of things, as well: his discussion is organized around a

> And see not ye that bonny road,
> Which winds about the fernie brae?
> That is the road to fair Elfland,
> Where you and I this night maun gae.
> But Thomas, ye maun hold your tongue,
> Whatever you may hear or see,
> For gin ae word you should chance to speak,
> You will never get back to your ain countrie.
> —"Thomas Rhymer"

kind of dooble economy—"a complex interaction of two contrastive, but not exclusive economies," one of them general and one

restricted, that shadow and intricately bind one another. As "re-
production" is for Phelan, so "equivalence" for McCaffery is the
demon stoking the furnace—the engine of the restricted economy,
of objectification and capitalization, sworn foe of freedom from
value. (The general economy, like "representation without repro-
duction," is a matter of no equivalence. It is instead a "space in
which meanings splinter into moving fields of plurality, establish-
ing differentials able to resist a totalization into recoverable inte-
grations that would lead to a summatable 'Meaning.' " Paint it
black, you devil!) And Equivalence gives to capitalism the form of
a potlatch—which in turn provides "an interesting analog system"
to the practice of writing:[13] for "writing," as Phelan says, is "an ac-
tivity which relies on the reproduction of the Same (the three let-
ters *cat* will repeatedly signify the four-legged furry animal with
whiskers) for the production of meaning, . . . a substitutional econ-
omy in which equivalences are assumed and re-established" (149).
So all of our threads are linked.

In potlatch, the great Haida-Kwakiutl-Tlingit ceremony of pro-
duction and consumption, equivalence attains its *jouissance*. McCaf-
fery calls this a "gift economy,"[14] and it's another well-known
(though mysterious) story (and the Haida-Kwakiutl-Tlingit anither
appropriated ither for the gallery at theory's place overlooking
Puget Sound). As Greil Marcus tells it:

> These tribes, the anthropologists discovered, had a strange practice:
> one chief met another and offered gifts. The second chief had to re-
> spond in kind, but on a higher plane of value. That was the potlatch.
> The game might begin with the presentation of a necklace and end
> with the burning of a town—with a tribe burning its own town, thus
> raising the obligation to an almost impossible level. . . . "The ideal,"
> sociologist Marcel Mauss wrote in 1925 in *The Gift*, "is to give a *potlatch*
> and not have it returned."[15]

In potlatch, the frenzy of returns (the gauging of equivalences),
one escalating into the next, ends with the unreturnable gift, the
gift that escapes all equivalents. "In Kwakiutl communities," Mc-
Caffery notes, "televisions are thrown into the sea, precious objects
broken and their parts distributed in order to catalyse the circula-
tion."[16] In capitalism this self-defeating expenditure is made avail-
able to all, in small but constantly renewed inoculatory doses.

What performance proposes instead is always a response—and
never an equivalence. Song seeks a response: not necessarily a re-
sponse in kind (the audience sings a song in return—though often

this *is* the case, people in public and private places taking turns singing songs, telling stories . . .) but a response of *some* kind. (Even the performance in solitude, singing to myself, seeks a response, an emotional/physical movement that answers the performance.) The point of a performance is not, like a potlatch, to negate all possible responses, but to engender responses without end—and responses can only be endless if they are not conceived in terms of equivalences: their own value is not fixable but disappears in the air and in the body.

Potlatch, like writing, worries the bone of equivalence until it implodes. But performance would eschew this bone altogether, and head straight for the great bottomless mystery of Death.

Expenditure without equivalence, representation without reproduction: in any event, performance is not sanctioned—it comes and goes, and however it might find itself contextualized, appropriated by producers and consumers (as in *The Scots Musical Museum* or *The Merry Muses of Caledonia*), the performative moment itself is neither produced nor consumed. The moment of performance would be an icon of freedom—if to say as much, to reproduce it as such, were not to miss the point: the moment is not to be used, it is only to be occupied and passed, by bodies in relation and response.

All Princes and Potentates are mock ones in the Song Zone. Nobody is king but the Worm, and even King Worm is mocked—in the joy of the moment. The joy is mocked, too (by thoughts and movements of the sensible flesh that often lie too deep for tears). "Life is all a VARIORUM," so "Let them rant about DECORUM / Who have character to lose." Performance is always already lost.

> Odds and ends, odds and ends,
> Lost time is not found again.
>
> —Dylan

Phelan and McCaffery are interested in Deep Economy, too, calling it Lacan and Bataille, respectively: what links performance to the Haida-Kwakiutl-Tlingit ceremony and the ceremonies of capitalist bureaucracy is a sex link. Sex is the ur-tale, the foundational myth of the Theory of Expenditure, the infrastructure's infrastructure: it's the site of the flesh's fullness of loss, and the imagination's Black Hole—what trumps every equivalence. It's the place of the nameless.

"The sexual relation cannot be written," écrit Lacan: "Every-

thing that is written is based on the fact that it will be forever im-
possible to write the sexual relation as such."[17] (Ditto the
performative relation.) Sexual and psychosexual development and
differentiation lie at the heart of the cosmic human mystery, and
elude every exegesis—eat every exegesis from below (as Blake's
plates show). Bataille is even more explicit.

"Now," Bataille notes, writing of Dr. Kinsey and his Reports, "it
is possible to discuss sexual conduct as one discusses things" (add-
ing "this is to some extent the
originality of the Reports"). But
sex, Bataille knows, is not a thing.
"Whatever has no meaning for it-
self is a thing"—that is, whatever
has a value assigned to it (which
masquerades as *its* value, but is
nevertheless always only as-
signed).[18] Sex has a value assigned
to it—marriage is one name for
this value, self-recognition is an-
other, *jouissance* another—but sex, for Bataille, is but barely per-
turbed by these feeble labels: jousts full of bravado but purely
symbolic, poor containers for the darknesses of mystery. To speak
of sex as of a thing is to measure both the poverty of our speech
and the depth of our need to ward off the terrors of existence.

> Our secret experience cannot enter directly the field of our conscious awareness, but at least our consciousness can know just when it shifts out of the way the thing it con-demns.
> —Bataille

Sex—or what Bataille calls "sexual exuberance" or "the sexual
plethora" (or "our secret experience")—is not a thing, "could only
be thought of as a thing if we had the power to abolish it and to go
on living as if it did not exist." ("We do indeed deny it but vainly,"
the mad librarian adds.) What sex is instead (or "eroticism" as he
calls it here) is "the way that an ordered, parsimonious and shut-
tered reality is shaken by a plethoric disorder," the Plethora a Type
of expenditure and excess—beyond the bounds of identities and
equivalences (in a land that isn't even debatable). The shuttered
reality of Production, Inc. is specifically shaken: "an undeniably
rigorous incompatibility . . . exists between awareness bound up
with work and sexual activity," for "erotic conduct is the opposite
of normal conduct as spending is the opposite of getting"—"The
truth of eroticism is treason."[19]

The politics of eroticism, for Bataille, like the politics of perform-
ance for Phelan and McCaffery—like the politics of eroticism and
of performance for Burns—is devoted to an order of "sovereign
attitudes in ourselves, . . . only useful for being what they are and
never subordinated to ulterior ends,"[20] subordinated only to the

gods of presence and immanent loss. This is the politics of free-
dom, too: the revolution will not be televised, angel, the revolution
will be live, because what's *live* is whatever might not be preor-
dained, or confined to a catalog of previously accounted-for possi-
bilities—whatever resists the Archive of What Is Done and How
(Derrida calls it "an archive determined as *already given, in the past*
or in any case only *incomplete*, determinable and thus terminable in
a future itself determinable as future present, domination of the
constative over the performative, etc.").[21] But here we're back to
Horse Island. . . .

All this is commonplace by now, if not commonly held. We yawn,
or busy our brains about the thought of sexual economy, but (if
our research is to be trusted) the case remains: sex has been deeply
transformed in the course of industrial capitalism—has been do-
mesticated, put to use, administered like nobody's business, and
has become in the process a rebellious angel. (Or not transformed
at all, Bataille would say: sex is always transgressive at the root—a
transgression against the order of a helpless identity—and the cur-
rent ministrations of marriage and reproductive property rights
represent but the latest acknowledgements of its transgressiveness.
Sex is the rebellious angel of *every* order.)

32
THE THING YE KEN

Burns himself identified songs and the sexual plethora, if not as
interchangeable (equivalent) terms, as congruent movements from
the beginning. As modes of contradiction, both Sang and Mowe
were effectively designed to agitate the Calvinists of Kirk and State
and what Habermas calls "the bourgeois public sphere." Edward
Cowan says that "John Calvin himself adopted a pragmatic atti-
tude to music as to many other subjects"[22]—but this is of course the
problem itself: pragmatism is one of the bourgeois public sphere's
loving nicknames for itself, and must prove equal to every chal-
lenge. Sang and Mowe persist, rattling their chains, hiding in the
hills from spiritual Excisemen and all the rest.

Song and sex represent renegade impulses in different ways
(even if the song is about sex—and not politics, or auld acquain-
tance), but neither is subject to a strict gauging: each disappears
into the people it sustains, and remains (if not out of law's and mar-
ket's reach) a land without rulers. (Adorno insists that "even in

[our] most secret innervations" we "are exposed to" the radioactive reach of Production, Inc.'s factors[23]—but to be exposed, even to be enslaved, is not to be negated, finally: what Bataille calls "our secret experience" cannot be excised as long as people live—or at least from Lascaux to the present. By definition, it resists every effort to define it.)

> That which distinguishes folk-song in the framework of a nation and its culture is neither the artistic fact nor the historic origin; it is a separate and distinct way of perceiving life and the world, as opposed to that of 'official' society.
> —Gramsci

In any event, Sang and Mowe persist, to worry the biggars o waas. "When Robert Burns turned 'The Merry Muses of Caledonia' into some of the most beautiful and most moving of Scottish songs," Cowan argues, "he was working within a long-established Scottish convention," noting also that "as early as 1449 parliamentary legislation decreed that 'bards and other runners' were to be nailed through the ear and their ears cut off before their owners were banished";[24] Currie adds that "the minstrels, whose metrical tales used once to rouse the borderers like the trumpet's sound, had been by an order of the legislature (in 1579) classed with rogues and vagabonds, and attempted to be suppressed."[25] Frederick II of Prussia takes his pretensions even further in a "rescript" of 1784:

> A private person has no right to pass *public* and perhaps even disapproving judgment on the actions, procedures, laws, regulations, and ordinances of sovereigns and courts, their officials, assemblies, and courts of law, or to promulgate or publish in print pertinent reports that he manages to obtain.

Indeed.

> For a private person is not at all capable of making such judgment, because he lacks complete knowledge of circumstances and motives.[26]

Unlike Frederick. Let us sing him a song of a mowe.

> O where hae ye been, Lord Ronald, my son?
> O where hae ye been, Lord Ronald, my son?
> I hae been wi' my sweetheart, mother, make my bed soon;
> For I'm weary wi' the hunting, and fain wad lie down.—
>
> What got ye frae your sweetheart, Lord Ronald, my son?
> What got ye frae your sweetheart, Lord Ronald, my son?

I hae got deadly poison, mother, make my bed soon;
For life is a burden that soon I'll lay down.

                                                    —Burns

Not even the sacred ballads, the national icons, are exempt (let alone the likes of a Prussian king—Frederick himself comes under the great levelling in "Why shouldna poor folk mowe?" ["When Princes and Prelates"]).[27] Mowe measures everything— nothing takes the measure of Mowe (except a jolly gauger/beggar queen).

So when we turn to Burns's Book of Mowe, we remember to begin with the fact that he never made a book of it. The bibliographic history of the object called *The Merry Muses of Caledonia* is itself a wee replica of the contention between bawdry and stable order—which is the contention the songs embody (amang ither bodies). Burns collected songs, wrote songs, turned bawdy into polite and vice versa. In or around 1800 (the date of the paper's watermark) a volume was published in Dumfries or Edinburgh: the title page read *Merry Muses of Caledonia; A Collection of Favourite Scots Songs, selected for use of the Crochallan Fencibles.* As Ferguson notes, "there is no proof that the title is Burns's," and further, that though Burns had a private stock of such songs, the *Merry Muses* "was printed from some other source than Burns's holograph collection."[28] (The Bard's own collection has never turned up, but a number of "jottings survive" among his posthumous papers— versions of "Brose an' Butter," "Cumnock Psalms," "I'll Tell You a Tale of a Wife," "The Fornicator," and "When Princes and Prelates"—which "all show numerous divergencies from the *Merry Muses* text" [*MM* 19].) A similar but not identical edition appears in 1827, and another, in 1911, with Duncan M'Naught's emendations based on W. Scott Douglas's marginal annotations, deviates even further. (This latter edition is subtitled "A Vindication of Robert Burns in connection with the above publication . . . ," and "Printed and Published under the Auspices of the Burns Federation. For Subscribers Only. Not for Sale" [*MM* 45–46].) A further edition, what Sydney Goodsir Smith (who co-edits it with James Barke) says "might be described as an 'ideal' *Merry Muses*" (*MM* 40), comes out in 1959. (I work from the 1964 first American edition: the cover shows Pan on the hoof with his pipes raised in song, wearing a tartan kilt.) This one includes most of the 1800 edition—omitting "ten songs . . . which are available in the ordinary editions," from "The Jolly Beggars" and scattered other sources—and includes sixteen songs "taken either from Burns's own MSS . . . or from printed sources such as the 1827 edition," as well as from something called *The Giblet Pye* (c. 1806, "being the / Heads, Tails, Legs and Wings, / of the Anacreontic songs of the celebrated / R. Burns, . . . / some of which are taken from the Original Manus / cripts of R. Burns, never before published"), and from *The Ancient and Modern Scots Songs, Heroic Ballads &c* (1769) collected by David Herd.

If we're looking for Burns's bawdry to assume a stable textual order, then, we are necessarily frustrated. As if to underscore the point, the 1959 *Muses* comes heavily wrapped in textual bona fides: there's a foreword and an introduction by Smith and an essay on "Pornography and Bawdry in Literature and Society" by Barke, "With a Prefatory Note and some authentic Burns Texts contributed by J. DeLancey Ferguson" ("a scholar," Smith affirms, "such as we are not" [*MM* 42]). Poet or Professor, the tone is serious and unapologetic throughout this prefatory material, confined to the bibliographic or to the moral reflections of sober modernity. (Barke: "The old Scots proverb that 'a standing cock has nae conscience' is profoundly true, but if civilization is not to relapse, as it has so often relapsed in the past, it must acquire a conscience. Burns, who knew the terrible strength of a standing cock, did much to supply it with such a conscience" [*MM* 36–37].) But the effect is to register, rather, the terrible power of the illegitimate, and the anxiety of the textual.

The 1959 *Merry Muses* (a centenary edition of the fruits of bawdry) falls into several categories: there are songs in Burns's holograph, either written or collected by him, some of which appear in the 1800 edition and some of which don't; songs by or attributed to Burns from printed sources but for which no holograph is extant; old songs collected by Burns but, again, not in holograph (all but one, which is from the 1827 edition, are from the 1800), and an additional group of such songs upon which Burns based polite versions (which are not included: also not included are alternative bawdy versions that Burns wrote of some of these old songs); a group of what the editors call "Alien Modes" which nevertheless fold into one of the categories above; and a collation, by Hans Hecht, of three manuscripts known variously as "Libel Summons," "The Court of Equity," and "The Fornicator's Court," which never appeared in any book.

It's a messy business, counting the categories, and in any event all talk of authorship is worse than beside the point. So maybe it's time for Burns to disappear again, right here before us—to become nothing but a name around which a certain resistance (and a certain pleasure) gathers in us.

33

Authorship articulates ownership, property, foreclosure in a
proper noun. The name as brand. Actor or performer sup-
poses spectacle, spectator and, for us, speculation—the practice
of a product, the theory of a production, the process of an ef-
fort (an effect), the play of a value and the value of play.
—The Kids of the Book-Machine (McCaffery & bpNichol)

Naming, owning, and foreclosing on the Author is not the only
difficulty: naming sex is another. Burns himself acknowledges the
problem—along with bawdry's antithetical standing—writing to
Provost Robert Maxwell, Esq., in 1789:

Shall I write you on Politics, or Religion, two master-subjects for your
Sayers of nothing? . . . —I might write you on farming, on building, on
marketing, on planning, &c. but my poor distracted mind is so torn, so
jaded, so racked & bedevil'd with the task of the superlatively
Damn'd—MAKING ONE GUINEA DO THE BUSINESS OF
THREE—that I detest, abhor and swoon at the very word, Business,
though no less than four letters of my very short Sirname are in it.—

Well, to make the matter short, I shall betake myself to a subject ever
fertile of themes, a Subject, the turtle-feast of the Sons of Satan, and
the delicious, secret Sugar-plumb of the Babes of Grace; a Subject,
sparkling with all the jewels that Wit can find in the mines of Genius,
and pregnant with all the stores of Learning, from Moses & Confucius
to Franklin & Priestly—in short, may it please Your Lordship, I intend
to write BAUDY![29]

Baudy or bawdy (and bawdry) are names, among others, for the
writing of the "Subject," but the Subject itself remains nameless.
What to name the subject?—always an instructive question to ask
(and one that subject peoples, with good reason, are perhaps wont
to ask, having been themselves/ourselves named as objects).
   The word *sex* has indeed been Kinsey'd into an abstraction (it's
been Marcuse'd, too); the Subject's chief appellation in these scien-
tific times, it's hard not to use it (without sounding precious)—but
there's no hair and blood to *sex*. (*Sex* is a book by Madonna.) *Fuck-
ing* is a bit closer to the meaning intended, though *fucking* seems
necessarily to include (if not exclusively to mean) genital inter-
course, and part of the point is that this was not always the point:
Henry Abelove's research indicates that "the earlier part of the
long eighteenth century . . . was an era of . . . very diverse sexual
practice"—that the monoculture, as it were, of "sexual intercourse

so-called becomes [with 'the onset of the Industrial Revolution'] discursively and phenomenologically central in ways that it had never been before," "the rise in the popularity of sexual intercourse so-called in late-eighteenth-century England [being] an aspect of the same phenomenon that includes the rise in production." "This phenomenon," Abelove adds, "could be called either capitalism or the discourse of capitalism or modern heterosexuality or the discourse of modern heterosexuality," and among other effects transforms what might be termed *play* into "foreplay," the invention of which is cognate with "the invention of industrial work-discipline."[30] *Fucking*, in this context, may be regarded as a form of Business, which is not the Merry Muses' mood.

Mowe is perhaps better, although Mowe seems to mean Fucking—Kinsley's glossary lists it as "*v.* copulate (with a woman); *n.* intercourse." Still, Mowe has the advantage of irreducible idiom—of adding, as Pater says in his definition of Romanticism, "strangeness to beauty"—and is certainly a word the Merry Muses come round to again and again.[31] Still again, this is only part of the story: Mowe is crucial to the Subject, but not its definitive name.

Lovemaking has a sweet ring—it's what Morris would call it—and the making of (undomesticated, unproductive) love is often close to the heart of these songs; but the term isn't fully consistent with the situations and events the Merry Muses sing— sometimes something else is being made (sometimes brutally), or nothing is being made at all. *Lovespending* maybe.

Passion and *desire* and *polymorphous perversity* are too general to serve; *lust* lacks play. *Houghmagandie* (which the Kilmarnock glossary defines as "a species of gender composed of the masculine and feminine united") and *fornication* smack of reprobation: these are the religious categories, and won't do at all. *Meeting*, perhaps. Can a body meet a body?

(How to name the *writing* of the Subject is problematic, too, of course. *Bawdry*, by now, has a purely classificatory thrust. *Erotics* won't do, either—though Bataille uses the word in something like the sense the Merry Muses celebrate: erotics has a leavening of culture in it, of the refinements of reflection, while the Muses [however refined and reflective in their way] strike a different chord. *Literary criticism* has obvious shortcomings.)

No doubt the best name is the "——" which appears throughout, the meaning of which is never (but for a moment, maybe, occasionally) in doubt, however unspelled it may be: "——" is the name of the unsayable. It comes harnessed to a rhyme (which is one way we know it, one way we learn to spell it), or it comes in the middle of a word ("m——e," often—or "c——t," "p——," "a——e," or "L——d") which context spells. Sometimes, as in "Eppie McNab," a bare "——" floats free in the middle of a line: "Thy breeks they were hol'd, and thy —— hung out, / And thy —— play'd ay did dod, did dod," Eppie says to Jock Rob, and cock and balls and arse keep trading places—though the drift, no doubt, is clear.

In "Supper is na ready" it's called "the thing you ken."

While Damon's a——se beat time, Sir.—

—Burns

The practice of the Merry Muses is less to name the Subject than to enter into it. (William Gass, speaking as Willie Masters' Lonesome Wife, writes "how close, in the end, is a cunt to a concept—we enter both with joy."[32] An old friend of mine, aye a preacher's daughter, said instead "how close, in the end, is a cock to a concept—both enter us in pain.") The Subject is— unnameable, only demonstrable (because *it* defines *us*), and stands for nothing but itself (like Burns and Scotland). Here in Caledonia, it's a matter mainly of body parts and their movements.

The word *mowe*, which is one of the central cyphers (appearing in many forms, as "——," "m——we," "m——s," and "m——g,"), is itself sometimes a noun and sometimes (more usually) a verb. Even considering all variants of Mowe, and including the numerous variants of *fucking* (f——s, f——'d, f——k'd, f——g, f——k, f——, f——t), the movements of the body are well outnumbered, among cyphers, by the body itself—or its parts, as if with lives of their own. Chief among these is "C——t" and its variants (c——, c——nt, c——ntie, wry-c——d, ——), the single most frequent reference, exceeding even Mowing & Fucking, exceeded only by the combined references to "a——" (a——e, a——se, a——elins), "pr——cks" (p——, p——s, p——ntle, p——e, c——ks, c——k) and "b——s" (b——ks, ——). (There's also "f——rted," "sh——ten," and "sh——" among verbs, the participial adjective "d——n'd," the noun "h——ll" and the ever so Proper nouns "Br——nsw——ck," "Pr——ss——a," "Emp——r——r"—their vowels like baudy holes—and "L——d," the ultimate obscenity.)

Beyond the cyphers, too, the songs are preoccupied less with abstractions than with spots of time, encounters and engagements, anatomy and a kind of perpetually surprised emotion. Not surprisingly, the Subject of the Merry Muses being effectively an unsubject gesture, the question of the independence of will (often constrained, even overwhelmed) figures prominently, too: bodies meeting bodies also means wills engaging wills—and this means Politics. "Curse on the word which ended the period!"

34

Ha, ha, ha, the girdin' o't.

—The Merry Muses

Consensuality is an ideal the Merry Muses honor, but it is not synonymous with their pleasure (aesthetic or otherwise). The Caledonia of the Merry Muses is (among other things) a place of some violence and dehumanization, where "No" is almost never taken to mean "No": rape, compulsion, social irresponsibility, and crass objectification—every dog here has his day. (A Scotland of the object-people: a variant Horse Island.) Not always a pleasant territory, it includes also the misery of The Jolly Beggars, the alienation (often) of affections, and the body driven (in countless ways, and in every sense) up against the wall: the impulse of free expenditure sings an unsocial order.

Why consensuality at all, then, in such an economy, with such a politics? Why not Übermensch and be damn'd t'ye? We must listen to the Merry Muses.

By Annan Side

In fact, consensuality is a more common preoccupation of the Exalted Nine than one might expect. But to frame the question in this way—consensuality or no consensuality—is inapt: the question may even be a luxury, available to those of us with sexual privacy and health sufficient to consider such matters in terms of choices to be made. In Caledonia, such privacy is catch as catch can, and "——" is rather like the weather (you can talk about it all you like, ain't goin' do nothing). Women and men both are subject to forcible sex here, and subject to sex itself, to the sexual plethora. In the end, the question is not consensuality yea or nay (which obviously, for plenty of good reasons, is *our* question), but rather (an anterior question) the nature and status of the power of self-will—a kind of renegotiation of 1707: these are not free wills, exactly, that meet in Caledonia, and how they manage the borders between them is another name for the Subject.

But as this subject's something kittle,
Our wisest way's to say but little . . .

—Burns

Reading the songs through, with an eye to the nature and status of volition, is an unsettling experience: if Caledonia is a politic model, all is not peace and pleasure. The Merry Muses' Caledonia is a place imposed upon (and a place in which being imposed upon is common) every bit as much as Georgian Scotland is: both are worlds of slavery, though to different masters (and in different "economies"). To speak of the consensual, then, in either context, is to speak a utopian language—to make all power equal.

All power is not equal in Caledonia, nor in British Scotland either, but the way each sovereignty makes sense of this plain fact differs radically. The Bourgeois Public Sphere, for instance, is itself concerned with redressing certain political/economic inequalities, and with fortifying others, in part on the basis of notions of consensuality. In Caledonia, however, the Utopian Consensual flowers in more fully democratic soil.

(Remembering too that—although many of the songs are cast as dialogues between men and women, and many as from women alone—The Merry Muses of Caledonia c. 1800 is an emanation of the Crochallan Fencibles, men one and all. Our subject here is not a demographic sampling of sexual politics—not a picture, or an oral transcript, of what you might call a sexual "reality"—but an imagination of such politics, answering to imagination's reality: a question, again, not of truth but of [in this case, male] troth, pledged in this case to the sexual plethora.)

By my count, over half of the items in the Merry Muses collection (fifty-four out of ninety-seven in the 1959 "ideal" edition) can readily be considered to describe—or to sing—situations of a consensual nature. You can try to consider the songs in terms of their consensuality quotient—it isn't easy, the categories slide around—and you'll come up with a different count from mine, but it's clear that in many of the songs consensuality is regarded as (a virtue) abiding by the heart of the holy mystery of —— (the thing ye ken)—that it's a "positive value." The Consensual may be achieved "in holy ecstasy" or "amang the creels," or may not be achieved at all, may be disappointed or betrayed, but in these songs at least some notion of consensuality is assumed. (My list, for the Archive: "Bonie Mary," "Nine Inch Will Please a Lady," "Ode to Spring," "O Saw Ye My Maggie?," "The Fornicator," "My Girl She's Airy," "Brose an' Butter," "Cumnock Psalms," "Green Grow the Rashes,

O" [versions A and B], "Todlen Hame," "Wap and Row," "The Pa-triarch," "Wha'll Mow Me Now?," "Had I the Wyte She Bade Me" [A and B], "Dainty Davie" [A and B], "Put Butter in My Donald's Brose," "Here's His Health in Water," "The Jolly Gauger," "Gie the Lass Her Fairin'," "Tail Todle," "Let Me In This Ae Night," "Eppie McNab," "Logan Water," "The Mill Mill-O," "My Ain Kind Dearie," "The Cooper o' Dundee," "Will Ye Na, Can Ye Na, Let Me Be," "Ellibanks," "As I Cam O'er the Cairney Mount," "John Anderson, My Jo," "Duncan Davidson," "The Ploughman," "How Can I Keep My Maidenhead?," "Andrew an' His Cuttie Gun," "Wad Ye Do That?," "The Reels o' Bogie," "Blyth Will an' Bessie's Wedding," "The Lass o' Liviston," "She's Hoy'd Me Out o' Lau-derdale," "Errock Brae," "Our Gudewife's Sae Modest," "Supper Is Na Ready," "She Gripet at the Girtest O't," "Duncan Macleerie," "Wha the Deil Can Hinder the Wind to Blaw?," "Cuddie the Coop-er," "The Linkin' Laddie," "O Gin I Had Her," "He Till't and She Till't," "The Bower of Bliss" and "The Plenipotentiary.") In some cases, specific performances might tip the balance one way or an-other—the texts may be ambiguous—but in every case the spirit is open to "no reward but fond regard," and all "as keen as oursels." (This isn't Britain.)

There's another category of songs (twenty-three by my count) which may or may not be regarded as concerned with the consen-sual—call them Either/Or, or Neither/Nor. In some cases (as in "They Took Me to the Haly Band" and "While Prose-Work and Rhymes") the subject simply doesn't come up; in most cases the situation sung is imaginable as either consensual or not. (Again, in-dividual performances, or recordings, may evoke one or the other possibility—in this category, even more plainly. My list: "I'll Tell You a Tale of a Wife," "When Princes and Prelates," "Muirland Meg," "Sing, Up Wi't, Aily," "Green Sleeves," "Our John's Brak Yestreen," "Two Epitaphs" [not songs, from *The Court of Equity, An Episode in the Life of Burns*, Printed for Private Circulation, Edinburgh, 1910," reprinted in 1959], "Ye Hae Lien Wrang, Lassie," "Comin' Thro' the Rye," "O Can Ye Labour Lee, Young Man?," "Jenny McGraw," "Yon, Yon, Yon, Lassie," "The Modie-wark," "Ken Ye Na Our Lass, Bess?," "We're a' Gaun' Southie, O," "Nae Hair On't," "There's Hair On't," "Johnie Scot," "Madgie Cam to My Bed-stock," and "Tweedmouth Town.")

Each song in another group—call it Both/And—clearly embod-ies both a consensual impulse and a violation of that impulse; often the "No" comes first and then the "Yes": sometimes they come in other combinations or together. All of them might be said to indicate at least an awareness of consensuality as a virtue—although sometimes forcibly attained: this *might* be Britain. (I count eleven such: "There Cam a Sodger," "The Trogger," "O Gat Ye Me Wi' Naething?," "The Tailor," "Duncan Gray," "She Rose an' Loot Me In," "Comin' O'er the Hills o' Coupar," "Jockey Was a Bonny Lad," "The Yellow, Yellow Yorlin'," "Ye'se Get a Hole to Hide It In," and "Una's Lock.")

Only three songs (among those gathered here) are given wholly to sexual encounters that are Not Consensual: "Godly Girzie," "There Cam a Cadger," and "The Lassie Gathrin' Nits." Even here, the violation of consensuality (in what can only be called rape in each case) is marked in such a way that consensuality itself appears *in absentia* (this is *Scotland*)—but the songs are turned, for the moment, in another direction.

Five pieces I would classify outside the categories of the Consensual altogether, and would call Reprobation Songs (and Epistles): "Act Sederunt of the Session," "To Alexander Findlater," "The Bonniest Lass," "I Rede You Beware o' the Ripples," and "Libel Summons." These pieces are concerned not with the will(s) of the Concerned Parties, but with the Will of Law—which is implicitly non-consensual, i.e., imposed by kirk and state.

Finally, and again altogether beyond questions of consensuality, two songs fall only in the category of Shit: "There Was Twa Wives" and "Grizzel Grimme" ("a mighty Dame" who seeks to lord it over "sh——," and who for her presumption is cursed by "hill and valley" all around, "Lincluden wa's amang"). These might be termed Anti-Imperialist Songs, embodying a mode of resistance to control that survives even Culloden.

35

"Cumnock Psalms" and "Wha the Deil Can Hinder the Wind to Blaw?" could fall into that latter category as well, both of them concerned essentially with farting. But both pursue this subject within the context of consensual fucking (and consensuality is my master category here, claiming any song that fits—even if it also fits another category, as the two above, or "The Fornicator," which is also a Reprobation Song). "Cumnock Psalms" (which Burns transcribes in a letter to George Thomson, "As there can be no harm in transcribing a stanza of a Psalm")[33] gives us the Consensual Transcendent, and places that category within another, consensuality submitted to another, more deeply rooted order—gives us a dialectic between the affirmation and negation of will.

The song is a Voyeur Song, too: "As I looked o'er yon castle wa', / I spied a grey goose & a gled"—that damn'd privacy issue, again, and the Gaze of the Other (other Species in this case!)—"They had a fecht between them twa, / And O, as their twa hurdies gade.—" The chorus is perhaps unmatched (even among the Merry Muses' songs) for the purity of its urge toward the musical—to sing without speaking:

> With a hey ding it in, & a how ding it in,
>   And a hey ding it in, it's lang to day:
> Tal larietal, tallarietal
>   Tal larietal, tal larie tay.

The scene is wholly consensual: "Between them twa they made a mowe." But there are other Laws that apply here too—and I don't mean Calvinist or Westminster Law. The Law of the Blowing Wind—with "ilka fart that the carlin gae"—trumps all consent. The carlin's partner invokes an old authority indeed—"Temper your tail by Venus' law"—but this is to no avail, just as the carlin's own will is to no avail: the wind says *won't*.

Still, the couple's consensuality is unimpaired: "Double your dunts, the dame replied," for "If the wind o' my arse blaw you out o' my cunt, / Ye'll never be reckoned a man o' weir.—" (A fly in the ointment: the man here, although he never withdraws his consent, is at least the object of persuasion—his willingness is not as ready as hers, or more readily compromised.) So:

> He placed his Jacob whare she did piss,
>   And his ballocks whare the wind did blaw,
> And he grippet her fast by the goosset o' the arse
>   And he gae her cunt the common law.

He bends to her will and she to his, and each one, bending, both gives and recieves "the common law"—which bends to nobody, not even "the deil." The Consensual is powerfully Transcendent here (helped along by a bit of shame) even as it is subsumed within a vision of the limits of will—a vision of the fart as Transcendental Anti-Transcendental, the fart as dialectic.

You could say that in "Cumnock Psalms" we have the wills of the two participants in mowetion, and the will of the body's parts themselves. ("Nine Inch Will Please a Lady"—a Lady indeed, and a "koontrie c—-t"—is another good example, giving us not so much Sex, let alone Love or Marriage, as a "length o' graith, when weel ca'd hame," a "wanton tail sae ready" and a "carlin" who "clew" it, "Tway roarin handfu's and a daud," "double drivin" and lots of nidging, nudging, lowsing, lugging, and thrashing at the gyvel. But such examples abound. "I learn'd a sang in Annandale," "Nine inch will please a lady" [sung "To its ain tune"]—as in the "Psalms" and elsewhere throughout, song is here specifically identified with this vision of bodies in motion.) So perhaps instead of talking about consensuality yea or nay, as if a will was something simply either imposed or opposed, assenting or resisting—as the borders of nations might be imposed or opposed—we ought to be talking always of a struggle of wills toward some shared imposition (another oxymoron for the Archive). In "Cumnock Psalms" as throughout, imposition is what's consented to: both he and she impose the common law on one another and consent, together, to submit to it themselves.

The "common law" includes and limits the consensual, but it does not seek to proscribe consensuality (quite the contrary)— this is one difference between Caledonia, where the common law applies, and Presbyterian Scotland or Jacobite Scotland or British Scotland or Imperial Britain, where other laws apply (class laws, capitalist laws) and where consensuality is a blessing only so long as it is politically and/or economically useful. All consensuality is sanctioned in Caledonia. But consensuality is never without imposition.

Bodies in Caledonia negotiate this difficult political terrain through a wide range of social relations: soldiers and prostitutes, the steward and the fit-man laddie, the patriarch and his young wife, Solomon and King Davie and their concubines, the gauger and the beggar, the Wife and the Priest, Godly Girzie and the "chiel' " "Amang the Craigie hills," the gudewife and her gudeman, Damon and Sylvia, the Cooper and the "baillie's fair daughter," Roseberry and his lady, Duncan and Janet Macleerie, lads and lasses—and sometimes (always) simply a body and a body. (Metaphors of "——" proliferate as well: fiddling, ploughing, tailoring, cooping and hooping, and other trades and practices come under the Sign of Mowe.) "O Gat Ye Me Wi' Naething," "Duncan Gray," "Jockey Was a Bonny Lad" (among Both/And Songs), "John Anderson, My Jo," "The Lass o' Liviston," and "She Gripet at the Girtest O't" (among Consensual Songs), all provide characteristic examples of the common law in action, and of a (Caledonian) politics not fit (perhaps) for Halls of Parliament—a devolutionary politics of the most radical sort.

> Gat ye me, O gat ye me,
>   An' gat ye me wi' naething?
> A rock, a reel, a spinning wheel,
>   A gude black c—-t was ae thing.

Thus complains Luckie Lang to his scullion gudewife. He's been tricked, which is to say imposed upon (though in this case unawares). But so has the gudewife, who tells him "had your tongue now, Luckie Lang:"

> I held the gate till you I met,
>   Syne I began to wander;
> I tint my whistle an' my sang,
>   I tint my peace an' pleasure . . .

Luckie Lang's very life imposes upon the woman, who would (in some subjunctive sense at least) in turn impose his death upon him: "But your green grave now, Luckie Lang, / Wad airt me to my treasure." There would seem no end of imposition here. Neither he nor she denies the charges of the other; at the same time, each sings within an assumption of the consensual—embodied in the subjunctive delicacy of that closing suggestion of a death threat, in the "tocher fine" that Luckie Lang falls for, and in the gudewife's erstwhile holding of the gate.

"O Gat Ye Me Wi' Naething?" is a Marriage Song, too, one of the few in Caledonia. Another, "Duncan Gray," sings a similar negotiation between the will and that which knows neither submission nor resistance. The story of Duncan and Meg is one of persuasion, consensuality, and weariness—one can imagine them, in the end, having the same conversation Luckie and his wife have. At the outset Duncan comes "O'er the hills an' far awa, / Ha, ha, ha, the girdin' o't" (in which " 't" may be taken to mean Cosmic Necessity, if not Duncan's own daud)—to woo Meg, who refuses his offer; she's being "nice an' wadna do," perhaps in accord with certain social conventions. By the second stanza, though, when "Duncan, he cam here again" and "A' was out, an' Meg her lane," and with the third stanza, the politics has shifted: "He kiss'd her butt, he kiss'd her ben, / He bang'd a thing against her wame," and "She took him to the cellar then, / Ha, ha, the girdin' o't, / To see gif he could do't again."

There is no indication here if Duncan kisses Meg butt and ben against her will or otherwise: even if taking him to the cellar suggests otherwise, any number of scenarios are possible. In any

event, the song is a kind of chart of impositions: Meg says won't,
Duncan says will, Meg says will and Duncan "gie[s] her the long
girdin' o't" (to "gie" here being either a thrust or an offering, it's
impossible to tell). The fourth stanza continues the pattern:

> But Duncan took her to his wife,
>   Ha, ha, the girdin' o't,
> To be the comfort o' his life,
>   Ha, ha, ha, the girdin' o't;
> An' now she scauls baith night an' day,
> Except when Duncan's at the play;
> An' that's as seldom as he may,
> He's weary o' the girdin' o't.

All wills are disappointed wills, as Duncan and Meg find them-
selves under the common law alone.

A third marriage song, "John Anderson, My Jo," tells the same
tale of mutual impositions and disappointment. In the polite ver-
sion Burns made of this song,[34] the woman singing imposes noth-
ing (old age having imposed itself on both her and her jo,
John)—the imposition is what makes the song bawdy. John's "tail-
tree," in the Merry Muses' version, is "waxen wan . . . / And wrin-
kles to and fro;" he stays up late (reading, it seems! "Ye'll bleer a'
your een, John"), and won't come to bed.

> O it is a fine thing
>   To keep out o'er the dyke;
> But its a meikle finer thing,
>   To see your hurdies fyke;
> To see your hurdies fyke, John,
>   And hit the rising blow;
> It's then I like your chanter-pipe,
>   John Anderson, my jo.

This is again neither consensuality nor its absence so much as—to
"hit the rising blow"—a meeting of free wills imposing themselves
on each other with pleasure. It's a meeting here desired and disap-
pointed: the singer offers herself, back, breast, wame, middle, tap-
knot and tae "a' for your convenience, / John," and promises "ye
shall hae the horns, John, / Upon your head to grow," if he doesn't
come through.

Marriage is no more a free lunch than mowe itself is: consensual-
ity is no more a legal matter than it is a simple submission:

> When ye begin to haud me,
>> See that ye grip me fast;
> See that ye grip me fast, John,
>> Until that I cry "Oh!"
> Your back shall crack or I do that,
>> John Anderson, my jo.

Yet another Marriage Song, "She Gripet at the Girtest O't," puts it even more plainly:

> Our bride flate, and our bride flang,
> But lang before the laverock sang,
> She pay't him twice for every bang,
>> And gripet at the girtest o't.

> Our bride turn'd her to the wa',
> But lang before the cock did craw,
> She took him by the b——ks and a',
>> And gripet at the girtest o't.

Bodies in motion, imposing on one another with pleasure, and submitting themselves together to what imposes on them both: this is the Caledonian politics of bawdry—an idealized patriarchy, like the United Kingdom without the king.

> Eroticism shows the other side of a facade of unimpeachable propriety. Behind the facade are revealed the feelings, parts of the body and habits we are normally ashamed of. It must be stressed that although this aspect has apparently nothing to do with marriage it has in fact always been present in it.
>
> —Bataille

Some of the songs are more pointedly connected with efforts to imagine the United Kingdom without a king: "Dainty Davie," for instance, has its origin in the escapades of a "Mr David Williamson (one of the most eminent of their ministers now in Edenburgh)," with "a party of King Charles II" after him "for the frequent rebellion and treason he preached then at field meetings"—the song celebrates one of the heroes of the resistance.[35] But the same resistance—or rather, a more general, more pervasive resistance to kingly rights and reasons—is implicit in all of these songs.

And you don't have to be married, either. In "The Lass o' Liviston," the contract is strictly without legal sanction, but binding nonetheless:

> And she has it written in her contract
>   To lie her lane, to lie her lane,
> And I hae written in my contract
>   To claw her wame, to claw her wame.

These are mutually exclusive contracts, obviously—another Jacobite negotiation—but both would seem, in utopian fashion, to be honored here:

> The bonny lass o' Liviston,
>   Cam in to me, cam in to me;
> I wat wi' baith ends o' the busk,
>   I made me free, I made me free.

I made me free: the man singing this song sings consensuality and imposition at once, as if he couldn't tell the difference—the dream of a border vanishing.

"Jockey Was a Bonny Lad" makes one last exhibit for this display at the Archive. Jockey is "just the lad for me," and another in a long line of rough wooers—full of soft words and fast, even violent hands—however "dainty" and "neat sweet pretty" he may be. He calls Jenny to stay one day, "Friskin' thro' a field," and when she resists—"Na, Jockey lad, I darena stay, / My mither she'd miss me away"—he imposes himself: "ay huggin' ay dawtin', / Ay clappin', ay pressin', / Ay squeezin', ay kissin'." This last is the refrain, which ends: "An' winna let me be." "Tho' I intreated, begg'd an' pray'd / Him no to touzle me," Jockey will not let her be, and tears her gown in the process; "But what cam o'er, I trow, at last, / There diel ane kens but me," and when "his dance" is done, and he "confess'd without romance, / He was fain to let me be" is when Jenny sounds sorriest. In the context of "———" (in this case "what cam o'er, I trow, at last"), the consenting will and the will imposed upon turn into one another—a dream of politics undone.

36

> Sae blyth the beggar took the bent, like ony bird in spring,
> Sae blyth the beggar took the bent, and merrily did sing.
> —The Merry Muses

The way power is negotiated—the context in which power is exercised—in Caledonia is marked (as with value) by a vision of entities without identities, of the absence (the obliteration, even) of identity, a vision beyond the politics of identity, the economy of equivalences, the powers of calculation. (Here we are back to the dreams of *Sharawaggi* and the nightmares of "Horse Island" and MacDiarmid's hamstrung struggle with the incubus of Scottishness.) This vision—this condition—is akin to an "objective order," as Marcuse puts it: "In the aesthetic imagination, sensuousness generates universally valid principles for an objective order." And citing Kant, he adds, "The two main categories defining this order are 'purposiveness without purpose' and 'lawfulness without law.' "[36] Entities without identities, however—like the aesthetic imagination itself—is a political black hole: not so much an alternative political model as an anti-politics, a mirror in which all models shatter. Vis-à-vis the real world, *The Merry Muses of Caledonia* is of no practical *use*: it's only a mode of contradiction.

"The Lassie Gath'ring Nits" indicates why the Merry Muses are no model (but a master only). The lass is tired from her gathering—"She pu'd them heigh, she pu'd them laigh, / She pu'd them whare they hang"—and lies down to sleep "the wood amang," when "Three lusty lads an' strang" come along. The pulling of the nuts cannot be said to be a sexual activity, exactly, signifying (perhaps) a degree of sexual readiness on her part— but in the metaphorical universe of Caledonia, the possibility cannot be discounted. Still, she sleeps: the first lad kisses her ("He thought it was nae wrang"), the second loosens her bodice ("Faced up wi' London whang")—

> An' what the third did to the lass,
>   I's no put in this sang;
> But the lassie wauken'd in a fright,
>   An' says, I hae sleept lang.

This is a Rape Song, doubtless—what the third did to the lass is not put in this sang but something put somewhere else— presented, at the same time, as a song of rest. Although she doesn't resist, she certainly doesn't consent to the lads—and though she wakes "in a fright," what she says is not what you'd expect: sextime here is a kind of dreamtime ("I hae sleept lang"), a world in which the individual's will hardly figures at all, subsumed within a story no songline can render and no politics govern.

Or would we like to meet up with "The Trogger," like the woman coming "down by Annan side, / Intending for the border," who meets him "Amang the Scroggie banks and braes"—? "Wha met I but a trogger. / He laid me down upon my back"—the man is nothing but an event of main force, not only because the peddling trade here suggests the troglodytic:

> What could I say, what could I do,
> I bann'd and sair misca'd him,
> But whiltie-whaltie gaed his a——e,
> The mair that I forbade him . . .

The woman singing this song never reaches the border she intends (or might as well not reach it), at least as far as the song is concerned: she reaches a different place instead, going "daft amang his hands" and accompanying the Trogger to Ecclefechan for some serious drinking—a celebration, as at a marriage. "Bedown the bents o' Bonshaw braes" they take their "partin' yokin' "— their farewell bout, or fuck—and separate: "But I've claw'd a sairy c——t sinsyne, / O the deevil tak sic troggin!" The question here isn't what women want but what the devil wants—hardly an adorable model.

"Godly Girzie" is the victim of similar treatment, although her response is less to gae daft than to gae haly: "I trust my heart's in heaven aboon, / Whare'er you sinfu' p——e be," she sings, when she ("faint wi haly wark" and with "na pith to say him na") is overtaken by her assailant. Girzie submits with Christian denial—it's a "haly night" in "Kilmarnock"—which buys her nothing but the comforts of abstraction: meanwhile, she is overpowered, and considered as naught. Even more terrifying is the first encounter collected in the song "Comin' o'er the Hills o' Coupar" (the second encounter being to all appearances a consensual affair): here Donald Brodie "wi' his Highland hand" accosts "a lass," and he "Graipit a' the bits about her": in the chorus, "in a sudden wrath / He ran his Highland durk into her." "Up she started in a fright," and flees, "Thro' the braes what she could bicker"—the object of nothing but wrath, a prey. "Let her gang, quo' Donald, now," lordly, "For in him's nerse my shot is sicker." (Smith's footnote explains "him's nerse" as a "joke at expense of Highlanders' traditional muddling of genders"—another wrinkle.) Mowe is murder here, plainly no model but a dread (fell) emptiness.

The Merry Muses of Caledonia is not where politics starts but where it ends. In "Green Grow the Rashes, O" (version B), Mistress Mary combs "her thing" and spins "the fleece upon a rock, / To waft a Highland mantle, O." Rocks abound in Caledonia, and this is one use to which they can be put—making something warm out of hair and stone. "The Lyon" is here too, with his lady and his "coat o' arms": "The crest was, couchant, sable c——t, / The motto—'*ready, ready,*' O." And "godly Leezie Lundie, O," who "m——s like reek thro' a' the week, / But finger f——s on Sunday, O," and "fisher Meg" selling "her carrot c——t, / . . . for a labster." Nobody here says "No" to Mowe, to themselves, or to each other, it seems: it is a place beyond even desire (in this sense even an elegiac mode), a different kip. Another Story of the One Story, too—the end of everything the way everything continues, and a negation of all imagination's otherwise.

> Love's records, written on a
> heart like mine,
> Not Time's last effort can
> efface a line.
>
> —R. B.

37

Loose Ends

Wi' a riddle come a ra,
Wi' a fal come a ra,
Wi' a riddle come a randy.

—MacColl

Of course all of my analyses (drawn from the "ideal" text) are susceptible to variant performances: it is the variance itself, and no one performance (let alone a text), that is ideal. Performance gives voice to a politics of endlessly shifting authority: it marks a limit of textuality, and of all the Powers of Calculation—because you never can know what's going to happen next in a performance that hasn't happened yet. (A recording can capture some of this shifting, but by no means all.) In the politics of the variant, there are no forms of power that cannot be broken—all forms of power are broken (in the end) in the plethora, in the farts of Death (the only sovereign), in bodies in motion. All power is presumption in Caledonia, sayeth the variant—even the power of analysis. "Singing responses order otherwise."[37]

Forget about reception history, forget about textuality—language itself only gets us so far, angel (sad word for us, who live by language). "My Girl She's Airy" spells it out effectively in Robin Laing's performance: a rather pedestrian catalog of my girl's charms breaks down into the unnameable but still spellable—"Her taper white leg, with an et, and a, c, / For her a, b, e, d, and her c, u, n, t"—with the tempo and the syntax prying loose from each other in opposite directions.[38] Language is at once the locus of and estranged from "——" (in this case "the joys of a long winter night!!!"). Language breaks down in the face of it. No language can tie a loose end: you can only ride with it.

(In "Todlen Hame" the point is to get wet and stay wet: Litcrit, like all language, is a dry fuck—with its own plethoric pleasures, to be sure, but dry as paper.)

Language in "My Girl She's Airy" is given to the formulaic, to tired metaphors, simple glosses, and lists, and breaks down on the threshold of joy. Breaking down—"Fal, lal, &c."—it is translated into the body in motion (into song and mowe, representation without reproduction, zigzag performance), and carried across that threshold.

Songs from Robert Burns' Merry Muses of Caledonia, Sung by Ewan MacColl came out on the Dionysus label in 1962, and "is intended to be a musical supplement" to the 1959 edition. ("The edition [of the recording] is strictly limited to 500 copies, . . . made available by subscription only to a selected group of 'adult, mature and responsible' individuals—scholars and students in the fields of literature, folklore and related disciplines," Kenneth Goldstein observes in his liner notes, adding, "May the scales show an equal balance of knowledge and pleasure.") MacColl sings, without accompaniment, twenty-four selections to tunes learned largely from *The Scots Musical Museum* or from his father (who himself had one tune "from a fellow iron-moulder, Jock Smyllie").

In "O Saw Ye My Maggie" (tune: "Saw Ye Nae My Peggy"), Mac-Coll sings the translation of language (and identity) into Bodies in Motion, in the fullness of holy ecstasy and then some—sings it explicitly here, as implicitly (absolutely) throughout these recordings. "What mark has your Maggie, / That ane may ken her be?" is the question, and the answer is "Wry-cunted is she, / And pishes gain' her thie."[39] Maggie's mark ("in below her sark, / A little aboon her knee"), her identity (like her "treasure, / A hidden mine o' pleasure"), is nothing personal, and is to be found only "in the dark," "When nane's to hear or see"—but MacColl enters the song and stays throughout in "Rapture trembling," in the prospect of

> Een that tell oor wishes,
> Eager glowing kisses,
> Then diviner blisses
> In holy ecstasy!

We don't have Maggie's voice, but Ewan's reaching for it in consensuality no text can deliver.

"Muirland Meg" (tune: "Saw Ye My Eppie McNab") is a related song—what's "the measure o' Muirland Meg" is the question this time. Sexual objectification (of the female by the male), a reduction even to statistical, utilitarian, politico-sexual terms, the old story: but in MacColl's performance this is objectification turned against itself, an objectification by common law. Meg is "Amang oor young lassies"—a collective entity, rather than the private treasure of Maggie's lad, but nonetheless consensual for a' that (as MacColl sings her).

> Love's her delight, and kissin's her treasure;
> She'll stick at nae price, and ye gie her gude measure,
> As lang's a sheep-fit, and as girt's a goose-egg,
> And that's the measure o' Muirland Meg.
>
> > And for a sheep-cloot she'll do't, she'll do't,
> > And for a sheep-cloot she'll do't;
> > And for a toop-horn she'll do't tae the morn,
> > And merrily turn and do't, and do't.

Something beyond even the animal husbandry frame of reference and the absolute reduction to cuntedness troubles the air (in the text as in MacColl's performance)—maybe it's "the door o' her cage" that "stands open yet," or that "She'll beg or she'll work, and she'll play or she'll beg": in any event, and although the absence of Meg's voice sounds more fully here than Maggie's absence above, listening to MacColl would put you in mind of no reward but fond regard.

Muirland Meg, for all her vaunted availability, is an object of some distance in MacColl's rendering, as in Davy Steele's younger man's recording of the same tune on Iona Records—Iona's folk instrumentation and Steele's performance reach for the mystery of Meg's presence, while MacColl's raw (Dionysian) performance suggests more a mystery well known (and loved). In either case what's most mysterious may be consensuality's own movements amang the muirland merrily turning.

Gill Bowman (on Iona) sounds a kindred note in another key: in "As I Cam o'er the Cairneymount" (tune: "Highland Laddie") she

sounds like some dream projection of the Crochallan Fencibles—
though certainly she sings for herself, from her own pleasures: it
doesn't sound like she minds being push'd fiercely in the center at
all. In "Nine Inch Will Please a Lady" she takes the "sonsy
p——ntle" for her ain, riding a surging fiddle. (Jean Redpath,
singing to Serge Hovey's art setting of the tune, keeps at a further
distance, but comes close to the Merry Muses with her "Cooper
o' Cuddy," hiding the man behind the door and under a basket.)
Bowman's "How Can I Keep My Maidenhead?" (tune: "The Birks
o' Abergeldie") is full of both the joy and "weary wark" of losing
it—she sounds resigned and eager at once, battered at once by
choices to make and by something inexorable, well beyond choice:
though she "ken[s]" the wark, she is still a maiden singing from
the near side of carnal knowledge. (MacColl's version of this tune
sounds more like a daft old woman singing a song while she works,
remembering herself young and urging herself along—a splendid
performance in its own way. He goes for the inexorable in his
weary, wanton "Modiewark.") There is no end of variations, com-
plications, border blurrings. Any word can be turned into its oppo-
site, but the voice we believe doesn't lie.

In "Ye Hae Lien Wrang, Lassie" (tune: "Up and waur them a',
Willie"), Fiona Forbes (also on Iona) sings an adult woman (al-
though the text can be imagined in any number of other voices): a
farmwife neighbor, maybe. She's circumspect, has gentle chiding
aphorisms at the ready, and in the end is as direct as can be. "Ye've
lien in some unco bed, / And wi' some unco man," she sings in the
chorus, with neither blame nor comfort in her voice—and when
she sings the last line of the last verse, "I fear ye've got a stang,
lassie," she knows there's nothing for it, no resistance, consensual-
ity not even an issue. It's the weary wark again, O—the work of the
plethora at work upon us, in us, between us. Forbes's "Dainty
Davie" carries a similar air, though without the weariness, regard-
ing this time not a nameless lassie but her own self when young.
When she sings "O leeze me on his curly pow" she rides the tune
like a gust of fresh feeling rising out of memory, what's done and
finished and can't be stopped.

One enters (a song) or one opens oneself (to a song): in perform-
ance (if not always in bed) it's all the same.

A song, like a sexual affair, like the pit of theory, has no bottom.

Representation without Reproduction—the fantasy of a Free
Scotland—the embodiment of something that is not interchange-
able—the imagination of an emancipated RB (thy devoted slave):

my horizon, the horizon of Romanticism too, is the "thing" (for lack of a better, unspeakable word) irredeemably itself. (Satan, oh National Endowment, is another word for't.)

> The pleasures of love lasts but a fleeting but the pledges of life outlusts a lifetime.
> —Joyce

Hamish Henderson discusses the research of Milman Parry and Albert Lord in *The Singer of Tales*, on "the techniques of oral composition . . . among the Yugoslav epic singers, the Homerids of modern Europe. These virtuosi," he says,

> are able to "compose" orally (i.e. recreate, using traditional techniques) songs which can be thousands of lines long. The Serb epic singer does not start out with an immutable text, but with a story and a highly flexible system of techniques for telling it.

(Sounds like sex.) He goes on to quote David Buchan's *The Ballad and the Folk*:

> Thus every new rendering is in a sense a new composition. "Oral poems frequently possess quite complex architectonic patterns. These latter patterns manifest themselves, structurally and conceptually, in all kinds of balances and parallelisms, contrasts and antitheses, chiastic and framing devices, and in various kinds of triadic groupings. A conceptual pattern called by Lord the 'tension of essences', whereby certain narrative elements automatically cohere, would suggest that there are other hidden patterning forces, as yet undissected, working within oral tradition."[40]

What this leaves us with is, in Buchan's words, "Not a *text* but a ballad: a fluid entity soluble in the mind, to be concretely realised at will in words and music."[41] Soluble on the tongue, too, and in the ear, I'd say, sensuously and always fleetingly to be realized, entered and opened to, by the will of the singer and the will of the song simultaneously.

Wha the deil can hinder the wind to blaw? Song is wind, too, and can't be hindered—except by the song itself constraining the singer's voice, as all songs do, both hindering and enabling, a matter always of vice versa. Singer and song, wind and word, are always bound in a shifting state of mutual impositions. When Doc

Watson's son Merle dies, and Doc dedicates a recording of tradi-
tional songs *in memoriam,* the performance betrays no sense of his
loss as a personal affront by Fortune: the music doesn't so much
seem to express his grief as to obliterate it, or absorb it, or fill it. (I
say this even though Merle's death was unknowably imminent at
the time of the recordings—he plays on the sessions himself, a gui-
tar and clawhammer banjo, a harmony. In the music Doc Watson
plays, death is always unknowably imminent, and known to be
so.)[42] The will of the musician and the will of the music together
compose the Mind of Music.

Where does this Mind reside? In a kind of full-throated humility
(another oxymoron)—a submission to some mystic formal site,
some greater rational/sensual order. Musicians know that they are
not the source of their creative power, know that they serve a mas-
ter greater than all pretenders—all others paling before Music, be-
fore that mystery that moves us. Leadbelly's first wife's name was
Lethe.

(Musicians are notoriously—at least mythically—free of class
prejudice: can you play? Like Burns approaching the Great Polite
etc. [and granting the real power of the discourse the G.P. com-
mand, and the judgments they govern] nevertheless remaining
unterrified, unimpressed—still just people [or unjust people] with
bodies moved by music this way and/or that.)

> Oh me and it's oh my
> What's gonna become of me
> What's gonna become of me
>
> —"Georgie Buck"

I've learned more about this from listening to Bob Dylan all
these years—variant performances, bad performances, live and
canned, electrified and meditative, wild and broken perform-
ances—and from my brother's guitar, too, than I've learned from
any book: not to arrest the passage of time but to engage it in the
Mind of Music. One of the great powerful paradoxes of folk song
performance (you could call it a political paradox) is the way in
which the freedom of the "irredeemably itself"—the self-embod-
ied moment—moves within forms and conventions and a voice de-
rived from sources beyond the individual performer, from the
great collective of history-from-below. The singer claims the song
he or she is claimed by, back and forth. One could say (as a title
from the *Merry Muses* has it) "He Till't and She Till't," were it possi-
ble to say that songs themselves have any gender. But gender is
just an invention. Ask Blake.

A Sermon for closing: Ewan MacColl performing "The Bonniest Lass," from the *Merry Muses* text (though "there is little room for doubt that this is by Burns"),[43] to the tune "For a' that" (no. 290 in *The Scots Musical Museum*). The tune itself comes to us now with a long history, "continuously popular since the middle of the eighteenth century," as James Dick writes in 1903, often associated along the way with (what Dick calls) "Jacobite effusion[s]."[44] Burns notes "a 'For a' that & a' that' which was never in print" ("Put Butter in My Donald's Brose" in *The Merry Muses*) and which, he adds, "I have been told . . . was composed by a lady—."[45] He himself makes free with the tune for the Bard's Song ("I Am a Bard of No Regard") in "The Jolly Beggars"—a song later written, says Goldstein, "for publication in SMM as 'Tho' Women's Minds Like Winter Winds"—and in "Is There for Honest Poverty?" (MacColl sings this latter as well [on a Smithsonian/Folkways release], in a searching, slow version, as if, knowing the words and the tune, he were making sure of himself as they unfolded him.)

On the Iona recording of "The Bonniest Lass," Tich Frier sings with bravado and sounds (to me) a bit bluff—it would do well as a marching song—but MacColl sings as if from a pulpit (a low pulpit, in among the very congregation) a sermon of angry stinging bitter satire, a Reprobation Song to end all reprobation songs.

> The bonniest lass that ye meet neist,
> Gie her a kiss an' a' that,
> In spite o' ilka parish priest,
> Repentin' stool, an' a' that.
>
>> For a' that an' a' that,
>> Their mim-mou'd sangs an' a' that,
>> In time and place convenient,
>> They'll do't themselves for a' that.

This is rational argument (because of this—and in spite of that—then this) with its base in the reference to a first necessity, a given, even a First Cause: the Presbytery should be pleased. But the Cause here is a kiss out of nowhere: "——," whether reasonable or not.

Citations from Scripture follow:

> Your patriarchs in days o' yore,
> Had their handmaids an' a' that;
> O' bastard gets, some had a score
> An' some had mair than a' that.

> For a' that an' a' that,
> Your langsyne saunts, an' a' that,
> Were fonder o' a bonnie lass
> Than you or I, for a' that.

Reverend MacColl's subject is the contemporary Calvinist insult to human nature, and the hypocrisy of the social order: and he has his texts right. (You could look it up, if it wasn't already plain to you.)

The argument continues, a formal exposition: first a specific example to substantiate the claim regarding your patriarchs—

> King David, when he waxed auld,
> An's bluid ran thin, an' a' that,
> An' fand his cods were growin' cauld,
> Could not refrain, for a' that.

Then an extension of that example—

> Wha wadna pity thae sweet dames
> He fumbled at, an' a' that,
> An' raised their bluid up tae the flames
> He couldna drown, for a' that.

("For, as to what we shall not name, / What could he do but claw that"—MacColl's voice rising and halting on "shall . . . not / name," as if to indicate that the prohibition is not his own.) Then one more example—

> King Solomon, prince o' divines,
> Wha proverbs made, an' a' that,
> Baith mistresses an' concubines
> In hundreds had, for a' that.

> > For a' that an' a' that,
> > Tho' a preacher wise an' a' that,
> > The smuttiest sang that e'er was sung
> > His Sang o' Sangs is a' that.

"Then still I swear," he concludes—the same "still" he's been voicing all along, "Tho' priests consign him to the deil / As reprobate, an' a' that"—"a clever chiel / Should kiss a lass, an' a' that."

> > For a' that an' a' that,
> > Their canting stuff, an' a' that,

> They ken nae mair wha's reprobate
> Than you or I, for a' that.

Amen, brother Ewan. For Everything that Lives is Holy.

৵   ৵   ৵

This will find your ear, angel, at least—though I will claim also in lieu of substantiation two references. In Poem no. 119B in Kinsley ("Robert Burns' Answer" [to "Epistle from a Taylor to Robert Burns"]), the Bard himself aspires to the rabbinate:

> King David o' poetic brief,
> Wrought 'mang the lasses sic mischief
> As fill'd his after life wi' grief
>   An' bloody rants,
> An' yet he's rank'd amang the chief
>   O' lang syne saunts.
>
> And maybe, Tam, for a' my cants,
> My wicked rhymes, an' drucken rants,
> I'll gie auld cloven Clooty's haunts
>   An unco slip yet,
> An' snugly sit amang the saunts
>   At Davie's hip yet.

And David Daiches, in *Two Worlds*, remembers that " 'Rabbi,' incidentally, was often pronounced in Edinburgh as 'Rabbie,' the familiar Scots form of 'Robert.' "[46]

In Hebrew, the alphabet is composed largely of consonants; vowels are, for the most part, indicated in print by diacritical subscriptions—wee dots and dashes. But these vowels do not, as a rule, appear: in the sacred texts as in an Israeli newspaper they are absent. The reader, the chanter, and the singer supply them. Maurice Olender:

> The Hebrew word is described as mute, an opaque substance whose occult meaning emerges only when it is voiced. In order to be read, the text must be chanted, infused with animating breath according to rules distilled from centuries of vocalization. The meaning of a verse becomes clear only when, with the help of this prolonged oral tradition, the light of the vowels is made to shine upon the dark body of the text.

It is a lovely phrase. This is Yahweh breathing life into clay over and over again (it's also reading *Finnegans Wake*).

> According to Simon [the Oratorian Richard Simon (1638–1712), author of a *Critical History of the Old Testament* (1678)], it was not until quite late (around the seventh century C.E., in fact), that the Jewish scholars known as Masoretes wrote down the vowel marks that fixed the vocalization of the text through a system of signs. . . . Now, this "Masora was in no sense divine" . . . and "the Masoretes might have been mistaken in infinitely many places." While they were no doubt learned men, they were not, Simon notes, "either prophets or infallible." . . .

Herder figures here too:

> For if the vowel is "what is primary and most vital, the linchpin of all language," in Hebrew it is embodied by nothing more than "airy breath," invisible to the eye but "captivating to the ear." So spiritual and ethereal is this breath that it cannot be encoded by any alphabet. A light emanating from the flickering, indefinite text illuminates the face of its reader. Its invisible structure manifests the unimaginable, untouchable face of God.[47]

It's anyone's face, singing—a terribly various face, the face of God. It comes before the text, and supplies breath to animate it. What we supply (vowels from the Masoretes, tunes from the *Scots Musical Museum*) is not the breath of original animators: our (sacred, beloved, unshakable) texts are an unstable thing in our throats, and our breath is both their burden and their release. A dooble tongue. Make it New.

> Sa is our Saull with fantasie
>   opprest,
> To knaw the thingis in nature
>   manifest.
>   —Robert Henryson

Coda

It is the country which is not quite a country, possessing a language which is not really a language.

—Herbert

Is history not the opium of the imagination?

—Morgan

SO WE RETURN FROM BURNS (FROM CALEDONIA) TO SCOTLAND (OR Notland). What are the borders we've crossed? What have we lost in the passage?

The path I've traced here begins with the dragon by the side of the road, Monologos, and with our demonic jockey, the incubus of Scottish national identity anxiety. It runs through the Polymorphous Perverse like there's no tomorrow, around and around (the well at the world's end) the sexual plethora; its signage speaks a tongue of material and performative impulses, a tongue decidedly problematic to the textual mind; and it makes (thus) a direct line from *Sharawaggi* through MacDiarmid back to Burns (e'en the father of a nation).

(Like no tomorrow: an apocalyptic tradition [concerned throughout, at least, with the phosphorescence of the Scots leid, what's diein north of the border], or, considered otherwise, a future insistently unknowable, endlessly open, not apocalyptic but rampant, not the end at all but something evermore about to be. Dooble tongue of the future.)

The path begins and ends with the Archive, too: the Archive at Horse Island, Dr. Currie, my own improvisations—in every case a matter of accounting for the "consequences, however far-fetched" of (Unnatural) History,[1] a matter of taking specimens and of recognizing what's forspoken and by whom, a matter of absence (of presence mocked), of the measurement of loss. The critical discourse of the Archive—another way of naming Monologos—is what links the various readings I've pursued: of "Horse Island,"

236

of *Sharawaggi*'s encounter with (what Herbert elsewhere calls) "the Anchises of the Scots Style Sheet,"[2] of MacDiarmid's mad, spitting and spinning vision, of Burns's long-gone bold/sly zigzags—each a dialectical dance with the impulses and presuppositions of the Archive, and each a mode of resistance to knowability.

"No archive without outside," Derrida reminds us, and then asks "But where does the outside commence? This question is the question of the archive. There are undoubtedly no others." Each of the Scottish exhibits I've arranged here stakes its ground around this question, in the faith, too, that "the archive always works, and *a priori*, against itself."[3] The archive transcendent and self-contradicted—the archive and its discontents—has in effect been the (only) subject throughout.

The critical discourse of the Archive is my own incubus, and yours too, gentle reader—the One Story we enter floating as a dream or mist, the broth that makes a soup of everything tradition throws in the pot. (Forgive me my fancies, and my rude speech.) The One Story of the Archive finds a meaning for every sparrow fallen and every grain of sand; it covers the globe, like some giant device of a(n imaginary) cybernetic Excise, accounting for all—as Scotland grows accountable over hundreds of years (and critically during Burns's time) to England, and then to its own incubus: an imperial (empirical) dream.

Nothing escapes the Archive, in principle—the principle being all that counts: the given to the imperial theorem that all phenomena—even social revolt, even the negation of the damn'd negation (Hegel translated into Scots)—are readily assimilable. But what the Archive does, too, like any poem, is to illuminate its own illusions. In the Scottish Wing, the haill clanjamfrie is lit with a Romantic glow, and these are Romantic illusions that reflect upon themselves here.

Burns, MacDiarmid, Crawford and Herbert: all fall squarely within a broadly recognizable Romantic tradition—the monad adrift, the Transcendental hampered, all happit in an alien gloom. It is the great tale, the deeply infrastructural tale, the great tradition of our revolutionary and post-revolutionary age these last two hundred years: the Author and Engraver William Blake, the solitary figures of Byron's gloom, Keats's rapture, Shelley's flight, Wordsworth's mind, and Coleridge's mind, right on up through the Victorians and Pre-Raphaelites, through Yeats and Pound and Eliot, and on through a myriad of forms from our own part of the century, through Ashbery and beyond—all embody this one condition, and contest it variously. And this is to name only poets, and only men, and only the most(ly) familiar; to speak of other, more marginalized and recently recovered texts and the figures behind them only underscores the point.

The Scots line of this tradition represents a particular understanding of both the (Romantic) condition and the (Romantic) contestation of it, in the northern light of Scotland's own political history and linguistic subordination; and the emanations of Burns represent an especially challenging case. The dooble tongue functions for each of the Scots writers I've looked at here as the flag, body, and soul of a Being unaccounted for (and unaccountable)—a grounding unavailable in English (though inconceivable without English): a new (ever unformed, unfinished) horizon.

The dooble tongue is a vision of synthesis, and of the synthetic—of the conjoined and of the new-made: a utopian tongue. Or, put the other way round, Synthesis is the transcendental value of the dooble tongue. The Scots line imagines a new leid, a braided leid, that speaks unimagined forms of power and pleasure. Crawford has it thus, in "Burns Ayont Auld Reekie," which begins with the note "(Burns speiks)" ("[Burns speaks]"):[4]

> Forspoken still in Embro, Scoatlan's douce
> Sly Purgatoary o thi randy yuppies,
> Ringin blak forst o closes ayont whilk
> Ma wurds sky oot wi Coancoard's soanic bangs
> Abune thi Mekong, Murray, Mississippi,
> Ah bide hamschakelled in a pokey hoose
> Dreamin o Adiroandacks, Perth, an Err;
> Ah scrug ma bunnit tae thi bourachin toon
> An speir oan luve.

Injured by immoderate praise and conjured up in Edinburgh, Scotland's respectably sly Purgatory of the randy young urban professionals, stone-hard black frost of enclosures beyond which my words skim out along the horizon with Concorde's sonic bangs above the Mekong, Murray, Mississippi, I endure defiantly like a cow whose head is fastened to its forelegs, in a cramped house, dreaming of Adirondacks, Perth, and Ayr; I cock my bonnet fiercely on my brow to the congested town and anxiously inquire after love.

"Injured by immoderate praise and conjured up" is a way of saying "Forspoken"—though one of these languages may well be found less than precise here. Burns, in any event, although it is he who (presumably) speaks, appears here at first blush to be someone who has no word of his own (someone previously spoken for—

whose "Burns-sprach," rather, is wholly the conjuration of a wholly modern officialdom, a young urban professional class). Even so, he speaks ("ayont whilk / Ma wurds sky oot"), and it is precisely his presumed wordlessness that he denies, in Crawford's ventriloquism, even as he concedes the point; conceding the power of the cultural capital to reduce him to a set of dates and a collection of moral certainties ("Either they caa ma mou a midden-dub, / Oar a demanit thocht-bane, prettified / Fur printit towels"),[5] he refuses the totality of that power.

Burns in fact (in fantasy) here is someone who has not stopped speaking, and who has not yet been heard, who is only *imagined* to be what we yuppies imagine him to be; rather, still around and sounding like he never quite sounded before, with things to say about Vietnam, Mark Twain, or American civil rights, he claims himself as an unknown (and most unexpected) entity. If we thought we knew what Burns was about, in other words, we were wrong, and our error a political one: "Ah bide hamshakelled in a pokey hoose" is an image of the politics of the forspoken still.

"Luve" is what drives Burns's engagement and critique of this condition, this place we inhabit ("the bourachin toon" ["the congested town"]), and "luve," needless to say, has a hard going here. It is a matter of cocking one's bonnet "fiercely" and inquiring "anxiously," a contested and doubtful project—but nothing else keeps him alive. And he bursts, for the purpose, into song (and italics):

> *Ah waant yon guid aucht that's weet as olours, rerr*
> *As spluntin acors thi Mojave—mair thumblickin,*
> *Prollin thumbs hurry burry aw owre yi, wi nae*
> *Hurkle-durkle; stramash o reists an shanks.*
>
> *Loup ourweillin inventars o loo:*
> *Loofs, lonyngs, skirdoch o orising, red.*

I want that good intimate possession that's wet as herbs liked by swans, rare as running after girls at night across the Mojave—more making of bargains by licking thumbs, licking and striking of thumbs in confused hurry all over you, with no sluggishness in bed; disturbance of restive waiting insteps and legs, leap exceeding inventories of love: palms of the hand, narrow passageways, flirting of arising, spawning place.

This erotics of the thumb is what Burns demands of Embro, and what Embro cannot supply—if it can even recognize it—which is why he has come ("Ah am in Embro noo") to demand it: the luve he seeks is the return, again, of the repressed, overleaping all the appropriate inventories.

This luve (a leid, too) is fraught with its own virtual impossibilities, a matter of

> Grapplin wi rift o leid that loups an jouks
> Seantacks oar keepirs, yit can aye git claucht
> Unkennin, sae thi makar, strenyeabill
> In Embro kens thi dawtit wurds . . .

struggling (as when catching salmon) with hearty free conversation of language that leaps and evades lines lined with baited hooks, and keepers, yet can always get suddenly laid hold on without knowing, so that the poet rich enough to have his goods seized to pay bail in Edinburgh knows the fondled words . . .

And no lover, in any event, is listening:

> . . . Daft ramishes an gowks
> Witter oan an oan as if thi nemm wiz Tam
> Aikenheid, no Tam o Shantir, as if aw
> Wir ramskerie leid wiz jist ane dour stane baa.
> Muck-wreistlin Scoatlaun, durt's yir histoarie,
> Naishunlet aye oabsessed wi kickin baas—
> Yi scum yir makars oar cute-gralloch thaim—Ach!

Thoughtless people driven by violent impulses and fools struggle on and on as if the name was Thomas Aikenhead, not Tam o Shanter, as if all language lustful as a ram was just one drab stone ball. Mud-wrestling Scotland, dirt's your history, nationlet always obsessed with kicking balls—you strike your poets on their mouths and prevent them from speaking, or you disembowel them to make them cute—ach!

Luve and leid persist, then, in Crawford's Burnsian fantasia, like a transcendental up one's sleeve, neither dead nor born, quite, yet bearing a considerable power (to "taw thi shurg o thi hert"), a

> Muckle rairin o thi leid, synthetic leid,
> Ane smeek o whilk can taw thi shurg o thi hert,
> Is whit's become mair Scoats than onythin
> Bicause it's neiver circuat-aboot
> By peught white-livers, bibliofoams, or proafs.
> It mudges oot, lik froe, like Noah's arks,
> Row-chow-tobacco in thi tweddlin goab
> Coammun as muck . . .
>
> . . . .

Ah am yir Burns. Ah am in Embro noo,
Phoanin thi warld, dialin an dialin
Thi future o this laun aye vieve wi sang.

Great roaring of the language, synthetic language, one whiff of which
can suck dry like a baby the wet, gravelly subsoil of the heart, is what's
become more Scots than anything, because it's never encircled by asth-
matic flatterers, bibliofools, or professors. It moves out, like sperm, like
boat-shaped clouds, loud, complex game of winding, unwinding, and
hugging in the mouth that weaves a cloth where woof vertically crosses
warp, common as muck. . . . I am your Burns. I am in Edinburgh now,
phoning the world, dialling and dialling the future of this nation al-
ways quick with song.

And so (like a Drunk Man) we shift, dialectically, between the ina-
nitions of our alien modern gloom, and the inexplicable affirma-
tions of anither order, at once persisting and as yet unborn: a
messianic vision, in effect, of a religion that doesn't exist.

Ah amnae cummin towards yi, Ah'm muivin awa
Doon thi lang perspective. Ah leave yous wi thi leid.
Ah'm stuck in Embro, tea-cosified, deid in Err—
But vivual acors thi haill gloab. Ah've sprang ma trap.
    Ma leid
's in thi spittle o thi livin an atween thi sheets o thi
    dictionars.
It's growin oan thi green screen an amang thi peeggirrin
    blasts,
Forthens an here. In Glesca an Embro, fae Dundee tae
    Rugglen,
Oan thi Solway, in thi Boardirs, amang too'ir bloacks an
    japanese lairches,
Tongue it an dawt it, tak it an mak. Mak luive.

I am not coming towards you, I am moving away down the long per-
spective. I leave you with the language. I'm stuck in Edinburgh, turned
into a tea-cosy, dead in Ayr—but alive across the whole globe. I've
sprung my trap. My language is in the spittle of the living and between
the sheets of the dictionaries. It's growing on the green screen and
among the heavy stormshowers, far in the distance and here. In Glas-
gow and Edinburgh, from Dundee to Rutherglen, on the Solway, in
the Borders, among tower blocks and japanese larches, tongue it and
fondle it, take it and create. Make love.

The dooble tongue as rock and redeemer, divine body of the Scot-
tish nation: a Presbyterian dream.

The monad persists adrift, the Transcendental remains problematic, the postmodern remains Romantic; and the dooble tongue speaks at once within this tradition and outside it.

> Men of grave, geometrical minds, the sons of "which was to be demonstrated," may cry up reason as much as they please; but I have always found an honest passion, or native instinct, the truest auxiliary in the warfare of this world. Reason almost always comes to me like an unlucky wife to a poor devil of a husband, just in sufficient time to add her reproaches to his other grievances.
>
> —Burns

Crawford and Herbert, MacDiarmid, and Burns all stake their wobbling poetic worlds in the shadow of the Archive, and all assume postures—enact figures—of distinctly Romantic alienation: raging, they pine, disconnected (and dreaming of COILA). This condition, and their resistance to it, they conceive in a figure of Synthesis: dooble tongues, synthetic Scots—a figure pointedly beyond the bounds of all English capability. They dream of an unformed horizon.

Thus the Scottish tradition carries Romanticism forward with the spasmodic benefit of its dooble (deid, undeid) leid. This leid foregrounds the intransigently material and performative functions of language, and threatens (however waywardly, comically, even pathetically) the presumptive power of textual authority. Thi leid, too, as a corollary to its performative conception—its purchase on the immediate, the local, the sensory, the material, the divergent, the fleeting—is conceived as a sexual body, an instrument not of imperial power ("which was to be demonstrated") but of deeply dialectical desire (of synthesis), of an unending blending. The linguistic politics of the Scots tradition lies in its resistance to the future as a known quantity.

(Do we think we know what is going to happen, just because we think we know what *has* happened? This is the question from the dark [Scot] side of the Archive.)

Among the major English figures, perhaps only Blake and Byron approach such a destabilizing position—such a sexualized anti-state of performative resistance to the (textual) world as we know it. (The position—the tradition—is a marginal one, though it lives at the center of empire.) And among the Scots figures, perhaps, only Burns takes this position to something like an apotheosis.

For as a political position, Synthesis is of course not without its limits; the dooble tongue is by definition a dubious prospect. *Shar-awaggi* embraces the faith with a bravado both hip and antiquated, and the *Drunk Man* is drunk with it (in equal parts zeal and embitterment). Even so, and paradoxically enough, in their refusal of certain fundamentally given limits (like English, or logic), these texts reflect the very limits of the synthetic as a political possibility. Both (or all three) of these voices must shout, more than occasionally, to be heard, and exhortation, often, is near the limit of what can be said.

Burns goes them all one better, perhaps. He shares with the others a kind of birthright (or incubus) of the borders that define and deny Scottish experience, and in denying, refusing, ignoring, celebrating, and (in submission) cursing these borders, in turn, he is as hamstrung as any of them. Yet Burns's project represents a more radical analysis of the condition than MacDiarmid or our living specimens provide—a less hopeful vision, too. Poetry (or shouting) cannot overcome, cannot even significantly undermine, the edifices of a centralizing power: so Burns disappears, and disappears, and each time we roll away the stone, a great absence is revealed. Sing tal larietal, tallarietal, tal larie tay.

Notes

Chapter 1. Something of an Incubus

1. The *PMLA Program for the 109th Convention* of the Modern Language Association in 1993, for instance, lists the one session devoted exclusively to Scottish literature under the heading "Literature in English Other than British and American." This is, of course, wrong in at least two ways: the literature in question, while in some cases written in English, in some cases is written in Scots, and in either case is nothing if not British. The panelists regarded the matter of this confusion with a good deal of mirth, but insisted on noting it—as, in fact, it represented in part the subject they had come to discuss.

2. Daiches, *Robert Burns*, rev. ed. (New York: Rhinehart, 1964), 1.

3. Unless otherwise noted, all references in the following discussion are from Herbert, "Horse Island," in *Three Kinds of Kissing: Scottish Short Stories, 1993* (London: Harper Collins, 1993), 176–204.

4. Herbert, *Dundee Doldrums* (Edinburgh: Galliard, 1991), 3–4.

5. Ibid., 3.

6. MacDiarmid, quoted by Herbert in his epigraph to *Dundee Doldrums*.

7. William Dunbar, "Lament for the Makaris," in *The Oxford Book of Scottish Verse*, ed. John MacQueen and Tom Scott (Oxford: Oxford University Press, 1966), 107.

8. Drink is another Scottish vector in the story's skewed construction of locality, and a trope, as well, of resistance to premature domestication: "It was the exceptional purity of the malt (the Island's own) that had stopped me fully taking in my surroundings," "a dominie of malts" that "taught you about itself as you took your third sip, and suggested, like all the best teachers, that beyond this beginning was more discrimination, and yet more vigorous detail," and that "was also, I realized, setting the glass down reluctantly, potent enough to cause instant blethering in the drinker." Overwhelmed by the menu, so "bulky that I assumed it would take another drink to get through," Dips adds: "Perhaps I could settle in to the intensity of life on the Island before cirrhosis got hold, but at this rate it would be a close thing."

9. Herbert is steeped in MacDiarmid, who writes in his "Author's Note" to the first edition of *A Drunk Man Looks at the Thistle* (1926; reprinted in Kenneth Buthlay's edition [Edinburgh: Scottish Academic Press, 1987], 196): "It would have been only further misleading these good folks, therefore, if I had (as, arbitrarily enough at best, I might have done) divided my poem into sections or in other ways supplied any of those 'hand-rails' which raise false hopes in the ingenuous minds of readers whose rational intelligences are all too susceptible of realising the enormities of which 'highbrows' of my type are capable—even in Scotland." This again, as above, is a matter of resistance to domestication, again

244

explicitly figured in terms of drink: "Drunkenness has a logic of its own with which, even in these decadent days, I believe a sufficient minority of my country-men remain *au fait*. I would, however, take the liberty of counselling the others, who have no personal experience or sympathetic imagination to guide them, to be chary of attaching any exaggerated importance, in relation to my book as a whole, to such inadvertent reflections on their own sober minds as they may from time to time—as in a distorting mirror—detect in these pages, and of attempting, in, no doubt, a spirit of real helpfulness, to confer, on the basis of these, a species of intelligibility foreign to its nature, upon my poem."

10. Herbert's gloss: "Peelreestie—the restless, youthful skin." Crawford and Herbert, *Sharawaggi: Poems in Scots* (Edinburgh: Polygon, 1990), 32.

11. Ibid., 137.

12. Morgan, *Nothing Not Giving Messages* (Edinburgh: Polygon, 1990), 78–80; from "Let's Go," a 1975 interview with Marshall Walker.

13. Morgan, *Essays* (Cheadle Hulme: Carcanet, 1974), 153–54.

14. Ibid., 166, 172–73.

15. Ibid., 160, 162–63.

16. Morgan, in *Saltire Review* 1, no. 2 (August 1959): 75–81.

17. Unless otherwise stated, in the discussion that follows all references are to Crawford and Herbert, *Sharawaggi*. The poets' own glosses will be provided here in the notes.

18. Crawford glosses "stour" (which is more conventionally and simply glossed—as in Kinsley's edition of Burns—as "battle; tumult; storm; adversity; dust") as "flying dust raised by the wind or by mechanical treatment": Crawford's language speaks to the dead, not to the living but to dust, and this tumultuous dust represents either a force of nature or an industrial manipulation.

19. The language is a dense tissue of linguistic and orthographic neologism, "&/or" "words pillaged from dictionaries in a deliberately anarchic way" (Craw-ford, personal correspondence, 6 September 1993), with heavy, often peculiar, or peculiarly elaborate use of glossary and sometimes (for Crawford, though not for Herbert) parallel English text on facing pages; Crawford notes "the effect of the parallel text poems" to be essential to his own reading, to be one measure of the "strength of Scots being its *fluidity* & resistance to control."

20. "Of unknown origin; Chinese scholars agree that it cannot belong to that language" (OED).

21. Crawford's gloss: "nyaff—trifle, anything small of its kind; fozie—unpleasantly damp and spongy."

22. Herbert's gloss: "allutirly—totally."

23. Herbert's gloss: "gurly—fierce; tyauvit—stubborn, sorely-tested."

24. Herbert's gloss: "habbilt—chatted, argued."

25. Herbert's gloss: "spangit—shook, vibrated, sang."

26. Crawford's gloss: "Wulcat—Wildcat; wallies—teeth; mixt— confused, dis-ordered, pale from illness; squaached—screamed; mumpy—whisper-like, *but also* like chewing without teeth; chaff—chaff, *but also* rage, ill humour, *also associated both with loquacious talk and chewing.*"

27. Crawford's gloss: "shugbog—a bog that shakes under one's feet; path—steep, narrow way, the world, the path through life."

28. Herbert's gloss: "Gnipper and gnapper—the sound of a millstone grind-ing, small particulars; pangin—cramming."

29. Crawford's gloss: "Deidleid—dead language; subfuscit—wearing dark suits; fowk—folk."

30. Crawford's gloss: "hamschakel—to fasten the head of a horse or cow to one of its forelegs; Puir Wees—those trapped in the concept of a Puir Wee Scotland; pluff—set fire to suddenly; hammerflush—the sparks which fly from red-hot iron when beaten with a hammer; scran—ability, or means for effecting any purpose; ew-gowan—the common daisy; fushionless—in a state of being without pith; seg-gin—falling (often under the influence of alcohol); Cambuslang—suburb of Glasgow; queezie— disordered, squeamish after intoxication; sterns—stars."

31. Crawford's gloss: "claucht—lay hold of forcibly and suddenly, clutch; chit-terin—shivering with cold; peak—a very small quantity, a person with a thin, weak voice."

32. Herbert's gloss: "causie—cobblestoned road."

33. Perhaps this is what "sharawaggi" means.

34. Herbert's gloss: "selkith—seldom; virr, verr—strength, virtue; havirs, clishmaclavirs—nonsense."

35. Herbert's gloss: "pirn—spool; prisk—ancient; guschet— corner of land; bi-forrow—before."

36. Herbert's gloss: "garron—a small, sturdy horse, an old, worn-out horse."

37. Herbert's gloss: "scarts, jenny-wullocks—hermaphrodites; pellack—the flesh of the porpoise; peltin-pyock—shabby garment, worthless rag, suitable for rough work."

38. Herbert's gloss: "cleuchs—rock-faces of narrow bays; peeried—grew fainter; toyts—fresh-water mussels found in the Tay; whifflan—playing of the fife or chanter."

39. Antonio Gramsci, *Selections from the Prison Notebooks*, ed. and trans. Quintin Hoare and Geoffrey Nowell Smith (New York: International Publishers, 1971), 333.

40. Herbert's gloss: "scrievan—writing; pitmirk—dead darkness; sornin—sponging, lamenting; wuntellan—shaking with uncontrollable pleasure; starn—stars."

41. Herbert's gloss: "crine—shrink; lave—rest."

Chapter 2. Subjunctive Scotland

1. Hugh MacDiarmid, *Lucky Poet* (London: Jonathan Cape, 1972), 23–24, xv, 36.

2. MacDiarmid, *Selected Poetry*, ed. Alan Riach and Michael Grieve (Manchester: Carcanet, 1992), 185, 142.

3. See Duncan Glen, *Hugh MacDiarmid and the Scottish Renaissance* (Edinburgh and London: William and Robert Chambers, 1964), 83, 100–102, 133, 137, 146, 149, 169.

4. MacDiarmid might enjoy the echo here of Popocatepetl.

5. Paulin, *Minotaur* (Cambridge: Harvard University Press, 1992), 2–3.

6. Terry Eagleton, Fredric Jameson, and Edward W. Said, *Nationalism, Colonialism, and Literature* (Minneapolis: University of Minnesota Press, 1990), 28–29.

7. Ibid., 23.

8. Ibid., 23–24.

9. Ibid., 27, 4.

10. MacDiarmid, *Selected Poetry*, 10–11. The editors, Riach and Grieve, provide this gloss: "gorlin'—fledgling; slee—sly; sliggy—cunning; whuram—crotchet or

quaver; syne—then; lift—sky; byous spatrils—wonderful musical sounds; wame—belly; airels—musical notes; alunt—alight."

11. Crawford and Herbert, *Sharawaggi*, 43–46. Herbert's gloss: "fizzog—physiognomy; paroachenin—the parochial twilight of Scottish thinking; scrievan—writing; pitmirk—dead darkness."

12. Hans-Georg Gadamer, *The Relevance of the Beautiful and Other Essays*, ed. Robert Bernasconi and trans. Nicholas Walker (Cambridge: Cambridge University Press, 1986), 2–3.

13. See Kenneth Buthlay's Introduction to his edition of MacDiarmid, *A Drunk Man Looks at the Thistle* (Edinburgh: Scottish Academic Press, 1987), x–xx, xxxvii.

14. Quoted in Buthlay, xvi.

15. MacDiarmid, *Complete Poems*, ed. Michael Grieve and W. R. Aitken, 2 vols. (Harmondsworth: Penguin, 1985), 293.

16. Herbert, "MacDiarmid: Mature Art," *Verse* 4, no. 2 (June 1987), 29–30.

17. MacDiarmid, *Complete Poems*, vi.

18. Herbert, "MacDiarmid: Mature Art," 30–31.

19. Ibid.

20. Or as the Drunk Man puts it (line 2270), "The woundit side draws a' the warld." For Benjamin, see "Theses on the Philosophy of History," *Illuminations*, 253–64.

21. Herbert, "MacDiarmid: Mature Art," 31.

22. McGann, *Black Riders* (Princeton: Princeton University Press, 1993), 75. McGann's specific reference here is to the pages of Poe, Baudelaire, and Morris.

23. Ibid., 98. The text in question is Howe's *Pythagorean Silence* (1982).

24. MacDiarmid, *Selected Poetry*, 20. Riach and Grieve gloss "gairmscoile" as "poets' school." For the epigraph to *Penny Wheep*, see *Complete Poems*, 43. The phrase "penny wheep" also appears in *A Drunk Man* (line 815), published that same year.

25. MacDiarmid, *Selected Poetry*, 19, 21.

26. Ibid., 22.

27. See Weston's edition of *A Drunk Man Looks at the Thistle* (Amherst: University of Massachusetts Press, 1971), xi.

28. Wesling, "Social Poetics of Dialect," *Papers on Language and Literature* 29, no. 3 (Summer 1993), 306.

29. "Yow-trummle" is typically glossed as "cold weather in July after sheep-shearing"—the season when the ewes tremble. "Houghmagandie" is typically glossed as "fornication," but this word exists in Scots as well, and would seem a pale synonym. Burns, in his glossary to the Kilmarnock edition (1786), renders "houghmagandie" as "a species of gender composed of the masculine and feminine united."

30. Wesling, "Social Poetics of Dialect," 308.

31. Ibid., 314–15. The same dialect, however, spoken or written or read unselfconsciously, *not* in consciousness of its relation to some normative Other, is not a dialect at all but simply *language*. MacDiarmid's interest in Gaelic and in the Norse-inflected dialect of the Shetlands may represent an attempt to step outside the bounds of this condition of Scots.

32. Deleuze and Guattari, *Kafka*, trans. Dana Polan (Minneapolis: University of Minnesota Press, 1986), 18.

33. Kafka writes of "the literature of small peoples" that "the independence of the individual writer, naturally only within the national boundaries, is better preserved." *The Diaries, 1910–1923*, ed. Max Brod and trans. Joseph Kresh and Martin Greenberg (New York: Schocken, 1976), 149.

34. MacDiarmid, *Complete Poems*, 236.

35. The poem carries three epigraphs: "Is cam's is dìreach an lagh. / (Crooked and Straight is the law.)"—an Ancient Gaelic Proverb; "To the consternation of the Seminaries, the last number of the review *God* reproduced photographs of God by Man Ray, side by side with fetishes from the Upper Oubanghi."—from Paul Morand; and "A gulf divides the exaltations of the mystics from the tachy-praxia of the micro-splanchnic hyperthyroidics or the ideo-affective dissociations of the schizothymes."—from De Sanctis.

36. MacDiarmid, *Complete Poems*, 181.

37. Ibid., 181–82. *Cassell's New Compact Latin Dictionary* gives, for "*no, nare*—to swim," and by extension "to sail, flow, fly"; for "*incrementum*—growth, increase"; "*meton*—the makings of anything, also offspring."

38. As glossed in MacDiarmid, *More Collected Poems*, 19.

39. MacDiarmid, *Complete Poems* (Chicago: Swallow, 1970), 189, 185–86.

40. Ibid., 183, 190, 184, 188.

41. Ibid., 186.

42. MacDiarmid, *A Drunk Man*, ed. Buthlay, lines 18–19, 5–7. Line references hereafter will appear parenthetically in the text. All subsequent references to *A Drunk Man* are to Buthlay's edition, and all glosses from his annotations, which also provide the section titles that MacDiarmid supplied for his *Collected Poems* (1962); Buthlay's edition otherwise follows (and provides line numbers for) the final text authorized by MacDiarmid, in the *Complete Poems* (1978), although, as Buthlay notes, the poet's "attitude towards the problem of Scots spelling was such that he turned the entire text of *A Drunk Man* over to John Weston to be respelled more consistently in accordance with a different system—a procedure which Weston incorporated in his edition of 1971" (ix). Gloss: "elbuck—elbow; fankles—entangles (itself), becomes clumsy; sheckle—wrist; thrapple—throat; deef—numb."

43. "Thow—thaw; ha'en—having; jalousin'—suspecting, guessing; fur't—for it."

44. "I'se—I'll; haud—hold; kip—brothel (and cf. 'play the kip', play truant); maist—most."

45. "Fu'—full; doited—confused (as in dotage)."

46. In Walter Benjamin, *Illuminations*, ed. Hannah Arendt and trans. Harry Zohn (New York: Schocken, 1969), 144.

47. "Gruntle—snout; wheengin'—whining; ugsome—repulsive; aidle—foul slop, urine of cattle; the lave; the rest."

48. "Haill—whole."

49. "Wrocht—wrought; winna—won't; ettle—aspire." In "Sea-Serpent" (*Penny Wheep*) with its epigraph from Milton ("The soul grows clotted by contagion, / Imbodies, and imbrutes till she quite lose / The divine property of her first being") we

> ken that the serpent is movin' still,
> A movement that a'thing shares,
> Yet it seems as tho' it twines in a nicht
> When God neither kens nor cares.

See MacDiarmid, *Complete Poems*, 50.

50. "Muckle—too much; wun—get, reach; het—hot; natter— nag."

51. James Joyce, *Finnegans Wake* (New York: Penguin, 1976), 215.

52. "Aiblins—perhaps; biggin'—building."

53. See Buthlay, 21.

54. "Hauflins—youths; 'yont—beyond; stounds—throbs."
55. "Ettles—guesses, suspects."
56. "Reid-een'd—red-eyed."
57. "Frae'r—from her; dwamin'—swooning."
58. "Forekent—foreknown."
59. "Hauf—half; youky—itchy."
60. "Fell—extremely; aiblins—perhaps."
61. MacDiarmid, *A Drunk Man*, ed. Buthlay. "Poulp (Eng.)— octopus; agen—against."
62. "'Thoot—without; breenges—plunges forward, bursts; mind— remind; lood—loud."
63. "Heilant—Highland; ava—at all; aneth—beneath."
64. "Geylies feart—rather afraid; heid—head."
65. "Muckle Toon—Langholm, Dumfriesshire."
66. "Swippert—agile; swith wi' virr—quick with vigour; howes—hollows; astert—on the move; levin—lightning."
67. "Laichest—lowest; ootloupin'—outleaping; starns—stars; howes—hollows; hert—heart; nocht—naught."
68. "Antrin—rare; haingles—state of ennui; atweenwhiles—in between."
69. MacDiarmid, *A Drunk Man*, ed. Buthlay, 45.
70. "Shairly—surely."
71. "Cross-tap—mizzen-mast (MacD. From Swedish 'kryss-topp,' the mizzen-top, as cited by J[amieson]?); monkey-tree—monkey puzzle? (But monkey spars are reduced masts and yards for a vessel devoted to the instruction and exercise of boys); spiel—climb."
72. MacDiarmid, *A Drunk Man*, ed. Buthlay, 47.
73. "Beddit—bedded; gars—makes, compels to; bane—bone (But the sense of English 'bane' is also relevant); sinnen—sinew."
74. "Courage-bag—scrotum."
75. "Jizzen—childbed, straw (J[amieson]); claith o' gowd— cloth of gold; orra duds—shabby, ragged clothes; bairntime—a woman's breeding time (MacD. But used here as if it referred, not to her child-bearing span, but to lying-in or parturition itself); bellythraw—colic; ripples—diarrhoea (MacD); worm-i'-the-cheek—toothache; marrow—mate, companion." Buthlay further notes of "A'e winsome marrow": "Glossed by MacD as 'a creditable limb.' Used as a ballad-style formula by William Hamilton of Bangour in 'The Braes of Yarrow' and echoed by Wordsworth in 'Yarrow Unvisited' and 'Yarrow Revisited.' In Hamilton's poem the unwilling bride rejects the advances of her husband and turns to the ghost of her lover, whom he has killed." Buthlay, 61.
76. "Drumlie—dark."
77. "Feck—most part."
78. Crawford and Herbert, *Sharawaggi*, 44.
79. "Happit—covered, buried."
80. Perelman, *Captive Audience*, (Great Barrington, Mass.: The Figures, 1988), 26.
81. "Eneuch—enough; goam—stare vacuously; jalouse—suspect; dottlin—becoming senile, crazy."
82. "Clear keltie aff—drink off a bumper, empty one's glass."
83. "Gantrees—support for barrels; cullage—male genitals (formed by MacD from 'cull,' testicle, when in need of a rhyme?); yill—ale; spilth (English)—spillage, overflow; ullage (English)—deficiency in contents of a vessel."

84. "Cratur—creature."

85. "Worn to the back-hauf—nearly worn out; bean-swaup—hull of a bean, anything of no value or strength; ferlies—wonders."

86. "Loups—leaps; chuns—sprouts; tatties—potatoes; blink— glimpse."

87. "Ahint—behind; ugsome—repulsive; dernin'—hiding; Deils—Devils; een—eyes."

88. "To chowl one's chafts—to distort one's mouth, often for the purpose of provoking another, to emit a mournful cry (J[amieson])."

89. "Argie—argue."

90. "Ootrie—outré; gangrel—vagrant; bleeze—blaze."

91. "Hings—hangs."

92. "Rumple-fyke—itch in the anus."

93. "Sinnens—sinew; muckle—much."

94. "To stick a fork in the wa'—to transfer, by doing this, the pains of a woman in labor to her husband." Buthlay notes further (121): "The couvade had particular historical associations on MacD's home ground. 'Near where the tower of Langholm stood is a piece of ground on which a number of witches were burned so lately as the eighteenth century. It is recounted of the witches of Eskdale that they were sufficiently potent to be able to transfer the labours of child-birth from the mother to the father. As several of them were able midwives, the belief in their powers was much emphasized.' (H. D. Gauld, *Brave Borderland*, London 1935, pp. 349–350.)"

95. "Stertle-a-stobie (Jock-startle-a-stobie)—exhalations rising from the ground on a hot day." A figuration of the waking dead, this is a source for Crawford and Herbert, who title the first section of *Sharawaggi* "Sterts and Stobies."

96. "Breenged—plunged; pleuch (plew)—to plow (Normally 'pleuch' would be the substantive, 'plew' the verbal form); sauted—salted; scunner—disgust."

97. "The lave—the rest; dree—endure; weirdless—futile." Another echo in Herbert, "Penis Envoi" (*Sharawaggi*, 45):

> and anerly touch thae minds
> that dinna crine at licht—
> thi lave belang i thi nicht!

98. "Dernin'—lurking; wad—would (that); poor'd—poured."

99. "Lourd—dull."

100. "Hauds—holds; raxed—stretched."

101. "Deosil—Sunwise; Widdershins—Contrary to the sun."

102. "Grugous—grim, grisly; widdifow—deserving to be hung (J[amieson]), perverse (MacD); ramel—small branches; sibness— kinship; coonter—counter; airts—directions; yince—once."

103. "Winna—won't."

104. "Wheesht—hush; whummle—overturn; dee—die; tine— lose."

105. "Tak' it to avizandum—defer decision (MacD. In Scots law, this applies to a judge taking a case for private consideration outside the court)."

106. "Croon—crown."

Chapter 3. Recitativo

1. R.D.S. Jack and Andrew Noble, eds., *The Art of Robert Burns* (London: Vision, 1982), 24.

2. David Daiches, *Robert Burns*, 1; *Two Worlds*(Edinburgh: Canongate, 1987), 84, 119.

3. Jameson, *The Ideologies of Theory* (Minneapolis: University of Minnesota Press, 1988), 117.

4. Jack and Noble, eds., *The Art of Robert Burns*, 8.

5. This version is in L. M. Angus-Butterworth, *Robert Burns and the Eighteenth Century Revival in Scottish Vernacular Poetry* (Aberdeen: Aberdeen University Press, 1969), 187. Kinsley has a different version, poem no. 272A. (Kinsley's edition of Burns's *Poems and Songs* comes in both a three-volume set with complete annotation [Oxford: Oxford University Press, 1968], and a one-volume format without annotation; each of the poems and songs is numbered, with the numbers from the single volume keyed to the multivolume edition. In subsequent citations from Kinsley's text, therefore, I will give the number of the poem or song, rather than the page number, for readiest reference.)

6. Gavin Sprott, *Robert Burns: Farmer* (Edinburgh: National Museums of Scotland, 1990), 28.

7. Burns, *Letters*, 1:39.

8. In 1993 the condition of Scotland is characterized by the panelists at the Modern Language Association Convention in Toronto, half-laughingly, as "approximately post-colonial," eliciting knowing, ironic, and bitter laughter from their scholarly audience.

9. Burns, *Letters*, 1:149. To George Thomson, Trustees' Office Edinburgh. Currie's edition substitutes *prostitution* for *Sodomy*, a practice retained throughout the nineteenth century.

10. See Luke, 9:62.

11. Burns, *Letters*, 2:182–84.

12. Ibid., 2:356. To George Thomson [May 1795]. The appellation "Kind, honest-hearted Willie" is from an earlier letter to Nicol (1:120), dated "Carlisle 1st June 1787—or I believe the 39th o' May rather," one of Burns's most extended pieces of prose in Scots: "I'm sitten down here, after seven and forty miles ridin, e'en as forjesket and forniaw'd as a forfoughten cock, to gie you some notion o' my landlowper-like stravaguin sin the sorrowfu' hour that I sheuk hands and parted wi' auld Reekie. . . ."

13. See Burns, *Poems and Songs*, ed. Kinsley, 3:971–72.

14. Adorno, *Minima Moralia*, trans. E. F. N. Jephcott (London: Verso, 1978), 16.

15. For Carlyle, see Donald Low, ed., *Robert Burns: The Critical Heritage* (London: Routledge and Kegan Paul, 1974), 364.

16. Kafka, *Parables*, trans. Willa Muir and Edwin Muir (New York: Schocken, 1947), 25.

17. White, *The Content of the Form* (Baltimore: Johns Hopkins University Press, 1987), 21.

18. Crawford and Herbert, *Sharawaggi*, 103; William S. Burroughs, *Nova Express* (1964; reprint, New York: Grove, 1992), 7.

Chapter 4. Scots

1. Dunbar, "The Goldyn Targe," in *The Oxford Book of Scottish Verse*, ed. MacQueen and Scott, 129.

2. Dante Alighieri, *A Translation of the Latin Works of Dante Alighieri*, (New York: Greenwood, 1969), 4.

3. Stevens, *The Palm at the End of the Mind*, ed. Holly Stevens (New York: Vintage, 1972), 149.

4. Burns, *Letters*, 1:65–66.

5. Donald Low, ed., *Robert Burns: The Critical Heritage* (London: Routledge and Kegan Paul, 1974), 63. Subsequent references to Low's invaluable collection of Burns's early reception history will be given parenthetically in the text with the abbreviation *CH*.

6. Burns, *Letters*, 1:17.

7. Mackenzie, *The Man of Feeling* (London: Oxford University Press, 1970), 5.

8. Burns, *Poems and Songs*, ed. Kinsley, Poem no. 166.

9. Burns, *Letters*, 1:220.

10. Ibid., 2:153.

11. Crawford and Herbert, *Sharawaggi*, 74.

12. We in the academy represent that Tongue, again, as well: but we are also that Ear—tonguing ourselves obscenely.

13. Burns, *Letters*, 1:70.

14. Burns, *The Works of Robert Burns*, ed. James Currie (New York: J. Booth, 1832), iii. All subsequent references to Currie's edition (in each case to vol. 2 of that edition) will be given parenthetically in the text.

15. I will be citing here the text of Burns's letter as given by Currie—to give the good doctor his due. The corrected text is to be found in Burns, *Letters*, 1:133–47; in this case it differs only slightly from Currie's, mostly in matters of spelling and capitalization.

16. *Pye-coated* turns up an interesting cluster of associations in the OED. *Pye* (or *pie*) derives from "The bird now more usually called a Magpie" and thus refers specifically to a characteristic pattern " 'of various colours' (like the black-and-white plumage of the magpie)"—but by extension as well to "a cunning or wily person, . . . a chattering or saucy person" (an obsolete usage but cited as lately as 1886). The prefix may also have called up in Burns's ear "A collection of rules, adopted in the pre-Reformation Church, to show how to deal (under each of the 35 possible variations in the date of Easter) with the concurrence of more than one office on the same day, accurately indicating the manner of commemorating, or of putting off till another time, the Saints' days, etc., occurring in the ever-changing times of Lent, Easter, Whitsuntide, and the Octave of the Trinity"—or "a mass of type mingled indiscriminately or in confusion, such as results from the breaking down of a forme of type," or "a disintegrated or confused mass; a jumble, medley, confusion, chaos; a 'mess.' "

17. Burns, *Letters*, 1:146.

18. The word Currie has disemboweled here is "scoundrel," which appears earlier, spelled fully, in the quotation from Pope: Currie apparently not objecting to the word per se, but here protecting this unnamed factor's pride.

19. Burns, *Letters*, 1:146.

20. Daiches, *Robert Burns*, 37.

21. Burns, *Letters*, 1:16–18.

22. Ibid., 2:38–39.

23. A (most wee free Scottish) Symposium. The question for debate at its first gathering: "*Suppose a young man, bred a farmer, but without any fortune, has it in his power to marry either of two women, the one a girl of large fortune, but neither handsome in person, nor agreeable in conversation, but who can manage the household affairs of a*

farm well enough; the other of them a girl in every way agreeable in person, conversation, and behaviour, but without any fortune: which of them shall he choose?" (26) Love and money, power in person or security of station, a conundrum for a dooble tongue.

24. Burns, *Poems and Songs*, ed. Kinsley, 3:978.
25. Ibid.
26. Carol McGuirk, *Robert Burns and the Sentimental Era* (Athens: University of Georgia Press, 1985), 27.
27. Ibid., xv.
28. MacDiarmid, *At the Sign of the Thistle* (London: Stanley Knott, 1934), 170.
29. My text in the following discussion is the facsimile reprint of *Poems, Chiefly in the Scottish Dialect* from AMS Press (New York, 1974); the poems, of course, are all readily available elsewhere as well.
30. Daiches, *Robert Burns*, 126.
31. Sprott, *Robert Burns: Farmer*, 14, 27–28.
32. In Burns, *Selected Poems*, ed. Carol McGuirk (London: Penguin, 1993), 239.
33. Daiches, *Robert Burns*, 148, 144.
34. Burns, *Poems and Songs*, ed. Kinsley, 3:1118.
35. Kinsley observes of "Epistle to Davie" that "it was probably not drafted as an epistle to Sillar" (3:1039)—and Burns didn't give "To a Mouse" to a mouse: but these poems are delivered *as if* to their respective ears alone, as the Cotter to Robert Aiken and the Auld Farmer to his Auld Mare—and it is this representation that concerns me here.
36. See for instance Seamus Heaney, "Burns's Art Speech," in Crawford, ed. *Robert Burns and Cultural Authority* (Iowa City: University of Iowa Press, 1997), 216–33, for a rich evocation.
37. Burns, *Poems and Songs*, ed. Kinsley, 3:1174.
38. Ibid.
39. Ibid., 1040.
40. Ibid., 1174, 1088.
41. Dick, *The Songs of Robert Burns* (Glasgow: H. Frowde, 1903; facsimile reprint, New York: AMS Press, 1973), 482.
42. Ibid., 483.
43. Burns, *Poems and Songs*, ed. Kinsley, 3:1180.
44. Burns, *Selected Poems*, ed. McGuirk, 237.
45. Burns, *Poems and Songs*, ed. Kinsley, 3:1036.
46. Ibid.
47. Ibid., 3:1005.

Chapter 5. Sang & Mowe

1. Burns, *Letters*, 1:220.
2. Burns, *Poems and Songs*, ed. Kinsley, no. 484: "The Dumfries Volunteers" (tune: "Push about the jorum").
3. Burns, *The Works of Robert Burns, with His Life*, ed. Cunningham, 8 vols. (London: Cochrane and McCrone, 1834), 1:344; *The Illustrated Family Burns* (New York: Collier, n.d.), xxv.
4. Burns, *Letters*, 1:58, 1:367, 2:446.
5. Burns, *Poems and Songs*, ed. Kinsley, no. 537.
6. Burns, *Letters*, 2:367.

7. Ibid., 2:426, 224, 318.

8. Edward J. Cowan, ed., *The People's Past* (Edinburgh: Polygon, 1980), 2.

9. Jürgen Habermas, *The Structural Transformation of the Public Sphere*, trans. Thomas Burger (Cambridge: MIT Press, 1991), 36.

10. Phelan, *Unmarked* (London: Routledge, 1993), 148. Subsequent references to Phelan's work will be given parenthetically in the text.

11. Baudrillard, *Seduction*, trans. Brian Singer (New York: St. Martin's, 1990), 17.

12. Only Adorno seems to lack a name for this possibility: sometimes he will name Schoenberg, or critical theory, as a mode of troth, but only in the most tentative, complicitous, self-contradicted way. He is the gloomiest and most splendid of angels down here.

13. McCaffery, *North of Intention* (New York: Roof Books, 1986), 203, 220–21.

14. Ibid., 219.

15. Greil Marcus, *Lipstick Traces* (Cambridge: Harvard University Press, 1989), 393–94.

16. McCaffery, *North of Intention*, 220.

17. In Phelan, *Unmarked*, 6.

18. Georges Bataille, *Erotism*, trans. Mary Dalwood (San Francisco: City Lights Books, 1992), 152, 157.

19. Ibid., 158, 104, 161, 170–71.

20. Ibid., 185.

21. Jacques Derrida, *Archive Fever*, trans. Eric Prenowitz (Chicago: University of Chicago Press, 1996), 51.

22. Cowan, ed., *The People's Past* (Edinburgh: Polygon, 1980), 34.

23. Adorno, *Minima Moralia*, 40.

24. Cowan, ed., *The People's Past* 36, 32.

25. Burns, *Works*, ed. Currie, 2:64.

26. In Habermas, *Structural Transformation*, 25.

27. Liam McIlvanney gives a useful Bakhtinian account of the matter in " 'Why should na poor folk mowe?': An Example of Folk Humour in Burns," *Scottish Literary Journal* 23, no. 2 (November 1996), 43–53.

28. Burns, *Merry Muses*, ed. James Barke and Sydney Goodsir Smith, (New York: Putnam's, 1964). Subsequent references to this work's scholarly apparatus will be given parenthetically in the text, with the abbreviation *MM*.

29. Burns, *Letters*, 1:462.

30. Abelove, "Some Speculations on the History of 'Sexual Intercourse During the 'Long Eighteenth Century' in England," in *Nationalisms and Sexualities*, ed. Andrew Parker et al. (New York and London: Routledge, 1992), 339–40.

31. Walter Pater, *Appreciations* (London: Macmillan, 1911), 246.

32. Gass, *Willie Masters' Lonesome Wife* (New York: Knopf, 1971), unpaginated.

33. Burns, *Letters*, 2:308.

34. Burns, *Poems and Songs*, ed. Kinsley, no. 302.

35. 'Jacob Curate,' *The Scotch Presbyterian Eloquence*, 1692, quoted in Hamish Henderson, "The Ballad, the Folk and the Oral Tradition," in Cowan, ed., *The People's Past*, 83.

36. Herbert Marcuse, *Eros and Civilization* (Boston: Beacon, 1955), 146.

37. In *Faber Book of Twentieth-Century Scottish Poetry*, ed. Douglas Dunn (London: Faber and Faber, 1992), 106.

38. Laing's performance is from the Iona Records release of *Robert Burns' The Merry Muses* (Glasgow, 1996).

39. No dashes in this case: my text here is from the Dionysus liner notes, which scruple not to spell things out.

40. In Cowan, ed., *The People's Past*, 67.

41. Ibid., 68.

42. Greil Marcus explores this territory with powerful delicacy in *Invisible Republic* (New York: Henry Holt, 1997).

43. Burns, *Merry Muses*, ed. Barke and Smith, 92.

44. Dick, *The Songs of Robert Burns*, 475.

45. Burns, *Letters*, 2:364.

46. Daiches, *Two Worlds* (Edinburgh: Canongate, 1987), 12.

47. Olender, *The Languages of Paradise*, trans. Arthur Goldhammer (Cambridge: Harvard University Press, 1992), 24–25, 32.

Coda

1. Herbert, "Horse Island," 192.

2. Herbert, "Radical Scots," *Verse* 6 (1986), 56.

3. Derrida, *Archive Fever*, 8, 11–12.

4. The poem is cast entirely in the Bard's newfangled voice— Burns again (we have seen him in the role before, writing to Willie Nicol) a kind of ventriloquist's dummy. *Sharawaggi*, 48–55, or respectively (Scots) 48, 50, 52, 54, and (English) 49, 51, 53, 55. On one facing page of English (53), a word is missing ("anything"), appearing instead in the analogous position embedded in the Scots of page 52—a braiding of braids.

5. "Either they call my mouth a hole into which a dunghill's sap is collected, or a demeaned merrythought of a fowl, prettified for printed towels." Crawford's English gloss is further glossed with the note: "the merrythought is a bone between a fowl's head and neck, sometimes used like a wishbone."

Bibliography

Abelove, Henry. "Some Speculations on the History of 'Sexual Intercourse' During the 'Long Eighteenth Century' in England." In *Nationalisms and Sexualities*, edited by Andrew Parker et al. New York and London: Routledge, 1992.

Adorno, Theodor. *Minima Moralia: Reflections from Damaged Life*. Translated by E. F. N. Jephcott. London: Verso, 1978.

———. *The Culture Industry: Selected Essays on Mass Culture*. London: Routledge, 1991.

Anderson, Benedict. *Imagined Communities: Reflections on the Origin and Spread of Nationalism*. Rev. ed. London: Verso, 1991.

Angus-Butterworth, L. M. *Robert Burns and the Eighteenth Century Revival in Scottish Vernacular Poetry*. Aberdeen: Aberdeen University Press, 1969.

Barthes, Roland. *The Pleasure of the Text*. Translated by Richard Miller. New York: Hill and Wang, 1973.

Bataille, Georges. *Erotism: Death and Sensuality*. Translated by Mary Dalwood. San Francisco: City Lights Books, 1986.

———. *The Tears of Eros*. Translated by Peter Connor. San Francisco: City Lights Books, 1992.

Baudrillard, Jean. *Seduction*. Translated by Brian Singer. New York: St. Martin's, 1990.

Beerbohm, Max. *The Poets' Corner*. London: Heinemann, 1904.

Benjamin, Walter. *Illuminations*. Edited by Hannah Arendt. Translated by Harry Zohn. New York: Schocken, 1969.

Bentman, Raymond. *Robert Burns*. Boston: Twayne, 1987.

Bernstein, Charles. *A Poetics*. Cambridge: Harvard University Press, 1992.

Blake, William. *The Poetry and Prose of William Blake*. Edited by David V. Erdman. Newly rev. ed., with commentary by Harold Bloom. Berkeley and Los Angeles: University of California Press, 1982.

Boland, Eavan. *Outside History: Selected Poems, 1980–1990*. New York: W. W. Norton, 1990.

Brown, Mary Ellen. " 'That Bards Are Second-Sighted Is Nae Joke': The Orality of Burns' World and Work." *Studies in Scottish Literature* 16 (1981): 208–16.

Buchan, David. *The Ballad and the Folk*. London: Routledge, 1972.

Burns, Robert. *The Works of Robert Burns, with an Account of His Life, and Criticism on His Writings*. Edited by James Currie. New York: J. Booth, 1832.

———. *The Works of Robert Burns, with His Life*. Edited by Allan Cunningham. 8 vols. London: Cochrane and M'Crone, 1834.

————. *The Merry Muses of Caledonia*. Edited by James Barke and Sydney Goodsir Smith. New York: Putnam's, 1964.

————. *Poems and Songs*. Edited by James Kinsley. 3 vols. Oxford: Oxford University Press, 1968.

————. *The Glenriddell Manuscripts of Robert Burns*. Edited by Desmond Donaldson. Hamden, Connecticut: Archon Books, 1973.

————. *Poems, Chiefly in the Scottish Dialect*. Kilmarnock: John Wilson, 1786. Facsimile reprint, New York: AMS, 1974.

————. *The Prose Works of Robert Burns, with the Notes of Currie and Cromek, and Many by the Present Editor*. Edinburgh: William and Robert Chambers, 1839. Facsimile reprint, New York: AMS, 1975.

————. *The Jolly Beggars, or Love and Liberty: A Cantata*. Barr, Ayrshire: Luath Press, 1984.

————. *The Letters of Robert Burns*. Edited by J. DeLancey Ferguson, 2nd ed. G. Ross Roy. 2 vols. Oxford: Clarendon Press, 1931, 1985.

————. *Selected Poems*. Edited by Carol McGuirk. London: Penguin, 1993.

————. *The Illustrated Family Burns*. New York: Collier, n.d.

————. *Songs of Robert Burns. Sung by Ewan MacColl*. Introduction and Notes by Ralph Knight. New York: Folkways Records, 1959, FW 8758, sound cassette.

————. *Songs from The Merry Muses of Caledonia. Sung by Ewan MacColl*. Edited by Kenneth S. Goldstein. Dionysus: 1962, D 1, sound recording.

————. *The Songs of Robert Burns*. Sung by Jean Redpath. 7 vols. Cambridge, Mass: Rounder Records, 1976–90, Philo CD 1126, 1187–1189.

————. *Songs of Robert Burns,—Sung by Andy M. Stewart*. Danbury, Connecticut: Green Linnet Records, 1991, GLCD 3059.

————. *Robert Burns' The Merry Muses*. Glasgow: Iona Records, 1996, IRCD 035, compact disc.

Burroughs, William S. *Nova Express*. 1964. Reprint, New York: Grove, 1992.

Carlyle, Thomas. *Essay on Burns*. Edited by Sophie C. Hart. New York: Henry Holt, 1912.

Carswell, Catherine. *The Life of Robert Burns*. New York: Harcourt Brace, 1931.

Child, Francis James. *"Lord Randall" and Other British Ballads*. New York: Dover, 1996.

Collinson, Francis. *The Traditional and National Music of Scotland*. London: Routledge, 1966.

Cowan, Edward J., ed. *The People's Past: Scottish Folk, Scottish History*. Edinburgh: Polygon, 1980.

Craig, David. *Scottish Literature and the Scottish People, 1680–1830*. London: Chatto & Windus, 1961.

Crawford, Robert. *Devolving English Literature*. Oxford: Oxford University Press, 1992.

————, ed. *Robert Burns and Cultural Authority*. Iowa City: University of Iowa Press, 1997.

Crawford, Robert, and W. N. Herbert. *Sharawaggi: Poems in Scots*. Edinburgh: Polygon, 1990.

Crawford, Thomas. *Burns: A Study of the Poems and Songs*. Edinburgh: Oliver and Boyd, 1960.

———. *Society and the Lyric: A Study of the Song Culture of Eighteenth-Century Scotland*. Edinburgh: Scottish Academic Press, 1979.

Creeley, Robert. Introduction to *The Essential Burns*. New York: Ecco Press, 1989.

———. *Echoes*. New York: New Directions, 1994.

Daiches, David. *The Paradox of Scottish Culture: The Eighteenth Century Experience*. London: Oxford University Press, 1964.

———. *Robert Burns*. Rev. ed. New York: Rhinehart, 1964.

———. *Two Worlds: An Edinburgh Jewish Childhood*. Edinburgh: Canongate, 1987.

Dante Alighieri. *A Translation of the Latin Works of Dante Alighieri*. New York: Greenwood, 1969.

Davis, Leith Ann. *Scotland and the Politics of Romanticism: The Representative Fictions of James MacPherson, Robert Burns, and Walter Scott*. Ann Arbor: University Microfilms, 1991.

Deleuze, Gilles, and Felix Guattari. *Kafka: Toward a Minor Literature*. Translated by Dana Polan. Minneapolis: University of Minnesota Press, 1986.

Derrida, Jacques. *Writing and Difference*. Translated by Alan Bass. Chicago: University of Chicago Press, 1978.

———. *Archive Fever: A Freudian Impression*. Translated by Eric Prenowitz. Chicago: University of Chicago Press, 1996.

Dick, James. *The Songs of Robert Burns*. Glasgow: H. Frowde, 1903. Facsimile reprint, New York: AMS, 1973.

Donaldson, William. "The Glencairn Connection: Robert Burns and Scottish Politics, 1786–1796." *Studies in Scottish Literature* 16 (1981): 61–79.

Dunn, Douglas, ed. *The Faber Book of Twentieth-Century Scottish Poetry*. London: Faber and Faber, 1992.

Eagleton, Terry, Fredric Jameson, and Edward W. Said. *Nationalism, Colonialism, and Literature*. With an introduction by Seamus Deane. Minneapolis: University of Minnesota Press, 1990.

Fanon, Frantz. *Black Skin, White Masks*. New York: Grove, 1967.

Ferguson, DeLancey. *Pride and Passion: Robert Burns, 1759–1796*. New York: Russell and Russell, 1964.

Flaubert, Gustave. *The Dictionary of Received Ideas*. Translated by Jacques Barzun. New York: New Directions, 1968.

Forrest-Thomson, Veronica. *Collected Poems and Translations*. London: Allardyce, Barnett, 1990.

Foucault, Michel. *The History of Sexuality, Volume I: An Introduction*. New York: Vintage Books, 1980.

Gadamer, Hans-Georg. *The Relevance of the Beautiful and Other Essays*. Edited by Robert Bernasconi. Translated by Nicholas Walker. Cambridge: Cambridge University Press, 1986.

Gass, William H. *Willie Masters' Lonesome Wife*. New York: Knopf, 1971.

Glen, Duncan. *Hugh MacDiarmid and the Scottish Renaissance*. Edinburgh and London: William and Robert Chambers, 1964.

Glissant, Edouard. *Caribbean Discourse: Selected Essays*. Charlottesville: University Press of Virginia, 1989.

Gordimer, Nadine. *The Essential Gesture: Writing, Politics, Places*. London: Penguin, 1989.

Graham, W. S. *Selected Poems*. New York: Ecco, 1979.

Gramsci, Antonio. *Selections from the Prison Notebooks*. Edited and translated by Quintin Hoare and Geoffrey Nowell Smith. New York: International Publishers, 1971.

Gray, Alasdair. *A History Maker*. New York and London: Harcourt Brace, 1996.

Habermas, Jürgen. *The Structural Transformation of the Public Sphere*. Translated by Thomas Burger with the assistance of Frederick Lawrence. Cambridge: MIT Press, 1991.

Harris, Joseph, ed. *The Ballad and Oral Literature*. Cambridge: Harvard University Press, 1991.

Henderson, T. F. *Scottish Vernacular Poetry*. Edinburgh: Grant, 1910.

Herbert, W. N. "Radical Scots." *Verse* 6 (1986): 55–56.

———. "MacDiarmid: Mature Art." *Verse* 4, no. 2 (June 1987): 29–35.

———. *Dundee Doldrums*. Edinburgh: Galliard, 1991.

———. *To Circumjack MacDiarmid: The Poetry and Prose of Hugh MacDiarmid*. Oxford: Clarendon Press, 1992.

———. "Horse Island." In *Three Kinds of Kissing: Scottish Short Stories 1993*, Introduction by Tom Adair. London: HarperCollins, 1993.

———. *Forked Tongue*. Newcastle upon Tyne: Bloodaxe Books, 1994.

———. *Cabaret McGonagall*. Newcastle upon Tyne: Bloodaxe Books, 1996.

Howe, Susan. *My Emily Dickinson*. Berkeley: North Atlantic Books, 1985.

———. "Pythagorean Silence." In *The Europe of Trusts*. Los Angeles: Sun and Moon, 1990.

Jack, R. D. S., and Andrew Noble, eds. *The Art of Robert Burns*. London: Vision, 1982.

Jameson, Fredric. *The Ideologies of Theory: Essays 1971–1986. Volume Two, Syntax of History*. Minneapolis: University of Minnesota Press, 1988.

Jamieson, John. *An Etymological Dictionary of the Scottish Language*. Edited by John Longmuir and David Donaldson. 4 vols. Paisley: Alexander Gardner, 1879–82.

Johnson, James, ed. *The Scots Musical Museum*. 6 vols. Edinburgh: Ross, 1787–1803.

Johnson, Samuel, and James Boswell. *A Journey to the Western Islands of Scotland, and the Journal of a Tour to the Hebrides*. London: Penguin, 1984.

Jones, John Paul III, Wolfgang Natter, and Theodore R. Schatzki, eds. *Postmodern Contentions: Epochs, Politics, Space*. New York: Guilford, 1993.

Joyce, James. *Ulysses*. New York: Vintage, 1961.

———. *Finnegans Wake*. New York: Penguin, 1976.

Kafka, Franz. *Parables*. Translated by Willa Muir and Edwin Muir. New York: Schocken, 1947.

———. *The Diaries, 1910–1923*. Edited by Max Brod. Translated by Joseph Kresh and Martin Greenberg, with the cooperation of Hannah Arendt. New York: Schocken, 1976.

Leonard, Tom. *Intimate Voices: Selected Work 1965–1983*. Newcastle upon Tyne: Galloping Dog, 1984.

———, ed. *Radical Renfrew: Poetry from the French Revolution to the First World War*. Edinburgh: Polygon, 1990.

Low, Donald. *The Songs of Robert Burns*. London: Routledge, 1993.

———, ed. *Robert Burns: The Critical Heritage*. London: Routledge and Kegan Paul, 1974.

Lynch, Kevin. *Scotland: A New History*. London: Pimlico, 1992.

MacCaig, Norman. *Collected Poems*. London: Chatto and Windus, 1990.

MacDiarmid, Hugh. *Albyn, or Scotland and the Future*. London: Kegan Paul, 1927.

———. *At the Sign of the Thistle*. London: Stanley Knott, 1934.

———. *Burns Today and Tomorrow*. Edinburgh: Castle Wynd Printers, 1959.

———. *Collected Poems*. New York: Macmillan, 1962.

———. *The Uncanny Scot*. London: MacGibbon and Kee, 1968.

———. *Selected Essays*. Edited by Duncan Glen. London: Jonathan Cape, 1969.

———. *More Collected Poems*. Chicago: Swallow, 1970.

———. *A Drunk Man Looks at the Thistle*. Edited by John C. Weston. Amherst: University of Massachusetts Press, 1971.

———. *Lucky Poet: A Self-Study in Literature and Political Ideas*. London: Jonathan Cape, 1972.

———. *Complete Poems*. Edited by Michael Grieve and W. R. Aitken. 2 vols. Harmondsworth: Penguin, 1978.

———. *A Drunk Man Looks at the Thistle*. Edited by Kenneth Buthlay. Edinburgh: Scottish Academic Press, 1987.

———. *Selected Poetry*. Edited by Alan Riach and Michael Grieve. Manchester: Carcanet, 1992.

Mackay, James. *A Biography of Robert Burns*. Edinburgh: Mainstream, 1992.

Mackenzie, Henry. *The Man of Feeling*. London: Oxford University Press, 1970.

Mackenzie, Robert. "Tearfilm: Lewis 1987." *Verse* 4, no. 2 (June 1987): 28.

MacLean, Sorley [Somhairle MacGill-Eain]. *From Wood to Ridge: Collected Poems in Gaelic and English*. London: Vintage, 1991.

MacQueen, John, and Tom Scott, eds. *The Oxford Book of Scottish Verse*. Oxford: Oxford University Press, 1966.

Magnusson, Magnus. *Bawdy Verse and Folksongs*. London: Macmillan, 1982.

Marcus, Greil. *Lipstick Traces: A Secret History of the Twentieth Century*. Cambridge: Harvard University Press, 1989.

———. *Invisible Republic: Bob Dylan's Basement Tapes*. New York: Henry Holt, 1997.

Marcuse, Herbert. *Eros and Civilization: A Philosophical Inquiry into Freud*. 2nd ed. Boston: Beacon, 1955, 1966.

Marquard, Odo. *In Defense of the Accidental: Philosophical Studies*. New York and Oxford: Oxford University Press, 1991.

McAfee, Caroline. "Dialect Vocabulary as a Source of Stylistic Effects in Scottish Literature." *Language and Style: An International Journal* 19, no. 4 (Fall 1986): 325–37.

McCaffery, Steve. *North of Intention: Critical Writings 1973–1986*. New York: Roof Books, 1986.

McCaffery, Steve, and bpNichol. *Rational Geomancy: The Kids of the Book-Machine*. Vancouver: Talonbooks, 1992.

McClure, J. Derrick. *Why Scots Matters*. Edinburgh: The Saltire Society, 1988.

McGann, Jerome J. *Black Riders: The Visible Language of Modernism*. Princeton: Princeton University Press, 1993.

McGuirk, Carol. *Robert Burns and the Sentimental Era*. Athens: University of Georgia Press, 1985.

———, ed. *Critical Essays on Robert Burns*. New York: G. K. Hall, 1998.

McIlvanney, Liam. " 'Why shouldna poor folk mowe?': An Example of Folk Humour in Burns." *Scottish Literary Journal* 23, no. 2 (November 1996): 43–53.

Montaigne, Michel de. *Essays*. Translated by J. M. Cohen. Baltimore: Penguin, 1958.

Montgomerie, William. "Robert Burns, Folk Song Editor." *Saltire Review* 6, no. 18 (Spring 1959): 56–59.

———, ed. *New Judgments: Robert Burns, Essays by Six Contemporary Writers*. Glasgow: William MacLellan, 1947.

Morgan, Edwin. "Modern Makars Scots and English." *Saltire Review* 1, no. 2 (August 1959): 75–81.

———. *Wi the Haill Voice*. Oxford: Carcanet, 1972.

———. *Essays*. Cheadle Hulme: Carcanet, 1974.

———. *Sonnets from Scotland*. Glasgow: Mariscat Press, 1984.

———. *Selected Poems*. Manchester: Carcanet, 1985.

———. *Nothing Not Giving Messages: Reflections on Life and Work*. Edinburgh: Polygon, 1990.

Muir, Edwin. *Latitudes*. New York: B. W. Huebsch, 1924.

———. *Scott and Scotland: The Predicament of the Scottish Writer*. London: Routledge, 1936.

Olender, Maurice. *The Languages of Paradise: Race, Religion, and Philology in the Nineteenth Century*. Translated by Arthur Goldhammer. Cambridge: Harvard University Press, 1992.

O'Rourke, Daniel, ed. *Dream State: The New Scottish Poets*. Edinburgh: Polygon, 1994.

Pater, Walter. *Appreciations*. London: Macmillan, 1911.

Paulin, Tom. *Minotaur: Poetry and the Nation State*. Cambridge: Harvard University Press, 1992.

———, ed. *The Faber Book of Vernacular Verse*. London: Faber and Faber, 1990.

Perelman, Bob. *Captive Audience*. Great Barrington, Mass.: The Figures, 1988.

———. *Virtual Reality*. New York: Roof Books, 1993.

———. *The Marginalization of Poetry: Language Writing and Literary History*. Princeton: Princeton University Press, 1996.

Phelan, Peggy. *Unmarked: The Politics of Performance*. London: Routledge, 1993.

Pound, Ezra. *The Cantos of Ezra Pound*. New York: New Directions, 1972.

Reid, Alexander. "The Dramatic Works of Robert Burns." *Scotland's Magazine* (January 1955): 47–48.

Renan, Ernest. "What is a Nation?" In *Nation and Narration*, edited by Homi K. Bhabha. New York and London: Routledge, 1990.

Robbins, Bruce, ed. *The Phantom Public Sphere*. Minneapolis: University of Minnesota Press, 1993.

Sampson, David. "Burns, Robert: The Revival of Scottish Literature?" *Modern Language Review* 80, no. 1 (January 1985): 16–38.

Saunders, R. Crombie. "Burns in Two Tongues." *Saltire Review* 1, no. 3 (Winter 1954): 41–45.

Shairp, J. C. "Burns and Scotch Song Before Him." *Atlantic Monthly* 44 (1879): 502–13.

Shklovsky, Viktor. *Theory of Prose*. Translated by Benjamin Sher. Elmwood Park, Illinois: Dalkey Archive Press, 1990.

Simpson, Kenneth. *The Protean Scot: The Crisis of Identity in Eighteenth Century Scottish Literature*. Aberdeen: Aberdeen University Press, 1988.

Singer, Burns. *The Collected Poems of Burns Singer*. Edited by W. A. S. Keir. London: Secker and Warburg, 1970.

Smith, Harry, ed. *Anthology of American Folk Music*. Washington, D. C.: Smithsonian Folkways Recordings, 1997, FP 251–253, 6 compact discs.

Smith, Iain Crichton. *Selected Poems*. Manchester: Carcanet, 1985.

———. "The Scholar and the Poet." *Verse* 4, no. 2 (June 1987): 3.

———. *Thoughts of Murdo*. Nairn: Balnain, 1993.

Smith, Sydney Goodsir. *Collected Poems*. London: John Calder, 1975.

Sprott, Gavin. *Robert Burns: Farmer*. Edinburgh: National Museums of Scotland, 1990.

Stevens, Wallace. *The Palm at the End of the Mind: Selected Poems and a Play*. Edited by Holly Stevens. New York: Vintage, 1972.

Tennyson, Alfred, Lord. *Selected Poetry*. Edited by Douglas Bush. New York: Modern Library, 1951.

Thomson, George, ed. *A Select Collection of Original Scotish Airs for the Voice*. 8 vols. London: Preston & Son, 1793–1818.

Trinh, T. Minh-Ha. *Woman, Native, Other*. Bloomington: University of Indiana Press, 1989.

Turnbull, David. *Maps Are Territories: Science Is an Atlas*. Chicago: University of Chicago Press, 1993.

Walcott, Derek. *Collected Poems 1948–1984*. New York: Farrar, Straus and Giroux, 1986.

———. *The Antilles: Fragments of Epic Memory*. New York: Farrar, Straus and Giroux, 1992.

Watson, Doc. *Riding the Midnight Train*. Durham, North Carolina: Sugar Hill Records, 1986, SH-CD 3752, compact disc.

Wesling, Donald. "Mikhaïl Bakhtin and the Social Poetics of Dialect." *Papers on Language and Literature* 29, no. 3 (Summer 1993): 303–22.

White, Hayden. *The Content of the Form: Narrative Discourse and Historical Representation*. Baltimore: Johns Hopkins University Press, 1987.

Wilson, Norman, ed. *Scottish Writing and Writers*. Edinburgh: Ramsay Head, 1977.

Index